WALKING ON THE GREEK ISLANDS – THE CYCLADES

About the Author

Gilly Cameron-Cooper's main career was as a journalist, non-fiction author and editor, but in 2002 she and her husband Robin gave up demanding London jobs and turned their hiking hobby into a lifestyle business. They set up Walking Plus Ltd, organising and leading walking holidays initially on Naxos, and later on Paros, Amorgos and Tinos. At the time, the islands offered untapped potential for adventure and exploration, as waymarking and mapping were minimal, and there was no competition from other tour operators. Gilly already had a foothold in Greek language and culture from living in Athens, where she wrote for the English-language press, ran a weekly magazine, and produced consultation documents on sustainable tourism for the Greek government. She has hiked all over the world, publishing articles for national magazines and newspapers, and books on walking London's waterways, Beatrix Potter's Lake District, and mythology.

WALKING ON THE GREEK ISLANDS – THE CYCLADES

NAXOS AND THE 50KM NAXOS STRADA, PAROS, AMORGOS, SANTORINI

by Gilly Cameron-Cooper

CICERONE

JUNIPER HOUSE, MURLEY MOSS,
OXENHOLME ROAD, KENDAL, CUMBRIA LA9 7RL
www.cicerone.co.uk

© Gilly Cameron-Cooper 2020
First edition 2020
ISBN: 978 1 78631 009 5

Printed by KHL Printing, Singapore
A catalogue record for this book is available from the British Library.

Route mapping by Anavasi www.anavasi.gr
All photographs are by the author unless otherwise stated.

Acknowledgements

Christoff Korovesis of www.walkingplus.co.uk on Paros, Nikos Boutsinis of http://santoriniwalkingtours.com, Panos Psychogios, deputy mayor and www.pensionpanos-amorgos.gr/greek on Amorgos, Tassos Anastasiou and Christos Sideris for their island knowledge and continuing battles to keep the paths open. Alex, Ilias and Peti of Casa Lengko, Santorini for generous hospitality; www.anavasi.gr for the best available maps for walkers; Mike and Russ of www.viewranger.com for excellent support; Blue Star Ferries, Zas Travel on Naxos, and Marko at Santorini Cars for help with travelling. My husband Robin, Stuart Thorpe and artist Cynthia Wells for companionship on the walks and general support.

Updates to this Guide

While every effort is made by our authors to ensure the accuracy of guidebooks as they go to print, changes can occur during the lifetime of an edition. Any updates that we know of for this guide will be on the Cicerone website (www.cicerone.co.uk/1009/updates), so please check before planning your trip. We also advise that you check information about such things as transport, accommodation and shops locally. Even rights of way can be altered over time. We are always grateful for information about any discrepancies between a guidebook and the facts on the ground, sent by email to updates@cicerone.co.uk or by post to Cicerone, Juniper House, Murley Moss, Oxenholme Road, Kendal, LA9 7RL.

Register your book: To sign up to receive free updates, special offers and GPX files where available, register your book at www.cicerone.co.uk.

Front cover: The path to the citadel of ancient Arkesini on Amorgos (Walk 31)

CONTENTS

Map key 7
Overview map 8–9

INTRODUCTION 11
History 12
Geology 16
Vegetation and wildflowers 17
Animal life 21
Climate. 22
When to go 23
Travel to the islands 24
Travel around the islands 26
Accommodation. 26
Eating and drinking. 27
Shopping and services 27
What to take. 28
Using this guide 29

PAROS 33
Walk 1   Parikia town to Cape Fokas 36
Walk 2   Northwest coast to Kolimbithres 43
Walk 3   Northwest peninsula eco-park. 49
Walk 4   Naousa port, inland to marble mines 53
Walk 5   West-coast hills to Parikia 59
Walk 6   Lefkes village and Byzantine Way 65
Walk 7   South from Lefkes to Dryos port 70
Walk 8   Southwest coast: Piso Livadi to Dryos 75
Walk 9   Angeria mountain circular. 79

NAXOS 83
Walk 10   Naxos town tour 87
Walk 11   Potamia villages and marble hills 93
Walk 12   South coast to Demeter's Temple. 100
Walk 13   Rural byways below Profitis Ilias 104
Walk 14   Wild lands around Apalirou 108
Walk 15   Central villages and Fanari foothills. 114

Walk 16	Filoti village and Mount Zas	120
Walk 17	Apiranthos to emery mines and port	125
Walk 18	Koronos, mountain and east-coast bay	132
Walk 19	Kynidaros, downriver to Engares	136

The Naxos Strada 141
Walk 20	Strada 1: Plaka to Kato Potamia	142
Walk 21	Strada 2: Kato Potamia to Filoti	148
Walk 22	Strada 3: Filoti to Apiranthos	155
Walk 23	Strada 4: Apiranthos to Koronos	160
Walk 24	Strada 5: Koronos to Apollonas	164

AMORGOS 169
Walk 25	Egiali and mountain villages	172
Walk 26	Remote north: monastery and mountains	178
Walk 27	Along the island spine to Chora	185
Walk 28	Inland capital to Katapola port	192
Walk 29	Old routes inland to the capital	199
Walk 30	Rollercoaster route: Katapola to Vroutsi	205
Walk 31	Ancient Arkesini and southwest farms	210

SANTORINI 215
Walk 32	Caldera rim: Fira to Ammoudi Bay	219
Walk 33	Ancient Akrotiri and southwest cape	225
Walk 34	Villages and vineyards to Emborio	229
Walk 35	Highest peak and Ancient Thira to Perissa	234

Appendix A	Route summary table	239
Appendix B	Useful Greek words and phrases	242
Appendix C	Bibliography	247
Appendix D	Useful contacts	248

Map key

Ⓢ	start
Ⓕ	finish
ⓈⒻ	start/finish
Ⓢ	alternative start
▬▶▬	route line with direction arrow
▬▬	alternative route line
▬▬	main asphalt road
▬▬	minor asphalt or concrete road
▬▬	dirt road
- - - - -	footpath
- - - - -	indistinct trail
――	watercourse
- - - -	seasonal watercourse
	seasonal lake, or marsh
▲	peak
○	spring, well
)	cave
⊙	threshing circle
✻	windmill, wind turbine
⊚	watermill, mill race
⌒	bridge
⚒	mine or quarry
	built-up area
✈⊕	international/domestic airport
- - -	ferry route
⛴	local ferry
🚢	main ferry port
☆	lighthouse
▲	campsite
Ⓜ	museum
▪	building
▫	ruin
⚰	church or chapel
✝	monastery
―	fortification wall
∴	ancient/historical monument or site
♖	tower
⊞	cemetery
Ⓟ	parking

WALKING ON THE GREEK ISLANDS

OVERVIEW MAP

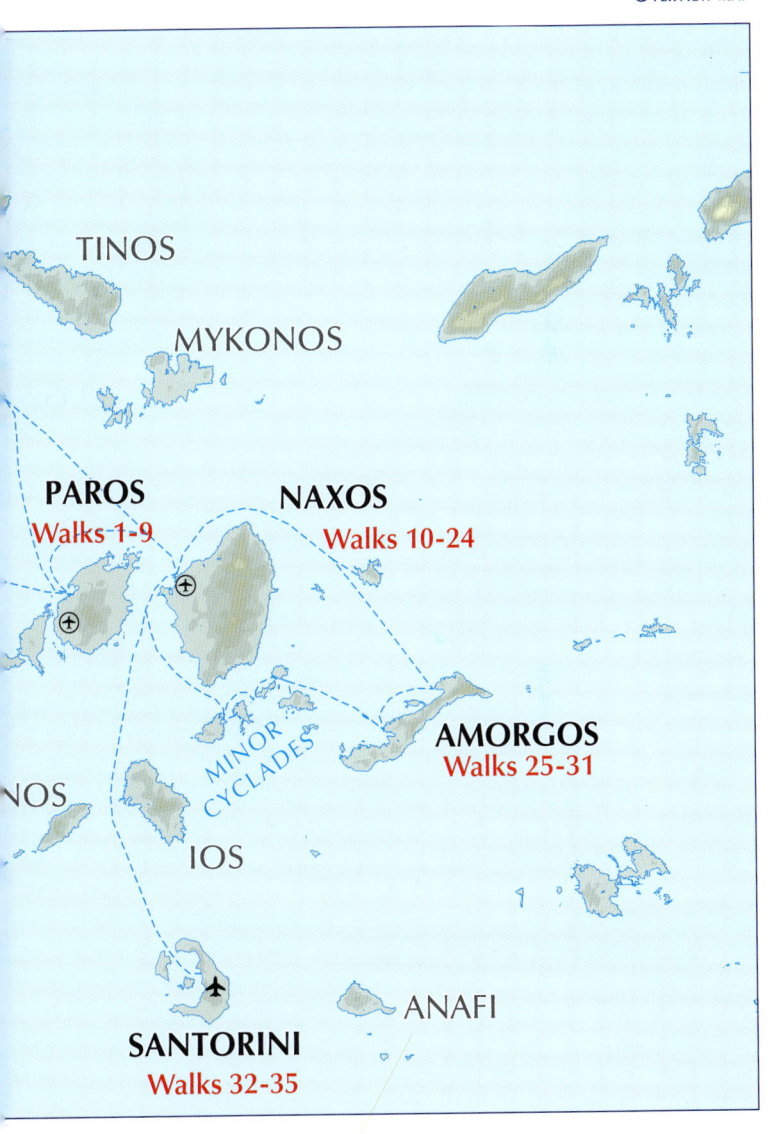

TINOS

MYKONOS

PAROS
Walks 1-9

NAXOS
Walks 10-24

MINOR CYCLADES

AMORGOS
Walks 25-31

IOS

ANAFI

SANTORINI
Walks 32-35

All four islands are networked with traditional working paths that link villages, churches and farmland, such as this monopati *on Naxos*

INTRODUCTION

Grotta Bay, Mount Zas (distant centre) and Naxos town (Walk 10)

Paros, Naxos, Amorgos and Santorini: the best of Greece in four islands. Each one gives you the whole intense Greek experience condensed into digestible areas that can be explored in a week or two – although you'll want to go back for more. Cragged marble peaks are bare and bleached against the sky, and startlingly white villages and monasteries are embedded in wild landscapes. Evocative remnants of ancient history lie in olive groves and hidden valleys, and always there is the encircling, glittering sea.

These islands are southern members of the Cyclades archipelago, a roughly circular scattering of treasure islands in the southern Aegean, linked by geomorphology, history – and ferry routes. From each island you can see at least one of the others, and yet each is a world of its own. Santorini's life and landscape are dramatically defined by its volcano; Naxos by its diversity of landscape and self-sufficiency. Paros has a gentler, more cosmopolitan ambience, and Amorgos is loved for its remoteness, stark beauty and potent shrubs. From a walker's perspective, Paros is a training ground for the much greater network of mountains and valleys on Naxos, while Amorgos is more rugged and exposed. Santorini is a warm-up exercise, too small for hikes of any length or a dedicated walking holiday, but a convenient launching-pad for the other islands, and has idiosyncratic natural and human-made

11

wonders quite apart from its spectacular caldera.

On most of the walks you are more likely to meet a lonely goatherd than troops of hikers, and may feel as if you are discovering places that other tourists don't reach. England has its bridleways, Spain its Moorish routes, and in rural Greece there are *monopati* and *kalderimi*, man- or mule-width paths paved with country rock, which carve their way into the heart of island life and landscape. They were built as vital lines of communication between villages, to reach a distant orchard or terrace of vines, a remote chapel or a mountain spring. Some wind crazily up vertical mountains like a collapsible ruler; others cut deeply between earthen banks thick with vegetation, or thread a route around age-old vineyards and farmland.

Although the walks are not long, they can be challenging, as they are less manicured and managed than in other countries. Even the most beautifully marble-paved *monopati* can disintegrate into oblivion, and although many routes have been opened up and waymarked, signing can be inconsistent and/or confusing – hence the value of a guidebook.

You could allow as many days for your trip as there are walks, but it's worth building in some time to soak in the Greek island lifestyle in a village *kafenion* (café) or taverna, or to swim in the Aegean blue. Paros, Amorgos and Naxos each give two weeks of satisfying walking, and four days in Santorini can be tagged on at either end.

HISTORY

The islands – and your walks – are littered with remnants of Greek history, so here's a quick guide to key dates and periods.

KEY PERIODS

Prehistoric Before the human story was recorded
Palaeolithic (Early/Old Stone Age) from 3.3 million years ago: Hominids use stone implements
Neolithic (New Stone Age) 7000–3000BC: hunter-gatherers, using stone implements
Bronze Age 3300–1150BC: Bronze is used for tools and weapons
  Helladic 2800–1600BC: Bronze Age in Greece
  Cycladic 3200–2000BC: Early Bronze Age culture centred on the Cyclades
  Minoan 2600–1200BC: Advanced Bronze Age civilisation based on Crete
  Mycenaean 1600–1100BC: Advanced Late Bronze Age civilisation centred on Mycenae in the Peloponnese

HISTORY

> **Geometric** 1100–700BC: A 'Dark Age' of limited development, with geometrical designs on pottery
> **Archaic** 650–480BC: a period of artistic development that laid the foundation for the Classical period
> **Classical** 480–323BC: Athens is the centre of artistic creation, philosophical and political thought. The Persian Wars (492–449BC) overlap, when the Persians annex a lot of Greece but then grant it independence
> > **Alexander the Great** 336–323BC: Alexander of Macedon builds an empire from the Adriatic Sea to the Indus River, and is granted generalship of Greece
>
> **Hellenistic** 323–30BC: From Alexander's death to the emergence of the Roman Empire
> **Roman Greece** 146BC–AD330: Greece is dominated by the Roman Empire
> **Byzantine Empire** AD330–1204: Constantine establishes Byzantium (Constantinople) as the capital of the Eastern Roman Empire, and makes Christianity the official religion
> **Frankish/Venetian occupation** 1207–1537: Follows the fall of Constantinople to the Fourth Crusaders
> **Turkish/Ottoman rule** 1537–1832: in the eastern Mediterranean, from Barbarossa's conquest to Greek Independence 1822–32

The particular history of the Cycladic islands is shaped by their location on the sea routes between mainland Greece, Asia and Africa, and their proximity to each other. Island-hopping has been going on since prehistory, when early humans in primitive dug-out canoes or coracles needed to keep in sight of land. Then, hunter-gatherers would have foraged in inland mountains and valleys. Their farming successors in the Early Bronze Age made small, permanent settlements on lower vales and coastal plains, and pioneering steps in crop cultivation and animal husbandry, skills and craftsmanship – a significant stage of civilisation that archaeologists call the Cycladic period.

As sea transport improved, the islands became a hub for trade routes and the exchange of influences and technology with the ancient civilisations of Egypt, Mesopotamia and the Middle East. Unfortunately, over the centuries, they also attracted invaders, from Minoans and Myceneans to Venetians and Turks, who exacted taxes and sometimes invested in island trade and economy. But the islands were remote outposts of empire, neglected when the ruling powers were under pressure. Then they were easy prey for pirates and privateers, sometimes whole fleets of

Ancient columns and a Byzantine chapel, Thira, Santorini (Walk 35)

them, who anchored in the sheltered bays and plundered land and people. Local populations were small, the people scratching out livings on the arid land, with no spare resources to defend themselves.

The Cycladic period's early achievements were superseded in the Middle Bronze Age by the powerful, prosperous and creative Minoan and Mycenean civilisations, notably and uniquely developed at Akrotiri on Santorini. When these empires declined, their glittering sophistication, craftsmanship, and the Linear B alphabet were lost, and the 'Dark Ages' began. Islands were depopulated, but tribal peoples such as Dorians and Ionians migrated from the mainland, bringing with them their language, customs and gods, and consolidating, in the Cyclades, a common Greek identity and character. In some places, such as Amorgos, city-states (*poleis*) were founded, with a fortified acropolis (high town) as the focal point of a scattered rural community, whose men could be called to arms.

The Hellenistic period was marked by war, unrest, and a plague of pirates, as Alexander's successors and city-states jostled for power, prompting the building of defensive towers and hilltop forts. The Romans took control of the South Aegean from 133BC, but didn't colonise. They installed local governors, exacted annual taxes, raised the cost of living, and used Amorgos as a place of exile. As the Empire weakened and Greeks and Romans fought for control, pirates and bounty hunters returned. Persistent, large-scale and devastating raids in the early Byzantine period prompted islanders to move their capitals away from the coasts to high ground inland, opening up the interiors for farming. Christian churches and chapels are the most visible legacy of the Byzantine period.

With the fall of Constantinople to the Fourth Crusaders in 1204, the Byzantine Empire crumpled, and in the carve-up of land the Cyclades were up for grabs. Venetian adventurer Marco Sanudo and his band of mercenaries took control of Naxos and Paros, Jacopo Barozzi took Santorini, the Quirini family Amorgos, and they moved the capitals back to the sea. Although the Venetians operated a feudal system, native islanders retained property and Orthodox religious rights. Over the years, the two cultures rubbed along together and even intermarried. When times were stable and good, olive groves, terraces for wheat, and marble quarries (for the architecture of Venice) were fully exploited, but persistent invasions, increasingly from Turks, led to depopulation as islanders were taken into slavery or left for safer shores.

In the late 1530s, Barbarossa, promoted from buccaneer to admiral by Ottoman ruler Suleiman the Magnificent, brought the Cyclades under Turkish control, which lasted for the next 300 years. The Turks didn't occupy the islands, but demanded an annual tax. They granted the Greek Orthodox Church administrative control over its people and many monasteries were founded under Turkish rule. This arrangement caused tension with the still-resident Catholic Venetians, who continued to act as lords of the manor. As a nation, the Venetians were still at war with the Turks, which triggered another period of piracy, disturbance and

Speliotissa, Virgin of the Cave chapel near Profitis Ilias, on Naxos (Walk 13)

depopulation on the islands from the late 17th to 18th centuries.

Island economy, with its focus on shipping, suffered with the coming of steam-ships and the opening of the Corinth Canal in the late 19th century. There was an influx of refugees from the Turkish-Greek population exchange in the 1920s, and more than 1000 opponents of the Metaxas dictatorship were deported to the Cyclades in 1936–1940. After World War II, however, populations were decimated, due to starvation and emigration. 'Let them perish as long as no German starves,' was the edict of Hitler's deputy, Hermann Göring in 1942. Supplies from Athens stopped, fishing boats were grounded, foodstuffs plundered, and outposts such as the Aegean islands carried on starving even after restrictions were lifted. Some village populations plummeted from 2000 to 200, and with rural depopulation to Athens and emigration to North America, never fully recovered. Package tourism in the 1960s boosted development and economy – at least around the main ports and coast.

GEOLOGY

The Cycladic landscape is dominated by the drama of rocks that have been shaped by fire and mighty earth movements. Domes and piles of boulders, infused with the colour and sparkle of minerals, command valleys that slice to the sea. The Cycladic islands are the peaks of mountains whose steep sides disappear into the ocean depths. They are high points of a continuous landmass called Aegis that was pushed up from the sea, stretching from the island of Evia and the lower part of mainland Greece to Crete and Asia Minor. Over geological ages, through mountain-building phases and glacial periods, parts of Aegis submerged and others uplifted. The pattern of island and sea that makes up the Cyclades archipelago as we know it today was established when the sea rose at the end of the last glacial period, some 2 million years ago (around the time when the first humans evolved).

The Earth's crust is relatively thin in the South Aegean, stretched out by shifting continents, and the Cyclades perch on a hotbed of tectonic activity. The Aegean oceanic plate pushed up against the African plate, forcing it to slump towards the molten core of the Earth and triggering, at the volatile collision point, a ring of fire – the Hellenic Volcanic Arc – of which Santorini is the most spectacular representative. The pumice, ash and lava that constitute most of the island were spewed out from beneath the Earth's crust by volcanic explosions. Naxos and Paros are on a central aseismic part of the subterranean landmass, but the whole area is creased by multiple fault lines where rock masses slide against each other and become fractured and deformed. Molten rock forced up from the bowels of the earth solidified on the surface as igneous

Lava has oxidised into red cliffs near Akrotiri, Santorini (Walk 33)

intrusions of hard, glittering granite and granodiorite, changing the country rock around them. Most of Naxos, Paros and Amorgos are made up of such metamorphic rocks changed by heat and pressure. Limestone recrystallised into marble; muds and shales turned into parallel-grained schists glittering with mica; granites and sandstones metamorphosed into banded gneiss.

VEGETATION AND WILDFLOWERS

'The riot of colour, scent and form which bursts from the landscapes of the eastern Mediterranean islands each spring is something that everyone with any interest in flowers should experience,' said botanist Fred Rumsey.

Paros, Naxos, and parts of Amorgos were forested with oak, juniper and cypress until the Venetians took control in early medieval times and used up the timber for ships to protect their Aegean territories and trade routes. Trees didn't regenerate on the steep, arid hillsides, where wind and winter rain scour away any thin layers of soil, and scrub became the dominant vegetation. On the islands, the rich diversity of the Greek flora is concentrated into a compact area. Their isolation also enabled endemic species to evolve and provided refuges for ancient plants lost elsewhere.

The predominant vegetation of the arid, rocky parts of the Cyclades is phrygana, the Greek version of the French *garigue*, and includes aromatic shrubs such as rosemary, lavender and thyme. Tough, bushy, and low-lying among bald rock with sand or thin soil, the shrubs have adopted survival strategies against summer drought (such as deep, anchoring tap roots), winds and grazing animals. Leaves are small, may be crinkled or needle-like to reduce surface exposure, and coated with sticky resin as in the rock roses (*Cistus*). Other surface finishes are tough and glossy as in the viciously spined buckthorn, felted as in sages, or scaly as in Phoenician juniper. Sweet-scented but spiny dwarf broom, spiny spurge and thorny burnet form rounded mounds to reduce wind damage and conserve moisture, and are armed against grazing animals. Poisonous milky sap deters animals from nibbling at the mounds of *Euphorbia dendroides*, which brings a tapestry of colour to mountain areas, from acid yellow through orange to coral, over the year.

Phrygana may merge into dense, dark-green thickets of maquis, bane of the path-clearer. Culprits include the determined *Pistacia lentiscus*, distasteful to animals because of its tannins but whose wood was used to make wheelbarrow parts and the cross-bars of lyres. The brooms, tree heather, box-like myrtle, and *Cistus* are its companions. Lower, sheltered or watered slopes may support full-grown trees, where the sturdy, bushy crowns of kermes oak (*Quercus coccifera*), host plant of the red-dye (cochineal)-producing scale insect, and evergreen maple form a counterpane of soft greens, and on drier, more exposed land are carob and olive.

Riverbeds wet and dry are marked by shocking pink and poisonous

Mountain colour palette, May, with Euphorbia dendroides *and* Phlomis

Mid-spring annuals – lupin, campion and margarita daisies

oleander, and higher, cooler spots by the oriental plane and maybe a valonia oak, hung with giant, spiky acorn cups and toffee-apple-like galls.

In the open ground of phrygana and mountain, flowering bulbs, rhizomes and corms, which serve as underground reservoirs, have an early spring show, with scatterings of anemone, and on sandy ground are the cream and yellow trumpets of *Romulea bulbocodium*, and dwarf iris. First autumn dewfall activates flowering, before leaves develop, of sea squill – spires of white florets on microphone stems – whose bulb juice raises blisters on human skin. Asphodel, said to have carpeted the floors of Hades, has similar big, naked bulbs but starry pale-pink or white flowers in spring. Chequered pink-mauve *Colchicum macrophyllum* stars on stony tracks, while in limestone crevices are pale rose-lilac *C. cupanii*, and butter-yellow *Sternbergia lutea*.

Orchids that have escaped goat-trample can be spotted among the phrygana in March–April, although the insect-mimicking *Ophrys* were very scarce following a recent, unusually wet winter. Most common are the pointed hoods of *Serapia*, the pink and white pyramid of the *Anacamptis lactiflora*, and muddy pink, late-flowering *Orchis*.

19

WALKING ON THE GREEK ISLANDS – THE CYCLADES

Cycladic wildflowers (clockwise seasonally) – Serapia *orchid, honeysuckle and* Cistus crispus, *dragon arum,* Colchicum autumnale

Annuals and perennials come into their own in meadows, groves and path-sides from March. Cream and gold crown daisies dashed with scarlet poppies, and cerise-pink gladioli, carpet fields in April and May.

Violet-blue lupins, margarita daisies or chamomile may colonise entire terraces or olive groves before ploughing, but can be swamped by acid-yellow *Oxalis pes-caprae*, introduced to the Mediterranean 200 years ago.

Country paths may have sudden scatterings of tiny, scented narcissus – there are early spring and autumn-flowering versions. In walls, look for the smallest of lilies, pearl-white *Lloydia graeca*, and from May, among the rocks, tiny, fringed pale-pink *Dianthus*, the flower of Zeus (*Dias*). Tall, top-heavy *Euphorbia characias*, its heads of acid-green leaf-bracts centred with tiny maroon flowers, leans over many a rocky way in early spring. Later, giant fennel reaches more than a metre high, its thick stems lined with a slow-burning pith in which Prometheus carried the gift of fire to humans. The erect and sinister, mottle-stemmed and maroon-spathed dragon arum smells of carrion to attract fly pollinators. By June, hillsides are brown and gold against summer-blue sky and sea, with spinning plate-heads of wild carrot and viciously prickly acanthus and thistles, such as the mauve-blue *Echinops* and spiky yellow-flowered Spanish oyster plant.

On the coast, sea stock, white-to-pale purple and sweetly scented, is first to spread over dunes and headlands. Later come tufts of trefoil-leaved sea medick, glossy yellow-horned poppies, sea lavender, and the starry, translucent white sea daffodil, *Pancratium maritimum*, whose charcoal-black seeds float to new destinations by sea.

A profusion of vibrant colour in the villages comes from hot-pink and scarlet pelargoniums, purple bougainvillea, powder-blue plumbago, flame-orange trumpet vines (*Campsis*), and brilliant-blue morning glory. The centre-piece and shade provider of a village square is often a stately *Platanos* (plane tree), or perhaps a mulberry, recalling a silk-worm industry, and in well-watered areas are citrus groves.

ANIMAL LIFE

Nice insects, such as butterflies, come with the flowers of spring and include pan-European species such as red admirals, peacocks, tortoiseshell and brimstones, with small blues in the marble mountains. Marbled Jersey tiger moths wallpaper damp streamside walls, conserving energy and moisture to extend their breeding season into the summer. High insect season starts in June, with grasshoppers breeding in ground-hopping millions, while spiders big and small sling webs across country paths and lurk in funnel webs in the shrubs. Grey/brown *Oedipa* grasshoppers flash red or blue hind wings on take-off. Big, blue-black and clumsy carpenter bees, potter wasps, and intimidating, 3cm-long (but not generally aggressive) oriental hornets fly around. Skinny and weird (but harmless) praying mantis stalk the phrygana in late summer.

Agama stelio, a North African species of lizard found on some Aegean islands

There are few snakes, and the only poisonous species is the rarely seen viper, like the adder of northern European heathlands. Lacertid wall lizards are common, but little house geckos are becoming less so with air-conditioning. The dinosaur-like, head-bobbing *Agama stelio* is the only African lizard to reach Europe, either transported on rafts of vegetation or a remnant from when the islands were joined up before sea levels rose. Terrapins and crabs swim in the freshwater streams and pools of Naxos, while various dragonfly species dart and helicopter above.

The range of habitats, from riverine, maritime to mountain, supports a variety of birds, many of them migratory, such as bee-eaters and hoopoes. White heron, little plovers and stilts visit the brackish seasonal meres on Naxos and Paros. Raptors include sleek Eleonora's falcon, which breeds in the Aegean mountains in summer and winters in Madagascar. Griffon vultures, with a wingspan of more than 2.5m, wheel above the mountain crags in loose groups, while smaller Bonelli's eagles are more likely to patrol in pairs.

CLIMATE

The islands' maritime environment modifies the classic Mediterranean climate of hot, dry summers and winter rain. They are exposed to prevailing northwesterly winds, refreshing at Beaufort 4–5, sand-whipping at Beaufort 6–7, and at force 9, ferries are cancelled. Rain that hits mainland Greece doesn't always move on to the islands, which are often dry from May to October. Winds from the south and west are usually gentler and more humid, bringing hazy skies, soft, heavy clouds, and

WHEN TO GO

sometimes red sand from Africa. From June to September skies are relentlessly blue and cloudless, with temperatures often above 30°C. The Meltemi wind, sucked from the north by low atmospheric pressure over Africa, funnels through the Aegean in July and August like a hairdryer set on high, but it does make the islands a few degrees cooler than Athens. The wind has usually abated by the end of August. In September and October the edge has gone from both heat and wind, but rain is more likely. While the islands have many days of sunshine from January to March, they can also be bleak, wet and chilly, with occasional snow.

WHEN TO GO

The classic Mediterranean climate hiking seasons of April, May, September and October apply, when the weather is usually sunny but not impossibly hot, although be prepared for occasional days of chilly winds and rainfall.

The winter months of November–March can have halcyon days of warmth and sunshine, and from February the profusion of early spring flowers is enchanting. But daylight hours are short, and there's nothing as cold and bleak as a Cycladic mountain village on an overcast windy day, when heavy rainstorms propel cascades of water down

Island villages seem deserted in winter, but tavernas in Koronos, Naxos, are open all year

WALKING ON THE GREEK ISLANDS – THE CYCLADES

steep-stepped alleys and mountain paths, and snow is not uncommon. Local transport runs on skeleton schedules and routes; shops, museums, sites, rooms and most tavernas, especially in the villages, are closed – apart for the weekend 40 days before Easter, when everyone comes out of the woodwork for *Carnivale*, to socialise, dance and feast before the Lenten fast.

April brings more sunshine and the first swim of the year for the bold, but can still turn a chill breeze and rainstorm. Annuals and perennials flood the land with colour. Enthusiastic spring growth makes country trails harder to spot, and those that double as stream-beds may be waterlogged after heavy or unusually persistent rain. May is usually sunny and warm, and aromatic shrubs are in bloom. In June, mid-summer drought locks in and much of the natural world, apart from insects, goes into aestivation. The only advantages of July and August are that cultural sites, seasonal shops, rooms and tavernas are open, and bus services more frequent and wider-ranging. Otherwise, the islands are too hot, crowded, expensive, windy, and beaten by fierce sun in an unrelenting blue sky. For the still blue of the Aegean autumn, when the weather is gentle and the sea warm, go in September and October, when autumn bulbs bloom and paths are at their clearest.

TRAVEL TO THE ISLANDS

Flights

Fly to Athens International Airport (official name Eleutherios Venizelos, AIA) and take a ferry to any of the islands. From 1 May to mid October there are international flights (with easyJet and Aegean Airlines) to Santorini and Mykonos, with shorter ferry transfers to your destination island.

Domestic flights operate from Athens airport to Paros (35min), Naxos (45min) and Santorini (45min). They may be cancelled in heavy rain, but usually operate in strong winds. Amorgos does not have an airport. If there are cancellations or delays due to weather or strikes, the airport or travel agent will usually transfer your ticket. See Appendix D for airport and port authority contact details.

Airport to ferry

Catch the X96 bus from the stop outside the Athens airport terminal to Piraeus port (www.athensairportbus.com/en; allow 1½hr). Alternatively there's the metro (details on the same website; 6.30–12.30am, 1hr), or taxi. The latter will cost at least €50 day rate and still take an hour in heavy traffic.

Ferries

Blue Star ferries from Piraeus balance reliability, stability, reasonable comfort and price, and take 4¼hr to Paros, 5¼hr to Naxos, and 7¾hr to Amorgos (with arrival and departure times at ungodly hours of the night) and Santorini. Superfast and Seajet hydrofoil ferries are faster (for example, 3½hr to Naxos) but more expensive and susceptible to bumpy conditions or to cancellation in high winds. These and other ferries serve all the islands; see www.gtp.gr and enter departure and arrival port to see available services, bearing in mind that schedules change with the seasons and are often unavailable until a couple of months ahead. See also Appendix D for ferry company websites.

Do check national holidays (try https://publicholidays.gr), when you need to book as far in advance as possible – especially at Orthodox Easter (which falls on a different date from the Western Church) and general elections, when many Greeks return to their home island. The first trips following a strike, by air or by sea, are crammed to the gunnels. Otherwise, until mid June, you can buy ferry tickets before departure at the port. Allow at least 30min to buy tickets, or to get a picnic salad and *souvlaki* (grilled meat pieces on a stick) from a portside takeaway, although there is fast food for sale onboard.

Island-hopping
Blue Star has year-round ferry services visiting Piraeus–Paros–Naxos–Santorini and/or Amorgos, although winter sailings are much reduced.

Ferries and cruise ships sail into Santorini year-round

Schedules are published some months in advance; see www.bluestarferries.com. There are also Hellenic Seaways, Seajets and the faithful all-weather 'Express Skopelitis' that plies daily between Naxos and Amorgos, and takes 5 hours. Websites can be found in Appendix D. The closer to the unfashionable edges of season, the fewer services there are.

TRAVEL AROUND THE ISLANDS

Buses
Each island has a bus service – reasonably reliable and efficient on Paros and Santorini, less so on Naxos and Amorgos – but not necessarily at the times or to the places you want to go. The services fan out from terminals in the main town/port to villages and resorts, most frequently and to the widest range of destinations in June–September inclusive. Schedules change once a month, or weekly in low season. Print out a timetable from the websites or pick one up from the terminal at the beginning of your holiday. The buses do not always run on time, especially during the summer. You can buy tickets in advance from the terminal, a kiosk or mini-market nearby, or from the driver, but make sure you have small change.

Most of the walks in this guide begin and end near a bus stop or are on a bus route, but drivers do stop en route if they see you signalling. See Appendix D for contact details for buses on each of the islands.

Hitchhiking
Hitching is acceptable and safe; old men and women from the villages do it. Timing is crucial. From May to the end of September, 2–6pm is siesta time and your main hope for a lift is from a tourist. In low season, just before dusk is the optimum chance of a ride from farmers returning from bedding down/milking/feeding animals.

Car hire
Check internet sites to compare car hire companies. Some, such as www.naxosway.gr and www.santorini-car-rental.info, will bring a car to the port or airport when you arrive, and you can leave it there on departure.

Taxis
Taxis operate from the main town, port(s) and airport on each island, so transfers from a distant village will be expensive. Each island has a central taxi call centre telephone number – see Appendix D for contact details.

ACCOMMODATION

Ferry passengers are greeted on disembarkation with a forest of signs for 'rooms' and 'studios' – the most economical and widespread accommodation, usually with en-suite shower and loo, fridge and electric hob. Many hotels are very reasonably priced in the shoulder seasons, include breakfast, and may offer transfer services to hikers. From mid October to the end of April accommodation is only generally available in the main towns, and even then is limited. It's best to check what's seasonally available on the internet, for example on www.booking.com or airbnb.com. In this guide, accommodation is only suggested in remote villages, where it is a rare commodity.

Campsites tend to be near the main beach resorts; just search 'campsites' along with the island's name online to see what's available. Wild camping is likely to incur the wrath of local property owners and contravene national law.

EATING AND DRINKING

On Naxos especially, local fresh vegetables are plentiful and cheap. Greek salad (*choriatiki*) with tomatoes, peppers, onion, cucumber and olives is ubiquitous.

Chips are often offered as a starter, so if you want them with your main course, ask! Portions are large – consider sharing. *Moscari* translates as veal or beef, but is something between the two. Fresh fish is expensive due to over-fishing, and is often priced per kilo. Fresh *kalamari* (squid) season is roughly November to March. Wine is ordered by the kilo, *misokilo* (half-litre) or *tetarto* (quarter-litre), not in litres. From Easter and in fine weather, tavernas are open at least from lunchtime (1pm) until 11pm.

SHOPPING AND SERVICES

Shops are open Tuesdays and Fridays 8.30am–3pm and 6–9pm. Other days (apart from Sunday, when closed), they're open 8.30am–3pm/5pm. Main supermarkets are open Monday–Saturday daily through to 9pm, and Sundays 10am–3pm from May to the end of September. Petrol stations on the main roads are usually open

Greek salad for one – portions tend to be big

Naxos shop, Tsiblakis, selling local (and some imported) products (Walk 10)

daily. Banks are open Monday–Friday 8.30am–1.30pm. There are ATMs in the main towns of each island, and maybe a couple of the larger inland villages. It's as well to carry cash, as many tavernas and shops still do not accept card payments.

A 'tourist information' office is invariably a commercial travel agency serving its selected tours and hotels. The municipality website for each island contains some useful information – see Appendix D, which also includes contact details for local medical centres.

WHAT TO TAKE

The following recommendations to carry in a day-pack take into account terrain and climate:
- Lightweight hiking boots with ankle support and thick soles; waterproof boots in early spring. Walking sandals or trainers are inadequate
- Trousers with detachable lower legs, for shorts and thorny scrub protection
- Lightweight layers, from sweatshirt to fleece
- Lightweight waterproof/umbrella in shoulder seasons
- Swimming gear and flip-flops if there's a river or beach en route
- Cover-up clothing for sun protection on exposed stretches, and for monastery visits
- Minimum 1L water, in refillable bottles or 'camel'
- Nourishing snacks (the Greeks do a good line in *pasteli*, nut/seed bars)
- Sunblock, sun hat, sunglasses
- First aid pack, including blister plasters (heat, sweat and downhills challenge the toughest of feet), sting/bite treatment

and insect repellent for summer evenings
- Walking pole(s) – not just for precipitous, uneven down-slopes but vital for cross-path spider webs, vegetation and unfriendly dogs
- Multi-tool with pliers, for excessively wired fence-gates
- Mobile phone and emergency/useful contacts, plus charger if you're using GPS
- Maps
- Compass
- Cash for public transport, taxis, tavernas and entrance fees

USING THIS GUIDE

Essential information – start/finish point, distance, ascent/descent, walking time, type of terrain, transport options – is given in the route summary at the beginning of each walk. Walking times are based on a pace of 3km/hour – because walking in Greece seems to take longer than on tame, temperate European paths – and they exclude stops, rests, picnics, sightseeing and detours. Check all of the walk's statistics and add on at least an hour for every three for negotiating fence-gates, admiring scenery, flowers and sights, retracing steps and so

Apano Kastro bastion commands the inland vale of Naxos (Walk 21)

WALKING ON THE GREEK ISLANDS – THE CYCLADES

on. Some detours are included in the total time because they are the main point of the walk but don't fit into a circular route.

Route maps are provided but it is useful to carry a detailed walking map with you for an overview of the route and terrain. Anavasi 1:40,000 (www.anavasi.gr) maps of the individual islands are the most detailed and reliable, and can be ordered online in printed or digital form. They are usually stocked in principal island book/tourist shops.

On the walks, signage varies from large boards with no orientation, scale or useful information – used for shotgun target practice – to engraved wooden signs (which may appear at the start of a route and never again), and small red-and-white plaques with route numbers. The numbered routes are also marked on Anavasi maps, and are reasonably consistent and useful on accessible, well-trodden trails on Naxos, Paros and Amorgos. In remote areas, however, and on Santorini (where local landowners removed many plaques), signs may be lacking at critical points.

Greek place names are confusing, as signs for places and sites may have both Greek and Roman spellings, but the latter can vary considerably. This is further complicated by a village or mountain being known by more than one name, such as the village of Tripodes/Vivlos on Naxos. (See the glossary in Appendix B for Greek words and phrases that may be useful for directions and map-reading.) In

Signs like this often lack follow-through at the next junction (Walk 21)

Traditional working paths can be rough going (Walk 17)

the route descriptions, if a signpost is a useful waymark the characters have been replicated, whether Greek or English, as written on the sign.

Monopati is a single, often traditional footpath, which might be paved or cobbled and/or between walls. *Kalderimi* is a slightly wider, paved mule track. A trail tends to be narrow, earthen, and sometimes frayed into several alternatives by the passage of animals. Keep an eye on the way ahead to check the course of the route, especially on sharp corners or at vegetation takeover. If the way is obscured, look ahead for the next clear bit and aim for it. If all else fails, in open scrub or on rocky heights, follow the stained trails and droppings of sheep and goats. Over the last decade, old ways have been reopened, signed and numbered, thanks to waymarking hero Tassos Anastasiou and local walking groups such as Walking Plus and Santorini Walking Tours, but keeping them maintained is a perennial challenge.

Do not be led astray by waymarks, cairns and paint splodges, as they may relate to a completely different route. Always follow the directions in the guide first, and use other signs only for reassurance (if in agreement), or if noted in the text.

Most walks are a mixture of levels, with long stretches of clear country path or dirt track, and a short section of steep, uneven and/or thickly vegetated ground. Do read the terrain summary at the start of the walk. Particularly challenging paths have bail-out options.

Distances between points are only given if necessary – to alert you

Deep enough to swim in, with freshwater crabs and terrapins (Walk 19)

to a sudden turn, for example. Don't panic if there's a long period or distance between directions; it means there's nothing to report and the way ahead is obvious. Use the text in conjunction with the route map for changes of direction. Significant features that are marked on the route maps are highlighted in **bold** in the text.

Things can change on the ground over time; on occasion a fence-gate may be mentioned in the text but no longer in existence, or one may appear that isn't mentioned. To open a fence-gate, go for the side with the fewest wire fastenings, a hook or piece of rope (if you're lucky) and re-fasten. If you do need to use pliers or wire cutters – local farmers may erect excessive barriers on official way-marked paths – secure afterwards, though perhaps to a lesser extent.

Altitudes and distances are given in metric. Abbreviations used are L(eft) and R(ight), and N, S, E and W for compass directions.

GPX tracks

GPX tracks for the routes in this guidebook are available to download free at www.cicerone.co.uk/1009/GPX. A GPS device and app such as www.viewranger.com are useful aids to navigation, but you should also carry a map and compass and know how to use them. GPX files are provided in good faith, but neither the author nor the publisher accept responsibility for their accuracy.

PAROS

A hiker at one of Paros' many isolated monasteries (Walk 9)

Walking on the Greek Islands – the Cyclades

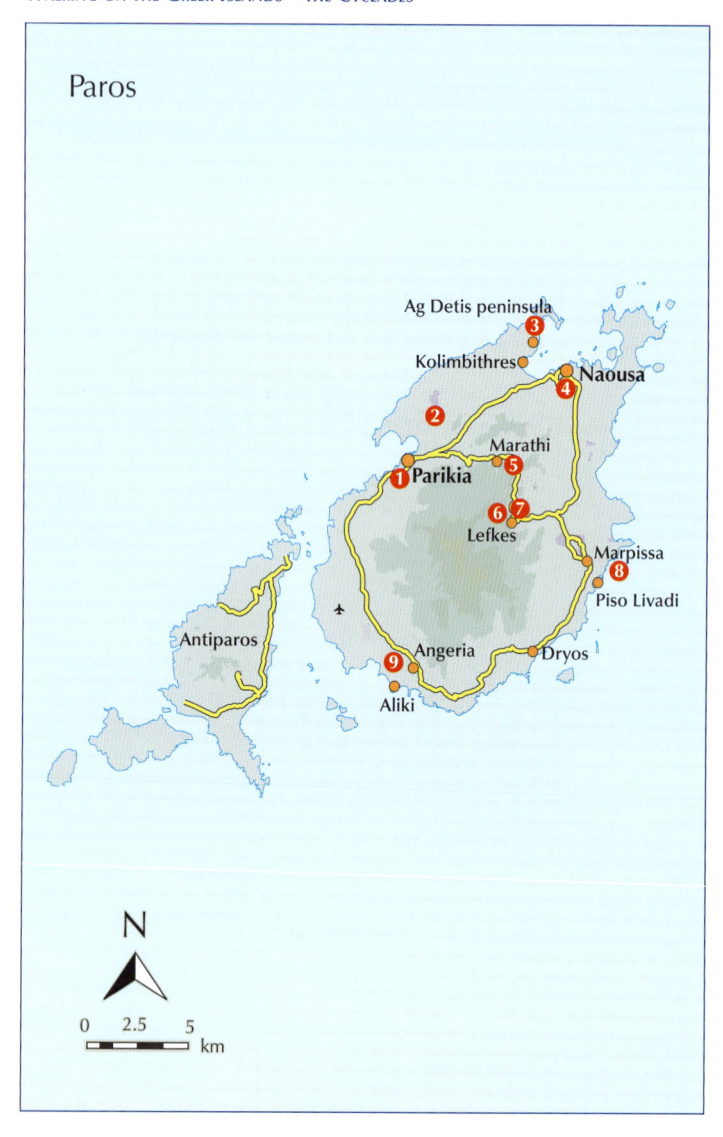

Paros

Paros is the geographical heart of the Cyclades. It is smaller (21 x 16km) and more cosmopolitan, cultural and crowded than its closest neighbour Naxos, 8km to the east, but still has wild places, hidden valleys and some of the finest examples of paved Byzantine 'ways'. The massif at its core rises to 765m and falls away to a near all-round border of coastal plains, although the northwest is a craggy world of its own. The island has the particular asset of having three big, sheltered bays – at the main port and town of Parikia in the west, Naousa in the north, and Molos on the east coast. Its marble and granite highlands were deforested by humans and their over-grazing animals, and soil washed onto the plains, enriching the main areas of cultivation that still exist today. Main products are olives – first seriously cultivated by the occupying Venetians – and wine.

The island's most prosperous period came when the rest of Greece was emerging from the Dark Age, when Parian trade links with the Phoenicians led to practically all Aegean trade flowing through its harbours by 800BC. Piracy and trading of captives as slaves followed, with Paros as a major centre. Colonisation of north Aegean lands rich in gold and silver, and exploitation of its own translucent white marble, made the island, for a time, the wealthiest in the Cyclades. Parian marble was said to be the finest in the world and was used by the leading sculptors of ancient Greece. The population was estimated at this time to be at around 12,000 free citizens (that is, excluding women, children and slaves). Today it is about 14,000 in total. There have been times in Pariot history, though, when the island has been all but deserted. Islanders were slaughtered wholesale by Slavs in AD675, recorded as being completely depopulated in AD1000, and again in the 16th century, after the Ottoman conquest.

Today, Parikia and Naousa are the island's most populous centres, although there are all-season shops and services at Aliki (in the south), and Marpissa (in the east). Bus routes go from the main terminal at Parikia, north and south along the main road that circuits the island, and cut across the centre via the former inland capital of Lefkes.

WALKING ON THE GREEK ISLANDS – THE CYCLADES

WALK 1
Parikia town to Cape Fokas

Start	Asklepion site entrance
Finish	Krios Beach
Distance	9km
Ascent	160m
Descent	170m
Time	3hr
Terrain	Paved alleys, beaches, easy coastal trails and dirt roads
Refreshments	Parikia town, seasonal tavernas along the coast to Krios
Transport	Water taxi, Marcello Beach and Krios to Parikia port, mid May–mid October

Practically every key moment in the island's history is represented on this circuit of wide Parikia Bay. Starting from an atmospheric ancient sanctuary, you thread through Parikia's old town via one of the Aegean's most significant and gracious churches, and an archaeological museum that will enrich your understanding of the island's history and sites. After a cultural morning (if you want to visit the museum) you stroll along the shore to a string of sandy bays and a low, rocky finger of cape, looking back to the port against its mountain backdrop.

The fourth-century BC **Asklepion** Sanctuary is unlikely to be officially open, so go to the ruin at the corner L of the entrance, and turn R. Take the first R and go past the hotel entrance, go up the *monopati* (footpath). Above the swimming pool, climb over the wall and cross to a miniature temple in the style of a Hellenistic mausoleum perching on a cliff-edge.

This is the uppermost level of the **Asklepion site**, where the earliest, archaic traces of a healing sanctuary to Apollo lie embedded in the ground. Apollo, for whom healing was just one of many items in

WALK 1 – PARIKIA TOWN TO CAPE FOKAS

Mausoleum-style building overlooking temple remains, Asklepion

his job description, was the father of Asklepios, god of healing and medicine. The Sanctuary was sufficiently out of town to provide isolation from infectious diseases, and water from springs. On the lower terrace, column bases remain of a Doric colonnade that supported the building where rituals invoked the god's healing powers.

From the little temple take the trail N and down to buildings, then turn L along the foot of the cliff past the marble spring basins. Drop to the colonnade and go L to and around the gate at the far end of the site. Turn R,

Walking on the Greek Islands – the Cyclades

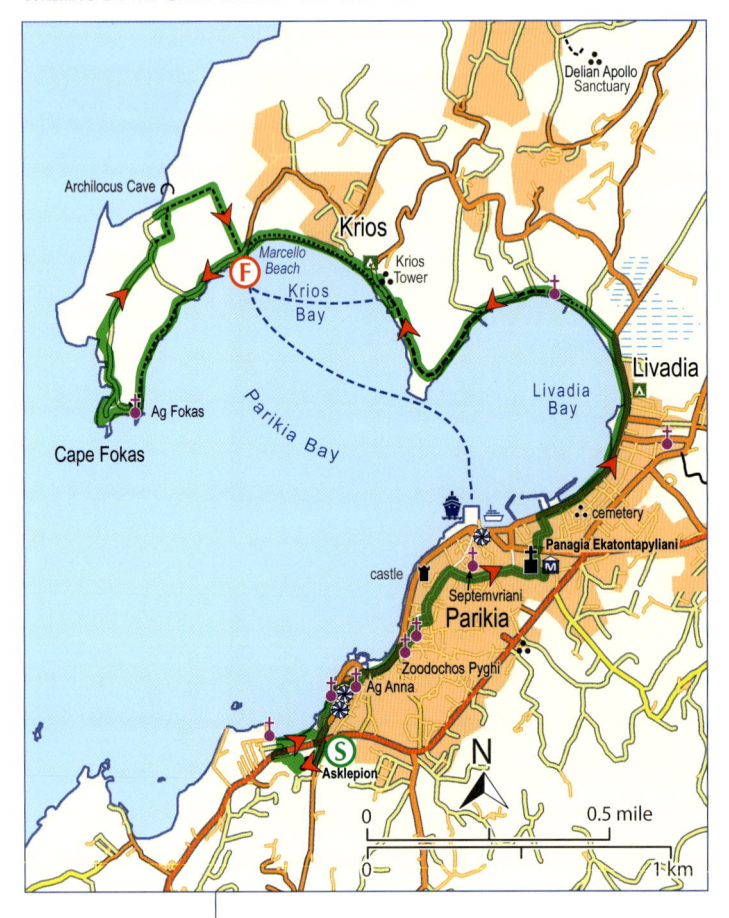

cross the road, go L down wide steps at the restaurant to reach the shore path, and turn R. Continue to a pine-wooded slope, go up to the road and turn L and immediately L again, past hotels to reach a paved cliff-top path.

Follow the path's rollercoaster way beneath council offices and a well-buffed Parian marble sculpture of an elongated head, to reach a road. Bear R and R again up

WALK 1 – PARIKIA TOWN TO CAPE FOKAS

steps through paved gardens around the tiny chapel of **Ag Anna**, encased almost entirely in recycled Parian marble. Back on the road at a bend, cross to a wide path, go down to a little marina and turn R along the seafront.

Cross to a marble-paved courtyard in front of the triple-blue-domed **Zoodochos Pyghi** (Virgin of the life-giving spring) church. Take the alley L of the entrance and wiggle R–L through the town, over a *plateia* (square) with a centrepiece of a boat's prow. When you see ahead a peeling ochre house with rooftop balustrade, turn R at the corner before it, then take the first L, soon coming to a dumpy chapel and a marble fountain. ▶

Continue to the next R–L kink under an arch, where embedded in the wall is the Taxiarchos church, which may be open for a peep inside at richly painted screens and an intense Orthodox atmosphere. Go L just before the arcaded building and R up stepped Odysseus Eliti street, named for a 20th-century Greek poet who loved Paros and its fountains (the second of which is at the foot of the steps), to the remains of the **'Frankish Castle'** – a liquorice-allsort construction of architectural salvage occupying the former site of a 525BC temple to Athena, many of whose

This is one of three fountains donated in 1777 by Paros-born Nikolaos Mavrogenis, who thrived under the Turks but later lost favour and was beheaded. His granddaughter, Manto, was a heroine of the Greek War of Independence.

Over Parikia Bay to Cape Fokas, giant fennel and oxalis

marble column fragments, cornices and beams can be seen in the 1260 tower and surrounding churches.

Return to the (probably 16th-century) arcaded building, which has Grotesque bas-relief male and female figures clutching their stomachs on its end columns. Go L to the junction and turn R into Gravari Street, past the colourful neoclassical Centre for Southern Aegean Fine Art, the twin-belled church of **Septemvriani** with marble salvage inside and out (key with the chemist, opposite), and the third Mavrogenis fountain. Go between Distrato café and shop, straight up and over a bridged alley, and along Manto Mavrogenous to the white block of **Panagia Ekatontapyliani** church.

> **Ekatontapyliani** (of the 100 gates, for its arcaded features) church is also known as Katapoliani (of the lower town), or simply Panagia (Our Lady). It is architecturally remarkable for a remote island church, and for being built by direct command of Byzantine emperors. The oldest part, the symmetrical, vaulted baptistery, is one of the earliest Christian buildings to have survived almost intact – for some 1700 years. The original church was founded around AD313 and expanded at the request of Emperor Constantine's mother, Helen, who had been shipwrecked and given sanctuary on Paros en route to the Holy Land. Most of today's building was added some 200 years later.

Go up the lane R of Ekatontapyliani to the **archaeological museum** (open 8am–3.30pm, closed Tuesdays).

> **Museum highlights** include a bas-relief of a symposium depicting the seventh-century Parian poet Archilochos (whose cave you will pass later on), the earliest examples of *kouroi* (monumental marble statues of idealised youths), and a headless but huge statue of the goddess Artemis from the Delian Temple (on Walk 2). Most exciting is a fragment of inscribed marble known as the Parian Chronicle,

which contained the only known written reference in antiquity to the epic poet Homer, as well as a catalogue of events including the Trojan War.

From the museum, go through the pine tree park to a gap in the wall, cross the road and turn L, then R and L again to reach the seafront. ▶ Turn R, and in the next block, behind railings, is a **cemetery** that served a large community for 1100 years from the eighth century BC, and included a *polyandrion* (of many men) tomb with funerary vases containing the washed bones of 200 men, probably soldiers.

Continue along the seafront, then taverna-backed strands. At the far end of **Livadia Bay** join a pleasant shoreline path and look back to the port with the white slice of the Anargyroii (saints without money) monastery wedged into the mountain. Cut across a headland of rock and wild scrub and just before the first house, drop down wide steps and turn R. Almost immediately, just before a road forks R, look R to a dirt slope, at the top of which is a long, windowless mystery building, its curved apse set abruptly into the rocky hillside.

Marble font for total immersion baptism, Katapoliani Church

This was where Minoans from Crete, the island's first colonists, established their port.

Ag Fokas church commands the entrance to Parikia Bay

No-one is quite sure what the **Krios tower** was used for, as there are no characteristics of a temple or church, or when it was built. Art historian Nigel McGilchrist says its construction suggests third century AD (although the marble ledge in the semi-circular apse is recycled from a fourth-century BC civic building) and it may have been used for storage or as an arsenal.

Walk the curve of **Krios Bay** to the jetty at **Marcello Beach**, another summer ferry stop, and join the sandy road. After two small beaches turn L onto the coastal trail to the dapper church of **Ag Fokas** and then the ruins of an 1867 lighthouse.

Head R to the main dirt road above a sea-bitten headland, then straight up past a large end-of-island property. Keep L past the entrance to another isolated house along the now stony track, then turn towards the cliff. ◄ Follow the clearly defined cliff-top trail NE to a junction, then turn R and follow the wall and track back down to **Marcello Beach** and turn L to **Krios**. May to mid October you can catch a water taxi from either; otherwise phone for a taxi or retrace your steps along the seafront to Parikia.

Go L towards the property boundary to look down the broken cliffs to the cave of Archilocus, named for the Paros-born pioneering lyric poet of the seventh century BC.

WALK 2
Northwest coast to Kolimbithres

Start	Delian Apollo Sanctuary
Finish	Kolimbithres
Distance	10km
Ascent	240m
Descent	360m
Time	4hr
Terrain	Exposed, wild and windy, with long stretches of dirt track, and rough cross-country trails among low, spiny shrubs
Refreshments	Kolimbithres
Transport	Parikia–Kolimbithres bus, summer only. Year-round Parikia–Naousa bus stops at the junction with the main road 1.8km SE of Kolimbithres along the bay. Alternatively, take two vehicles to Kolimbithres and return in one of them to the start, or use taxis.

The high ridge of the northwest coast drops down steep, ragged cliffs to an infinity of sea. It is wild, exposed country, with wind-carved rocks, a regiment of wind turbines, and an ancient acropolis on a granite tor. Inland, you look down to a wide vale that cuts a swathe northeast–southwest between mountain ridges from one big bite of bay to another, at Parikia.

From the stony footpath leading up to the **Delian Apollo Sanctuary**, go ENE along the dirt track.

> There's a direct sightline north from this platform of jumbled rock to the island of Delos, the spiritual heart of the cult of **Apollo**, god of music and healing. The god was worshipped here from the ninth century BC, with ritual dancing on a paved path around a rock altar. Later, in the fifth century BC, it was dedicated to Apollo's sister Artemis and became the

Walking on the Greek Islands – the Cyclades

Walk 2 – Northwest coast to Kolimbithres

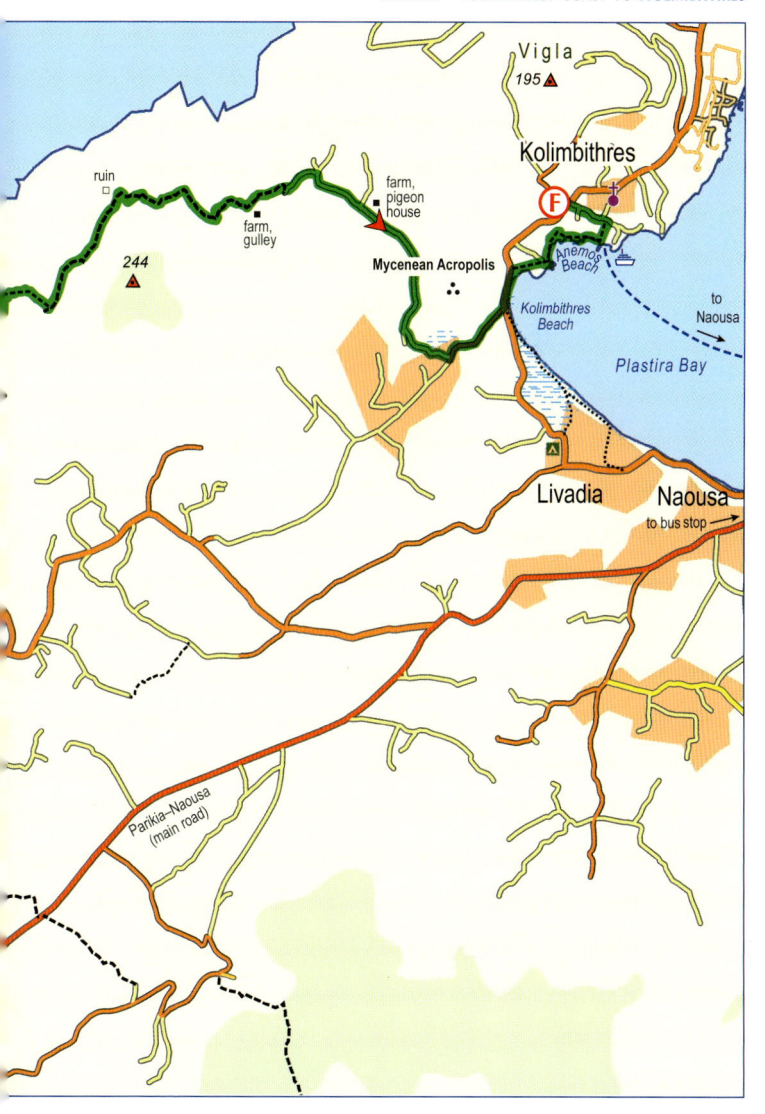

island's second most important sanctuary. It was a neat, square temple with a façade of Doric columns at the southwest corner of the site, but the most obvious remains are rows of rectangular marble blocks. The altar was at the east end, and a building for feasting, with marble benches and a portico, just to the south. Steps lead to a level area where worshippers watched for a light from Delos, the sign to ignite their own beacon and launch the annual festivities.

Keep L on the main track, passing a dumping area shaded by a weeping mimosa tree. Keep R at two forks with other dirt roads, heading E then NE on the main track and keeping straight ahead at R turnoffs. ◂ Beyond an immaculately cemented stone wall enclosing a **property** with an ornamental dove house and a personal chapel, look ENE, to Naousa. At the T-junction turn R downhill to reach an asphalt lane and go L up through the hamlet of **Kalami** – up to the L are authentic pigeon houses.

At the next T-junction, signposted 'Χοχλακας', turn L past a smart property, then R onto a dirt track opposite scruffy **farm** buildings. Continue for some 1.6km, past a large house and keeping L at a fork, to reach a small **chapel** crouched in the scything shadows of the **wind turbines**. ◂ Turn L, joining a gravel road and passing a small power-house up R. Round a corner to see a working **quarry** opposite and continue down until, just before

Below is a wide trough of productive farmland, which in the 19th century was fever-ridden marsh.

From the 20th-century chapel of Ag Ioannis you get a sense of Paros as the geographical heart of the Cyclades, with Naxos E, Mykonos NE, Syros NW, and Serifos NNW.

Remote farmstead with working pigeon house

WALK 2 – NORTHWEST COAST TO KOLIMBITHRES

a paved platform over a spring, you turn sharp back L onto an earthen track along the valley.

At the fork go R up a brown rock track, and then L through a fence-gate into a field. Keep R and go up to cross over a fence-gate onto a wide, walled path and turn L. Beyond the next fence-gate the route diminishes to animal trails, veering R at an animal shelter beneath a sloping rock. Descend past layered rock outcrops, following a discernible but overgrown path that dissolves into old terraces beneath a **ruin**, which you aim to the R of. Beyond, go through the space between rock and wall, turn sharp R up through another gap, then L alongside the seaward wall, crossing it at one point, to its end. Climb over the loose facing wall and head up R along a clear but rough path around spurs. ▸

After cornering R, look L immediately for cairns at the start of a track leading obliquely down the valley side. Cut down towards a path you see ahead below a rocky outcrop, and turn L onto it at a cairn. There's now a straightforward trail to a wire fence, and a R turn down to an inviting gap in the wall, which you do not go through, but turn L along a stony field and through a grey metal gate.

Pass a **farm** (R) and at the end of its low wall go through a **gulley** of slabbed pink rock to reach the track

View to the north tip of Paros

A prospect opens of scattered farm buildings, Plastira Bay, Naousa and Naxos.

below. Turn R through the gap in the wall, L through the gate, and L again along a lane bordering the marshy course of an upland stream. Go through the double gate at the end and turn R along a lane, past a **farm** with a **pigeon house**. At the next fork, keep L downhill to reach a T-junction and turn L to the coast.

MYCENEAN ACROPOLIS

A grassy path leads off L past a brown sign for this site, known as Koukounaries, which means pine kernels – suggesting there were once more trees here. The ascent is unclear but the rocks are easy to scramble over. There are great views but a confusing jumble of foundations. An outer defensive wall of polygonal blocks demonstrates Mycenean construction skills. Rectangular blocks on a flattish area near the summit were the bases of connected buildings, including storerooms.

The upheaval of weather-worn granite at Koukounaries was a prime location for the Myceneans. The acropolis is not high, but it is protected by a deep cleft to the north and commands the fertile coast and valley, and sea – ideal for a seafaring civilisation whose ships reached as far as Egypt and the Baltic Sea. Some 3300 years ago the Myceneans established the first important civilisation on the Greek mainland by a mix of aggression, conquest and trade. Their empire was made up of several small kingdoms with fortified citadels like this one. The Myceneans came to Paros in the 12th century BC and, according to some, left less than 100 years later. Ash in the former storage rooms suggest fire was involved. The whole Mycenean civilisation was crumbling, plagued by earthquakes, wars, and economic recession. Koukounaries did not become a sought-after piece of real estate again until the late Geometric period, when Paros as a whole was prosperous.

Follow the road L to Kolimbithres for tavernas and the bus, or go along the beach, through the sailing centre and around a little headland to **Anemos Beach**. From the beach, cut inland up a rocky gulley and look R for a low route over the boulders to the next bay. Repeat this boulder and bay pattern until you reach the Kolimbithres Beach jetty, a stop for the Naousa ferry (mid May to end of September). Turn L up a trail to the dirt road, which leads L to the road into **Kolimbithres**.

WALK 3
Northwest peninsula eco-park

Start/Finish	Boatyard, Ag Ioannis Detis
Distance	6.5km
Ascent/Descent	190m
Time	2¼hr
Terrain	Mostly clear trails over undulating, rocky ground with low scrub
Refreshments	Seasonal taverna, Monastiri Beach
Transport	Summer-only: bus service between Parikia and Kolimbithres, 1.2km south of boatyard, and ferry between monastery and Naousa

It is tempting to dismiss the gnarled jumble of rock at the northwest tip of Paros as too small and tame for a proper walk. In fact there's an astonishing diversity of interest condensed into the 80ha Ag Ioannis Detis peninsula, including a turbulence of metamorphic rocks, wave-cut inlets and sheltered bays, lowland heath and pockets of marshland, plus a dash of military history. The peninsula was made a protected 'eco-park' in 2009, and thanks to an annual programme of planting, a landscape once denuded by overgrazing now has a wonderful diversity of native flora, with goats and sheep banned.

At the end of the Ag Ioannis Detis **boatyard** turn L up a sandy track through low-growing maritime scrub. Fork L where you can, along a narrow, stone-lined path that rounds the headland. Wind down via a rock outcrop, a stone footbridge, a hooded rock, and a paved circle with stepped seating. At the signposted turnings go L, then meet a junction where the route goes R but there's a signed option L for a short detour to the **'rock park'**. ▶

Descend R to a shallow trough of land crossed with dirt tracks and follow lighthouse signs L, around cut-out wedges of inlets. Divert L at the next junction, up

It's hardly park status but has cliff falls of different metamorphic rock, compressed and contorted layers of schists, mica minerals and banded gneiss.

The calm of an autumn evening in Ag Ioannis Bay

Plastira Bay gave its name to a key archaeological period in the Early Cycladic period, after a 3200BC cemetery was excavated on its shores.

Geologists found shards of obsidian here – possible indications of a Neolithic arrow-making site.

to the **lighthouse**, which was built in 1887 by French mechanics.

Return to the start of the lighthouse diversion and head SE uphill, keeping R at the first fork and then L at the fork with double poles. Look ahead for the line of path with big stones, and at a sign for Κορυφυ Βουναλιτης Στερνας turn L for Detis peak. Turn L at the first crest, L around a high point, then follow 'red 7' and an arrow on a trail that hugs the rocks then goes R up a surprise wedge of marshland. The final climb, over the pitted rocks R to the summit of **Detis**, is not clear.

Back on the col beneath the summit, go S towards Plastira Bay, heading as directly as possible among the confusion of trails for the tiny beach and stone jetty of **Perikoptera**. ◄ You may pass a stone-lined pit with vitrified lower levels indicating its use a lime kiln.

From Perikoptera, go SE towards the low-lying tail of the peninsula, across a barren neck of land. ◄ At the start of the narrow curve of **Turkou Ammos** (Turks' sand), go L inland for a clockwise circuit of the headland, where marble is now the bedrock. Look across to the peak of Mount Zas on Naxos, the highest point in the Cyclades. At a signpost, fork R and follow the red-earth-stained trail around **Cape Tourkos**, site of a Russian naval yard, and perhaps nip off-piste at a sign directing you to the Russian **gun battery**.

WALK 3 – NORTHWEST PENINSULA ECO-PARK

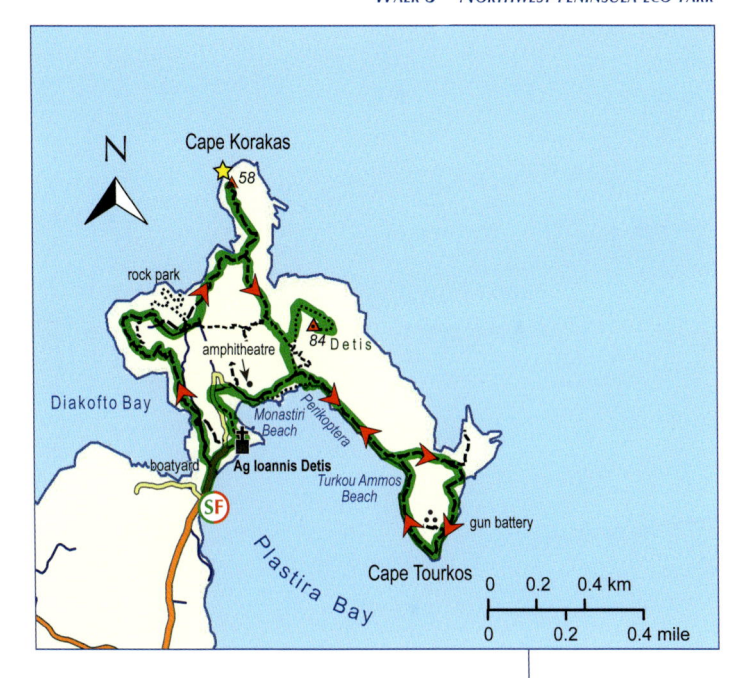

From 1770 to 1775 the **Archipelago Squadron of the Russian Navy** used Naousa Bay as a base in the second Turko-Russian War. At one time there were 42 ships, most of them anchored off this peninsula. Catherine the Great, Empress of Russia promised permanent liberation from the Turks in return for co-operation from the Greeks.

The path, bordered by pungent pincushions of soft grey, feathery leaved cottonweed, returns to **Turkou Ammos** and **Perikoptera** beaches, then continues along the shore to the monastery. Just before the beach, swing up R to the **amphitheatre**, go L beyond it to the car park and L down to the beach. At the far end take the path R, branch L through a blue gate to the **monastery** and then return along the road to the **boatyard**.

Looking over Perikoptera Beach and Plastira Bay to Naousa

Old maps show a church to St John on the **monastery** site in 1530, but today's building dates from 1806. The name Detis comes from the Greek to tie or to heal – which may refer to the sheltered anchorage it overlooks, or perhaps because it was a refuge for malaria sufferers in the 18th and 19th centuries. In the former monks' cells, a permanent exhibition of maps and storyboards illustrates the Turko-Russian War (open 10.30am–3pm except Mondays).

WALK 4
Naousa port, inland to marble mines

Start	Supermarket, Naousa
Finish	Bus stop, Marathi
Distance	9.5km
Ascent	325m
Descent	180m
Time	3½hr
Terrain	Steep rise up country lanes to maquis-covered hills, a rough dry riverbed, paths and dirt roads in an agricultural vale
Refreshments	Naousa, and seasonal tavernas and small store at Marathi
Transport	Parikia–Naousa bus route via Marathi

You could begin by wandering round Naousa, an attractive, arty resort and port with the largest fishing fleet in the Cyclades, then take the road about 1km south to the start. A climb is rewarded by a widening view across the water to Naxos. After a beautiful wild section, where folds of land fall to the east coast, you go inland to a broad agricultural valley framed by *garigue* hills. The cultural climax is a thrilling flashback of ancient history concealed in a cliff face, where the finest Parian marble was quarried.

Take the lane leading S beside the supermarket and follow its sage-scented way beside a river course. Keep L where the road turns R, then shortly L again onto a sandy track. At a major cross-tracks, go straight ahead and up. Pass a concrete road leading R and take the next fork R, by an exposed bank of rusty coloured rock, then fork L onto a dirt track. Below and to the L is a rather plain monastery – **Ag Antonios** – founded in the 1970s by the daughter of a wealthy family, who changed her name to Antonia and lived there until her death.

Continue straight up until the fading vehicle track veers L, and go straight ahead down a rough path that

WALKING ON THE GREEK ISLANDS – THE CYCLADES

leads obliquely L then along the edge of an old terrace, initially below power lines and meeting them again at an animal trough. Bear L beneath an olive enclosure, over a broken section of wall, then R to the L side of a blocked path. At an apparent dead-end, climb down into the rocky, vegetated but passable path to its top, into sharply scented **juniper forest**. Head downhill to a wall and turn R towards a three-tiered building. Go through the gate into a short section of walled path, then R up a **marble path** to the L of a grey gate.

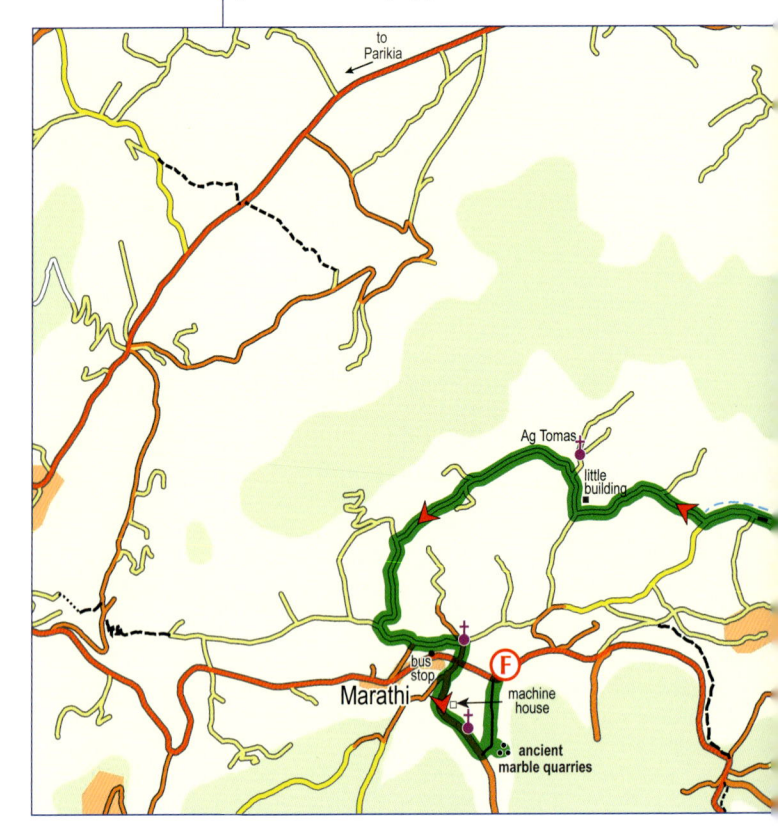

WALK 4 – NAOUSA PORT, INLAND TO MARBLE MINES

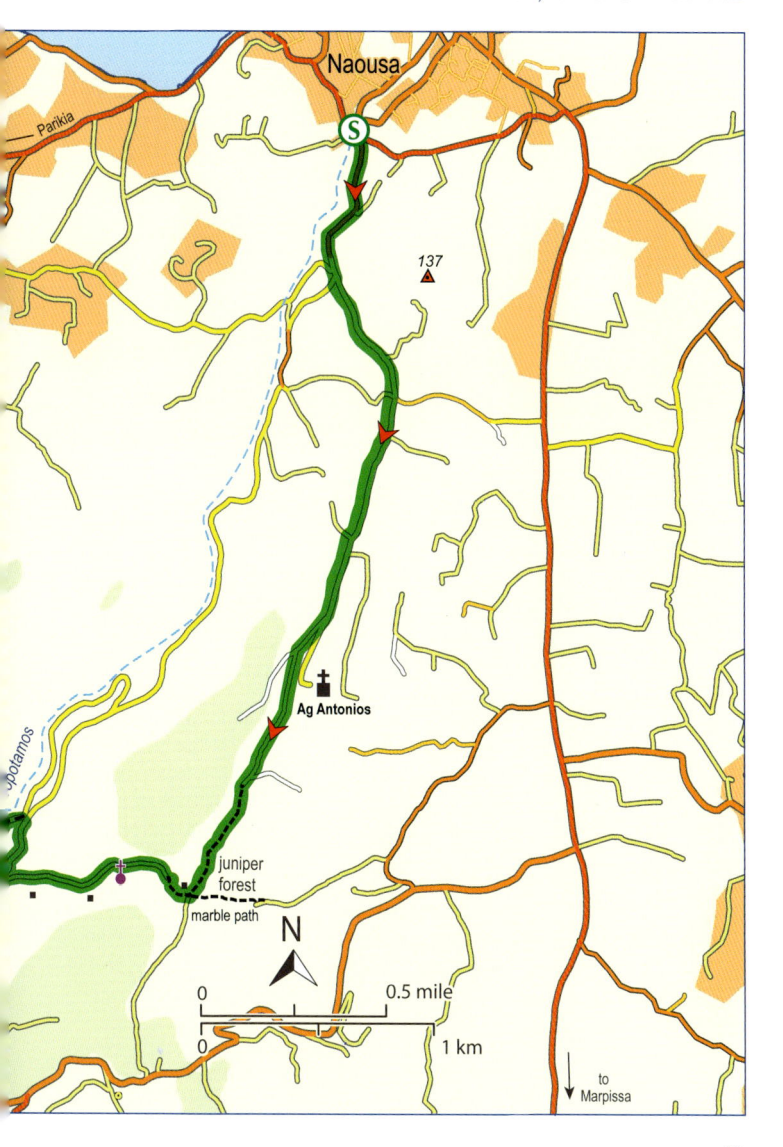

A short but perfect marble path leads towards the vale of Marathi

> The lane is bordered with velvet-leaved *Ballota*, whose seed vessels are traditionally used as floating wicks in olive-oil lamps.

The marble path becomes a dirt road. Crest the hill, and after a turnoff L to a pigeon house, head towards a **threshing circle** and turn R at the junction above it. ◄ As the way curves gently R, look for a steep cut in the vegetation, L, and step down into **Xiropotamos** (dry riverbed). Keep straight on at a dirt track L and an open area where tracks come in from uphill.

At a **little building**, take the track R, then keep straight on. Turn R at the junction, and L at the Y-fork (picnic spot at **Ag Tomas** chapel, R). Follow the main lane up and swing L. The route is soon bordered by dense, dark maquis on the hillside, and ordered groves of almond trees and olives, pastures and massive greenhouse tunnels in the vale.

At the next fork, go L and keep on the main track to a T-junction then turn L and go downhill across the valley. Turn L at the next T-junction and, just past a big house, go L along a path flanked by boulders towards a **chapel**. Turn R to the main road and cross it to reach the lane signed 'Ancient marble quarries'. Fork L towards honey-coloured shells of buildings that housed steam-powered marble-cutting machinery installed by the French in 1844. Beyond them, go straight along the dirt road to a

WALK 4 – NAOUSA PORT, INLAND TO MARBLE MINES

small cube of a hut, turn sharp L to a track-crossing and go obliquely over to a path signed 'CAVE', which leads to a fence with warning sign. ▶ Follow the fence R to a gate, beyond which you can scramble down to the dark gash beneath an overhang.

The next section is steep and loose, and the cave is dark, uneven and low. Proceed with care.

In the L corner behind a wire guard is a fourth-century BC bas-relief with an inscription dedicated to the nymph guardians of the caves. In the **tunnel** itself, look for chiselled grooves on the sides and ceiling, a dry-stone retaining wall on the right, and chambers off the main shaft. Victorian adventurer Theodore Bent recorded that when the Greek King Otto visited the mines in the 1850s he had to remove his epaulettes before crawling through the low galleries. The steep gradient followed the course of the marble vein but also acted as a chimney to draw the fumes from the lamps. Rubble was laid on the floor to ease the movement of marble slabs.

Return to the CAVE sign, turn R and reach a marble brick avenue of uncertain purpose, at the end of which is the main road. The **bus stop** is in **Marathi** village to the L.

Looking southeast over wild Paros

MARBLE OF LIGHT

Parian marble from the Marathi shafts was unique in its fine structure and translucency to a depth of 4cm or more, compared with the 2.5cm of the Carrara marble used by Michelangelo. The purest stone, extracted from the deepest shafts, was called lychnites, from the ancient Greek *lychnos* (lamp). Marathi marble was used by the ancient world's most gifted sculptors for such works as the Venus de Milo and statues at the Acropolis in Athens. Marble exports became the main source of the island's wealth from the sixth century BC, but the mines fell into disuse from the AD600s. They were not reopened until the 1840s, when a French enterprise extracted marble for Napoleon Bonaparte's tomb in Les Invalides, Paris. In 1879 a Belgian company took over the business but went bankrupt in the early 1900s, and today the lychnites marble vein is exhausted.

4th-century bas-relief at the ancient marble mines

WALK 5
West-coast hills to Parikia

Start	Bus stop, Marathi
Finish	Parikia
Distance	9km
Ascent	280m
Descent	445m
Time	3½hr
Terrain	Gradual climb to a high vale, along country lanes and a lovely old path, then down a youthful V-shaped valley cut through a coastal range
Refreshments	None on the route; spring water at Thapsana
Transport	Bus route Parikia–Marathi–Naousa

This walk passes an atmospheric old monastery, and a monstrous younger one with far-reaching ridge-top views inland and along the west coast. Idyllic country paths for much of the route more than compensate for lanes at beginning and end. In spring they're a festive procession of wildflowers and luscious green. A high, rolling inland vale is embraced by the massif of Ag Pandes and the ridge of west-coast hills, and for a time, as you wind among giant spurs of bare rock and phrygana, there is no sign of civilisation at all. There's potential for more old paths to be opened on the approach to Parikia, which are currently lost beneath dense vegetation.

From the **bus stop**, go W along the road to turn sharp L up the concrete lane. At the fork bear R and go steeply uphill. Turn R at the T-junction and go through the hamlet, bearing L at a kink, and go L again along a dirt track signed 'ΠΡΟΣ ΑΓΙΟ ΜΗΝΑ'. After a steep hairpin bend look L for steps to the splendidly solid **monastery of Ag Minas**.

> **Minas**, an Egyptian military officer, resigned because of the Roman persecution of Christians. He was later beheaded for his own faith and

Walking on the Greek Islands – the Cyclades

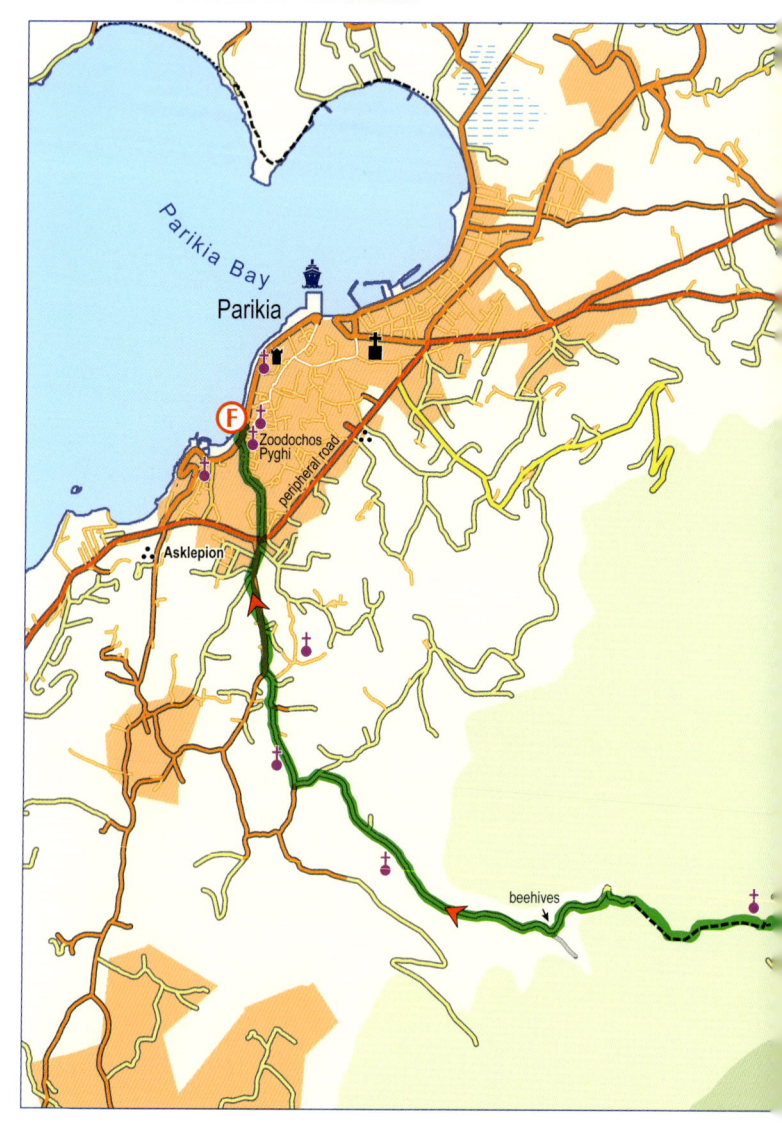

WALK 5 – WEST-COAST HILLS TO PARIKIA

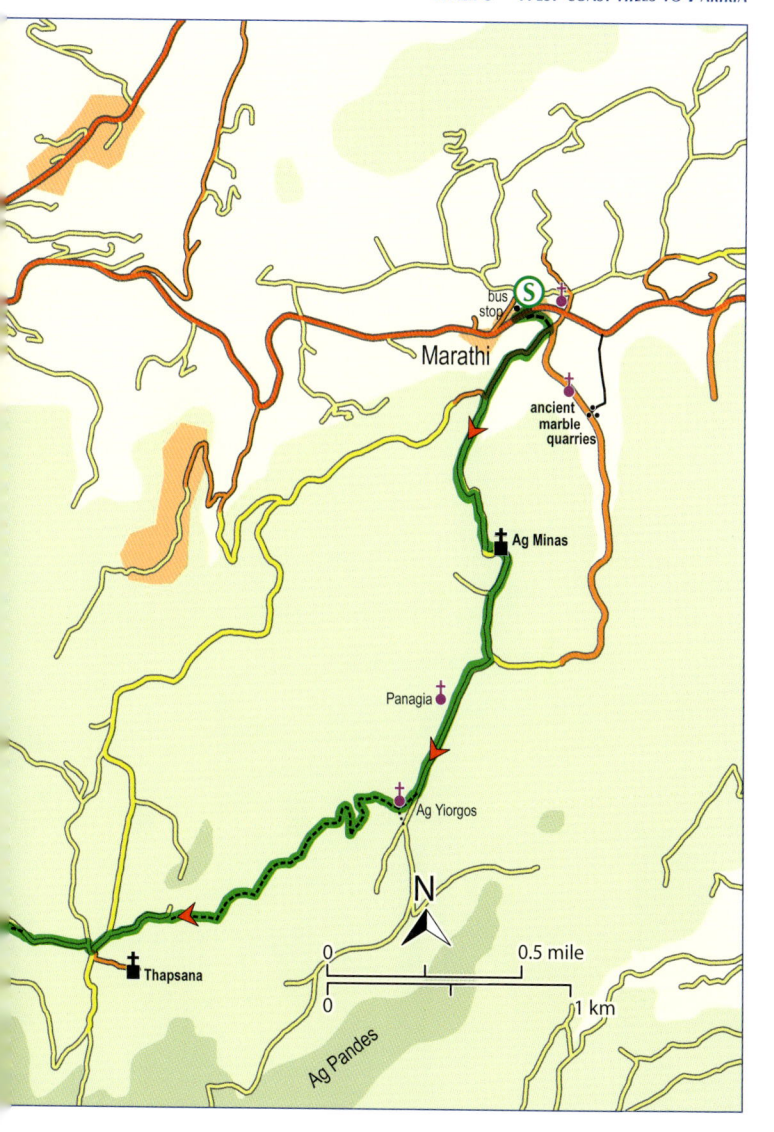

61

appealed to for help in healing, exorcism, protection in battle… and finding lost property. The monastery, founded in 1594, was largely rebuilt in the 17th century. Knock, in case the caretaker's there to take you into the courtyard dwarfed by a two-storey cypress, the church with damaged but richly painted frescos, and living quarters. Embedded in the fabric of the building are columns from a pagan temple, and a fragment from the fourth-century BC bas-relief at the nearby marble quarry.

From the monastery go down the gravel road, which has stands of giant fennel, with opening fists of sharp yellow flowerheads in spring. At the junction, turn R and follow the lane uphill, past a turnoff to the **chapel of Panagia**, then turn R at the fork to the next chapel (**Ag Yiorgos**). Kink through farm buildings and a low fence-gate, onto a path down to a wide stream-bed (the last metre or two may be overgrown, but push through).

Turn L along the stream-bed, and around the bend take the dirt track that forks back sharply R and up. Follow this towards a cube of ruined building and continue

The monastery walls conceal a huddle of courtyard, cells and chapel

WALK 5 – WEST-COAST HILLS TO PARIKIA

above the valley until the track ends at a low fence-gate, beyond which is a country path. Keep R where a couple of other old paths join from the valley, and eventually reach a stony dirt track. Turn L, passing well-managed olive groves R, and the orange-roofed, fortress-like **monastery of Thapsana** is ahead on the L.

> Dedicated to Theotokou Myrtidiotissa (Mother of God, Lady of the Myrtles), the **monastery** is one of the richest on the island and receives nuns and women visitors only. The current 1929 building is on the site of a 16th-century foundation.

At the top of the lane, turn L, and opposite the first brown metal monastery gate, turn R, then L down a concrete lane. Keep downhill where the track to the field goes up R, then, at a fence-gate across the track, drop L to a walled *monopati*. Follow it to a junction below a **chapel** up R, then turn L to cross a stream-bed and swing R on the other side, taking care of crumbling path-fall.

At an open triangle of worn land with olive terraces ahead, bear R downhill, above a gorge. Drop to cross

High vales and beehives beneath the limestone massif of Ag Pantes

Over the ridge to the W coast and Parikia

a stream-bed at a small concrete block of building and climb downstream for a few metres before picking up the trail again on the hillside R, marked by a red splodge. The path dips in and out of the stream-bed, then at a pipe junction becomes a track which rises past pastel-painted **beehives**.

Gradually the coastline opens out ahead: an aerial prospect of Parikia Bay to Cape Fokas. On reaching a sandy road, keep L downhill, passing a pigeon house up R. At the junction, turn L, then R at stepped, single-storey houses, then follow the main lane to a main junction and turn R, then L at 'stop' sign. Cross the **peripheral road** to go past Cine Rex and follow the lane through residential Parikia to the beach at **Zoodochos Pyghi church**.

WALK 6
Lefkes village and Byzantine Way

Start/Finish	Bus stop, Lefkes
Distance	12km
Ascent/Descent	445m
Time	4½hr
Terrain	Village alleys, then open hillsides and coastal lowlands via dirt tracks, and gradual climb on a paved path through phrygana
Refreshments	Lefkes, Prodromos (depending on time and season)
Transport	Bus service Lefkes–Parikia

Lefkes is a delightful village perched on the upper tiers of a valley that plunges panoramically to the east coast. Once you've found your way through the maze of alleys, you stride out around the hills to a lone monastery embedded in a valley-side, a haven of wildflowers, bees and butterflies among the rocks, and a perfect shady picnic spot by a hidden spring. From there it's a gentle ramble down to the coastal plain and gradually uphill to Lefkes along the paved Byzantine Way.

LEFKES IN HISTORY

Lefkes is the island's third most important town, and was some-time capital when the population moved inland from Parikia to escape periods of serious pirate raids in the eighth, ninth, 17th and 18th centuries AD. In-between, the Venetians established Parikia as their capital after their conquest in the early 13th century. By the end of the 19th century, Lefkes was the heart of olive oil, wine and dairy production for the south of the island, with nine windmills and nine olive presses. In the 1840s its population was boosted to 2000 by workers at the newly reopened marble quarries in Marathi, and many of the village's elegant neoclassical houses date from this time. Today, the population is closer to 500.

From the bus stop, go along the paved avenue into the village and in 20 metres fork L. Go L of a corner building

Walking on the Greek Islands – the Cyclades

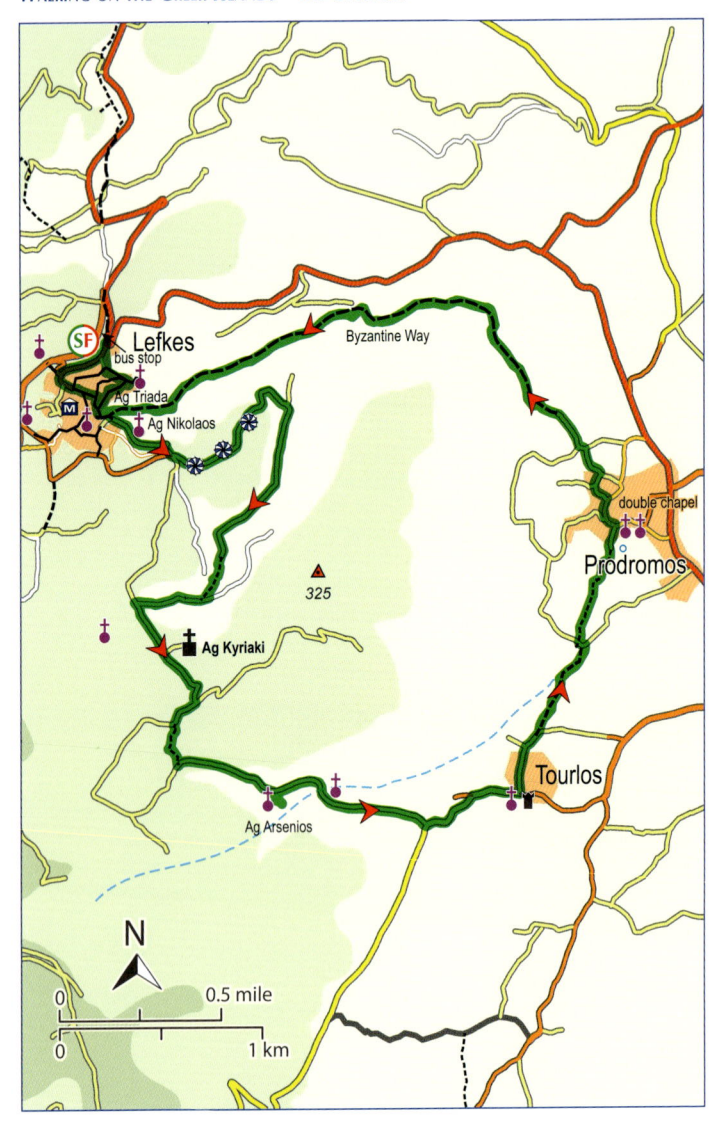

WALK 6 – LEFKES VILLAGE AND BYZANTINE WAY

with a small walled balcony, and L at junction opposite a lemon tree. At a cross-paths go straight uphill, then take the middle of three paths, towards the honey-coloured stone and marble, twin-belfried **church of Ag Triada** (trinity), which has one of the biggest areas of tiled roof on Paros.

Turn sharp R below the church, past Μαριγω café, go L at a junction with a small wooden sign for the Βυζαντινος δρομος (Byzantine Road), then continue to the next sign L and go down to a bridge. Go straight over up the lane, past the pedimented entrance to **Ag Nikolaos chapel** in a pine and cypress grove. Pass by the start of an old path and a well, above terraces where grain was once grown to feed the windmills you see ahead. Take the next (brief) relic of original footpath R, and go R again onto the asphalt road, then turn L turn onto a sandy track towards the **windmills**.

> There are no working **windmills** on Paros today. To maximise wind-power, the miller could adjust the tilt of the wooden roof as well as the sails, which were attached to a wooden shaft. As the sails turned, they activated a wooden cogwheel in the upper part of the mill, which transferred movement to a vertical shaft attached to the millstone. The grains of wheat or barley were poured onto the millstone for grinding into flour.

At a bend, where a track leads to a more intact (but locked) mill on a rise, keep L on the main track, go around and over the brow of the hill, then descend past a farmstead on a sharp bend. ▶ At a fork with a faded sign R to 'Αγ. Κυριακι', keep R along the level track. Pass a walled grove of heavily pruned olive trees and a small house with a large water tank before the track ends at a field. Go through the wire gate and keep to the top of the rough pasture, below the terrace guarded by a solitary, stumpy olive tree, with the monastery of Ag Kyriaki in your sightline.

Go L of a bamboo copse and follow the line of a wall pierced by prickly pear towards an olive tree at the end

A craggy limestone ridge dominates the view ahead.

Ag Kyriaki monastery

> The monastery was founded in the 1600s and closed in 1831. If you go down for a closer look you can cut up R cross-country to rejoin the main route at a sharp R bend.

of the field. At the corner of the wall on the R, go steeply down to cross the stream-bed obliquely L and scramble up to a rocky track, turning R uphill. At the junction, turn L along the marble-chip lane, passing above the **Ag Kyriaki monastery**. ◄

At a junction, turn R. On a R-hand curve with a tubular metal and mesh gate, go sharp L down a steep *monopati* disguised by (mainly soft) vegetation, which conceals deeply eroded gulleys and marble paving. Emerge onto a vehicle track and turn L. Some 85 metres beyond a turnoff to a smallholding, go down R to the **chapel of Ag Arsenios**, and beneath it L, to shaded planes of smooth rock and a spring for a perfect picnic spot.

Go on down the dirt track over a stream-bed with tilting slabs of rock, one with a miniature **chapel** perched on it. ◄ Keep L at the junction with a sign for 'St George's Monastery', then, on the outskirts of the scattered settlement of **Tourlos**, look for a walled enclosure with a crumbling Venetian tower, mini-monastery, chapel and cypress. Just before this, take the path L.

> In the valley L is a high block of wall, probably a mill chase. Farther on are the walls of a never-completed dam, and ahead is the conical peak of Kefalos, the town of Marpissa at its feet.

Keep R where another track forks L, and farther on turn L onto a surviving stretch of mule track, then keep down L to cross a riverbed. Go R along the far bank, soon meeting a gravel road, which you cross L and then immediately go R to an overgrown but passable *monopati* between low-lying walls. Take the L option at a concrete

WALK 6 – LEFKES VILLAGE AND BYZANTINE WAY

cistern on the outskirts of pretty **Prodromos** (forerunner), named for its 17th-century church dedicated to John the Baptist.

At a junction with a **double chapel**, turn L, then go R along a paved way to a wide fork and turn L. Follow the lane around R, and at the junction with open land opposite, go L. At the next junction go L, then go R onto the **Byzantine Way**. Now you can have a break from directions as the path is perfectly straightforward for around 4km through low-growing phrygana.

> Before the asphalt road was built in the 1970s, this path was still the **principal route** from the east coast and Molos (the island's main port until World War II) to the central villages. Its name suggests it was built during the Byzantine Empire – perhaps when Lefkes became the administrative centre in the eighth–ninth centuries AD.

The Byzantine Way ends in the **Lefkes** parking area by the stream you crossed at the start of the route. Go straight across it, past eucalyptus trees, swing to the R and wend your way up L–R to a *plateia* with a raised terrace shaded by a pine, and a colourful neoclassical building. Go L up a stepped alley in the top corner, past a splendid Byzantine door with carved marble surrounds. Go over a crossing of alleys to the village 'balcony' square, and along the main avenue back to the **bus stop**.

The Byzantine Way is the island's best-maintained path

WALK 7
South from Lefkes to Dryos port

Start	Bus stop, Lefkes
Finish	Dryos
Distance	12.5km
Ascent	505m
Descent	705m
Time	5hr
Terrain	Steep climb out of Lefkes, then little-used country lanes and tracks on scrub hills with little shade. Long descent via a sometimes steep, mostly paved path with brief rough sections.
Refreshments	At start and finish only – take a picnic. Springs at Kaparou and at halfway point.
Transport	Bus services Parikia–Lefkes, Dryos–Parikia

This walk, from the heart of the island to the sea, takes in a wonderful variety of bare mountain and hidden vales. You round high above a monastery on a knoll of orchard and deciduous trees, then surf the crest of a hill, in a landscape of stone shelters and monumental, wind-weathered rock. Spread below is a panorama of falling land, sea and neighbouring Naxos spread along the horizon. Superb coastal views switch to the south as you descend above the island's biggest valley on an ingeniously laid and cambered Byzantine path.

From the bus stop, go along the paved avenue into the village, swinging L at the balcony of a *plateia* that looks down to the E coast. Go straight on at a cross-paths, under an arched alley and turn R at the top of a pretty square with a colourful neoclassical building.

Continue up R–L, passing to the R of a two-belled **chapel**. Go L at a house with a spiral stairway, and up the main alley to the asphalt road. Cross to the concrete road opposite, and where it bends R, cut up the rocky path

Neoclassical building in a Lefkes square

and at the road, turn L. At the sharp bend R, go L onto the rock-slabbed path. ▶ Keep straight on at a staggered cross-paths, and at the fork. The path narrows towards a little house L with an underground spring just beyond.

At the road, cross to continue along the lane, signposted 'Άγιος Ιωαννης Καπαρου'. (Above the high bank L is a little square building with a circular opening, which once housed a spring of running water and sinks for washing laundry.) Round the bend beyond, see Ag Ioannis Kaparou monastery in a cluster of trees. Keep straight on at the next concrete road, round a bend, and pass L of and above pine trees to reach the **monastery** down R. ▶

Go S from the monastery on a path lined with fruit trees, dog and chicken pens. After about 350 metres, where a vehicle track continues L, go straight ahead up the R of the hill. Follow the trail beside a low broken wall to a stony vehicle track and turn L, then almost immediately L again onto a track that gracefully rings the hillside above the monastery.

Keep up and L where other tracks lead off, and nearing the top, pass below the **double chapel of Ag Yiorgos**.

The bulk of Ag Pandes (All Saints) mountain is ahead, its summit bristling with aerials.

Long vacated by monks, Ag Ioannis ('Kaparou' is the name of the landowning family) is rarely open, but you can fill water bottles here.

Walking on the Greek Islands – the Cyclades

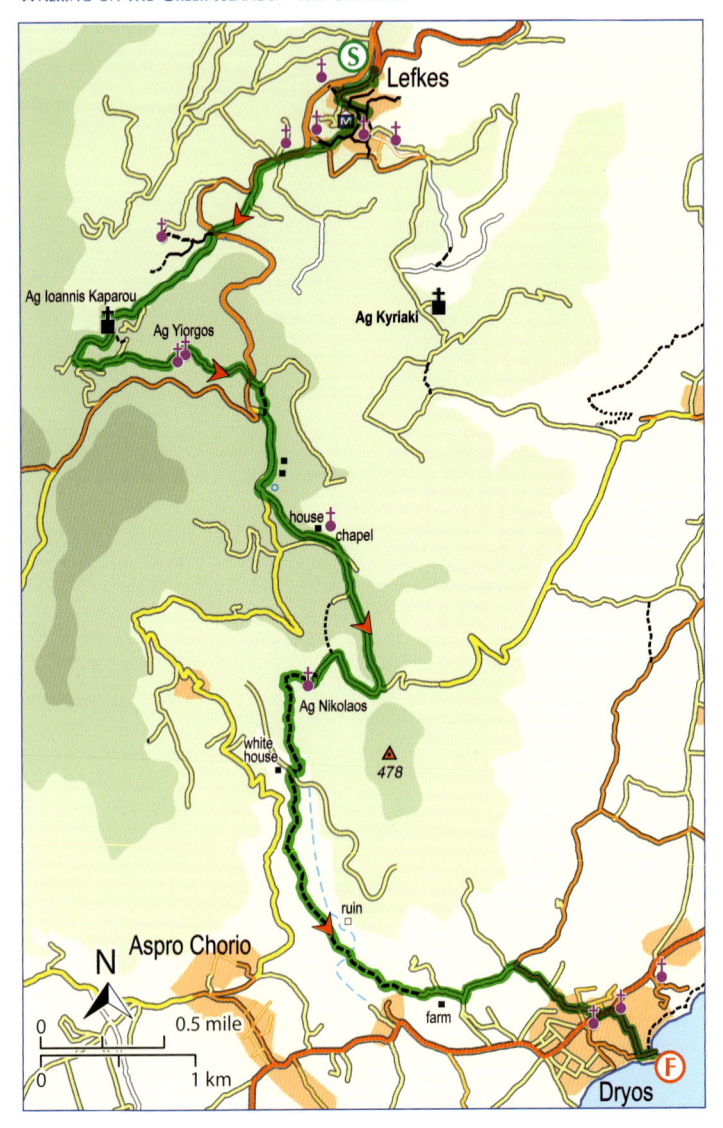

The path waltzes around spurs of hill to a junction where you turn R along a stony track to the road, and cross to the lane opposite. Turn R at the first junction, towards a house perched on the hillside, and go up the path R of its gate to the dirt road and turn L.

Continue for about 450 metres, and shortly after a group of **buildings** with stone slab and pottery chimneys, reach a dip by cypress trees. ▶ Take the first fork L down a gravel track, which you now follow for about 1.3 kilometres, with stage-set views of valleys opening to the coastal plain and the cone of Kefalos topped by a monastery. Pass a **house** with a roof-top water tank and **chapel** beyond, and another with cypress and pine trees, keeping straight up R. Rise to a spur and keep straight on.

After another spur, on a level stretch, a stony track leads up R; this is a possible shortcut over the hill to Ag Nikolaos but the path is not clear. Better to stride along the dirt track with enthralling views unfolding of sea and islands. After a saddle, the track rises, and far below R the pale orange of your future path snakes through grey-green scrub. To the L of the dome of hill ahead, the view plunges to the resort of Tserdakia and the oblong islet of Makronisi. To the R, the biggest valley on Paros opens up.

Overlooking the oasis of the Kaparou monastery

There's a well in a miniature courtyard L, complete with bucket for drawing water.

> After the first major bend L, and just before the chapel turnoff, a path marked by cairns falls from the R; this is the other end of the shortcut.

Reach a wide crossing of tracks and turn R to curve down towards **Ag Nikolaos chapel** on its head of land. ◄ Rough-cut paving marks the start of a Byzantine way, which after a junction with a path from the R, turns L to head for the coast.

Continue until you cross a stream-bed, then turn L onto a track leading uphill. At a bend beneath a **white house**, turn sharp L onto a rock path that crosses the stream-bed then rises to a fork. Go R downhill and keep L, then L again at the wall. Proceed uphill along the main track, which levels out then reaches a low **ruin** with a white window frame but no roof. Go straight down a very steep path to L turn alongside a new wall. The trail is single, but clear, as it winds seawards then swings E, eventually opening onto a track to a small **farm**. Go through the yard L of the house to a concrete lane that curves across a small valley.

Continue along the main lane, and at the crossroads turn L. It's about 450 metres to an asphalt road, which you cross to go down to the village and wend your way to **Dryos**, with its seafront tavernas, fishing boats and mysterious channels in the rocks that may have been cut for hauling marble blocks to ships in Archaic times.

> Dry docks from ancient Greece, or interesting rock formation?

WALK 8
Southwest coast: Piso Livadi to Dryos

Start	Piso Livadi harbour
Alternative start	Marpissa
Finish	Dryos
Distance	6.5km, or 9.5km including monastery
Ascent	70m, or 255m including monastery
Descent	70m, 125m including monastery
Time	2½hr, or 3½hr including monastery
Terrain	Easy coast-path walk with little shade. Optional steep, hot lane climb to monastery and road walk to main route.
Refreshments	Seasonal tavernas at most beaches
Transport	Bus services Parikia–Lefkes–Marpissa–Piso Livadhi, and Naousa–Marmara–Dryos

The conical peak of Kefalos, rising suddenly from the flat coastal plain, looks over the coastline you're about to walk. It's worth climbing to the monastery at the summit for the plummeting view of the east coast, spread below like a map (see optional route). The main walk starts at the delightful harbour of Piso Livadi and goes from one sandy bay to another, with low, rocky headlands in-between. Inland is the abrupt surge of the island's central massif, and out to sea are floating islets, and Naxos.

Optional addition to Ag Antonios Monastery from Marpissa

Start from the **windmill** in **Marpissa**, from which the monastery is signposted up a concrete lane. At a turnoff R to a block of concrete building, go up the signed path beside it through the pines that leads to the **Ag Antonios monastery** entrance. ▶ Unless you want to risk a **near-vertical scramble** via dense scrub on the E side, you must return the same way and road-walk to Piso Livadi to start the route described below.

Dating from 1597, the monastery (open Easter–24 September, 11am–3 or 4pm) towers at the summit of Kefalos, ringed by a topknot of pines, with an eagle-eye view of the coast from Molos Bay (N) to Dryos (S).

Walking on the Greek Islands – the Cyclades

Walk S along the beach from **Piso Livadi** to the rocks at the far end and up steps to the road. Go L along it and go down to the next beach, **Logaras**, which you walk the length of. Join the path that rounds **Cape Pounda** to reach the eponymous beach, and at the end go up paved steps to continue the coastal trail. ▶ Beach no. 4 is the shallow, tamarisk-fringed bay of **Mesada Beach**. On reaching a branch of dirt roads on a flat area, take the L (seaward) option, which leads to a narrow trail to **Tserdakia Beach**. It's a perfect strand, especially outside the summer season, and the rash of holiday homes is largely out of sight.

Leave Tserdakia at its far end to follow the road briefly past ranks of holiday apartments, then rejoin the coast path edging around **Cape Choni** to **Golden Beach**. At the far end, the path leaves the beach and the trappings of tourism to go through a rural haven of olive grove and vineyard, with glimpses of small and perfectly formed bays through the bamboo. Continue alongside **Boundari Beach**, then down to the bay and harbour of **Dryos**.

Dryos is a small resort and fishing village today, but plentiful fresh spring water and sheltered shores appealed to early settlers. The most evocative

From Kefalos summit to Molos, one of the island's 'big three' bays

The islets of Prasonisi (green island), Makronisi (long island) and Dryos float offshore.

Empty Tserdakia Beach and warm sea, October

relics of Dryos' history are deep, regular channels cut into rocks, which may have been dry docks. Marine biologist Peter Nicolaides discovered that the channels continued underwater to southern Antiparos and suggested they might have been haulage tracks for transporting marble blocks to the Despotiko sanctuary in the Archaic period. During the Ottoman period, Turkish officials anchored at Dryos once a year to collect taxes.

WALK 9
Angeria mountain circular

Start/Finish	Bus stop, Angeria
Distance	13km
Ascent/Descent	580m
Time	4½hr
Terrain	Country paths and trees near the coast, which rise via a long country lane to wild, remote open hills, and some rough sections through low shrubs
Refreshments	Angeria
Transport	Bus service Parikia–Angeria

This circuit touches all the essential elements of the island. You look down onto coastal plain inland from the pleasant resort of Aliki, then broad sweeps of farmland falling to the west coast. Civilisation is left behind for a while as you walk into wild, high phrygana and limestone country with precipitously perched monasteries and dizzying views down to the coast.

From the bus stop at **Angeria**, walk W towards the **church** and turn R up the lane on the corner beneath it. Follow this around to the R then wiggle up between buildings until you reach a walled path that opens out at the top of a dirt and rock track. Turn R uphill past a metal mesh gate, onto a narrow path that winds immediately R. Keep R at the first fork, joining a delightful path that levels out above a deep-cut valley of dark-green juniper and then swings N to meet the wide unsurfaced road to Kamari. ▶

Turn L and walk along the main dirt road, via R and then L right-angle bends, to reach **Kamari village** in roughly 1.3km. Head W through the village to the junction then curve up R and go R again onto a long, uphill exposed road. Beyond the drive to a big property on the R, the lane turns to sand and stone and you follow it around to the R and then keep L at the next fork. ▶

> You'll return to this point at the end of the walk to retrace steps back to Angeria.

> The hill you're walking beside (E) is called Skafi (boat) for its upturned hull shape.

WALKING ON THE GREEK ISLANDS – THE CYCLADES

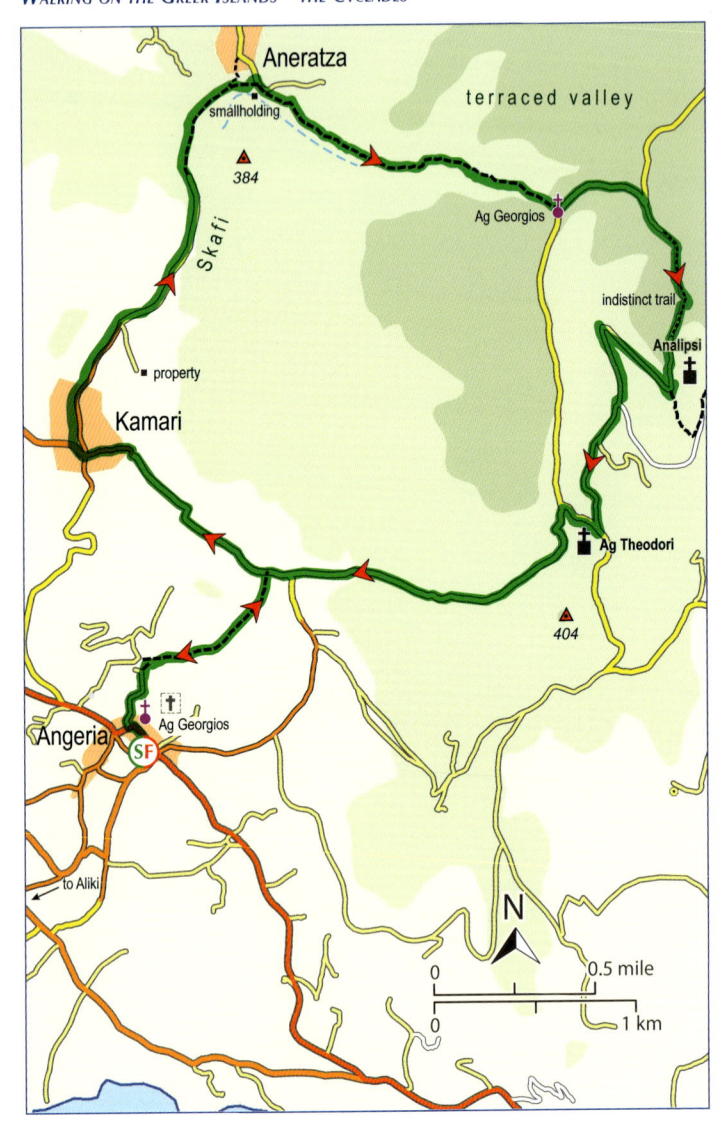

Round the head of the valley towards a saddle, where you can see the continuance of the path ahead. Where a drive leads to properties on the L, keep R up a rough stony rock track, which soon turns into a *monopati* among the phrygana, keeping R. The antennae-pierced summit of Ag Pantes rears ahead, and across the valley N lies the abandoned village of Aneratza.

Dip to cross a stream-bed, and beyond a **smallholding** turn R onto a concrete lane. After about 20 metres, just beyond a small building, look for cairn on the broken wall R among grey-leaved *Phlomis* bushes. This is the start of a great little mountain path scented with dwarf cypress and Mediterranean herbs, which follows a rocky, deep-cut stream-bed winding between the interlocking spurs of a high valley.

Join the stream-bed and rise, keeping R. There's a **valley** stepped with terraces ahead on the L, falling from the heights of Ag Pantes. Keep R and uphill on the narrow but occasionally paved trail along the side of another small valley. Where goat-trodden trails go down L, keep R and up, then follow the path along the top of a low wall L and higher wall R. Soon there are signs of cultivation, a little terrace of neatly planted vines, and a section of identifiable mule track, albeit studded with enthusiastic

Goat file through the phrygana above Angeria

shrub growth. After a wire fence-gate, the track runs uphill between widely spaced walls to the **chapel of Ag Georgios** astride its col.

Leave the chapel and go L along a wide, bleached sandy road until, right on the point of a paperclip L bend, you turn R onto a wide, rough stony track. This reaches a gate that blocks the old track to Analipsi (ascension) monastery, and you must go up L around it to follow a skinny, **indistinct trail** through the scrub, with the overgrown phantom track tantalisingly below. Look for small cairns marking ways to cut down to it after 100 metres or so, and go along the edge of a steeply descending dark juniper thicket. Follow cairns R to where the old path becomes more defined (albeit still briskly vegetated), to reach another cairn on a bend of the original path.

Shortly before **Analipsi monastery** (closed), which juts out over a sheer drop of mountain against a backdrop of sea and sky, the path clears. Continue on the steep and stony dirt road downhill, around a sharp hairpin, and then go L, accompanying a wee valley dense with dark green. Kink R–L over the stream-bed and head up to the next monastery, **Ag Theodori**, visible on the hill. The first wire fence-gate opens easily; if the one at the top is locked, you can climb over the hinged L side. Turn R and go uphill past the monastery via a steep concrete lane.

> **Agioi Theodori** is a nunnery of the strict Orthodox order of the followers of the Old Calendar. It's a 20th-century foundation with 10–15 resident nuns, who cultivate the surrounding land. Visitors are not particularly welcome unless they also believe in the Old Calendar.

At the junction, turn L to descend on a concrete lane, compensated by bordering terraces of vines and olives, an ever-widening 'V' of sea, then more healthy juniper-clad maquis. At a hairpin bend, where the concrete road continues L, go R onto an unsurfaced road. Soon, opposite a double gate on the R, you'll reach your return footpath, L, to **Angeria**.

NAXOS

Over the olive vale to Mount Zas, highest peak in the Cyclades (Walk 15)

WALKING ON THE GREEK ISLANDS – THE CYCLADES

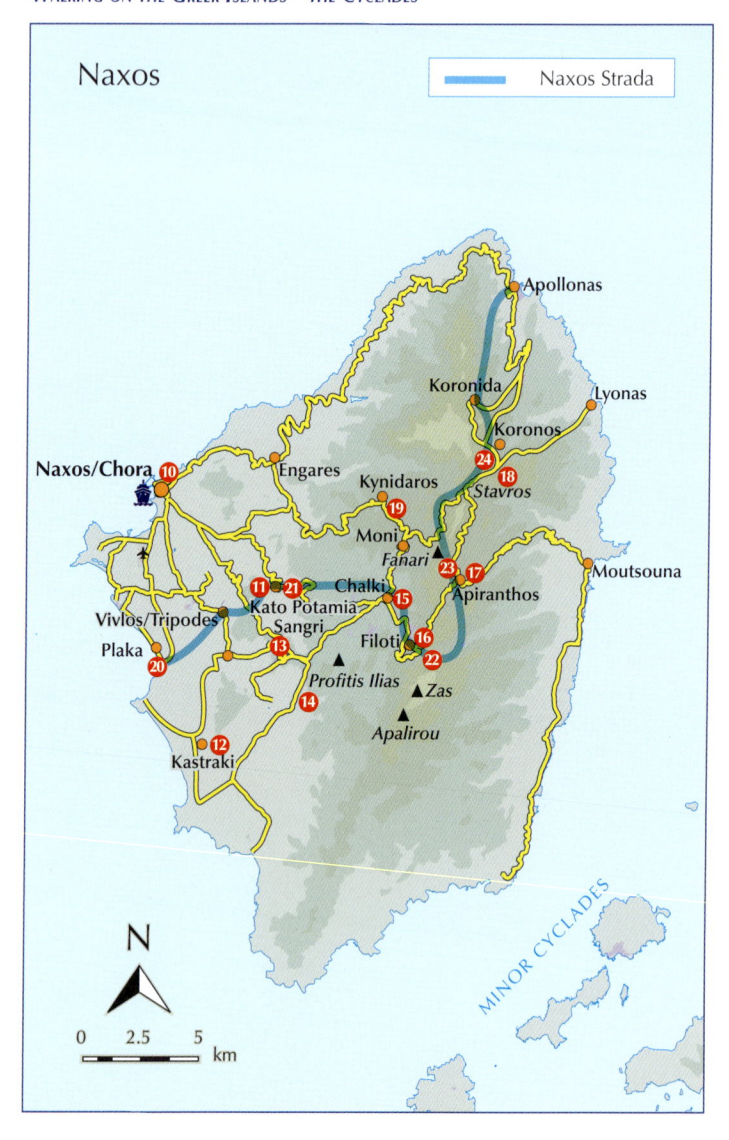

Naxos

Bigger, better watered and more diverse in resources and landscape than all the other Cycladic islands, Naxos has a working life quite independent of tourism. Its landscape soars from maritime plains to the archipelago's highest mountains, with broad vales of farmland and olive groves in-between. It was the favoured home of the Olympian god of wine, Dionysos, where he lived happily with the Cretan princess Ariadne after she'd been abandoned by minotaur-slayer Theseus. Not surprising, then, that archaeologists have discovered the earliest evidence of olive oil use and vine cultivation on Naxos. On the cusp of the late Stone Age and Early Bronze Age the island was a pioneer in farming methods and craftsmanship, and had an organised society, a thriving port and a metropolis. Another peak came in the sixth century BC with the export of its fine marble, and, with the slave-centre of Delos as a colony, the population was around 30,000. Today it is closer to 20,000, with a third of the people living around Naxos town (referred to by locals and on bus and road signs as Chora, pronounced 'Hora'), the port and capital.

The island's rich history left its marks on the landscape. Monumental marble sculptures destined for the ancient world's top shrines lie abandoned in the open near where they were quarried. There are hilltop Hellenistic and Venetian fortifications, and the greatest concentration of chapels with rare frescoes in the Aegean. Most significantly for walkers, a network of traditional paths developed over the mountains and between settlements.

The island's breadth and size (450 sq km) encompasses several mountain

Mid-path threshing circle en route to the east coast (Walk 17)

and valley systems, where, sheltered from the scouring effects of wind and sea, soil deposits built up and land became used for pasture and cultivation. Surface water is scarce, but there are enough subterranean water sources and the occasional year-round stream to sustain a thriving farming economy. Naxos is self-sufficient in meat, dairy produce, oil and vegetables, and exports cheese and potatoes. Taverna fare is invariably home-grown or reared, with generous portions of local specialities such as cheddar-like *graviera*, sharp-tasting *kefalotyri* and soft, mild *mizythra* cheeses, fresh vegetables and *chorta* (greens).

The accessible, fertile belly of the south and west is framed by a backbone of rugged mountains that drops in deep-cut valleys to the east coast. Few roads dare cross this wild land. One swerves around pinched valley-heads to link the northern villages; others snake hair-raisingly down to just three little ports on the entire east coast.

Urban life, shops, facilities and tourist accommodation are concentrated on Naxos town and, late April to September, the west coast to Ag Anna. Filoti and Vivlos/Tripodes are the only other villages with an all-season, practical range of shops. All bus services head from the main terminal in Naxos port to some main villages, and in summer to more distant beach destinations.

Naxos, a farming island, exports its cheeses throughout Greece

WALK 10
Naxos town tour

Start/Finish	Bus station, Naxos
Distance	4km
Ascent/Descent	80m
Time	1½hr (but add on cultural stops)

Naxos town (Chora) is clustered around a hilltop citadel overlooking harbour and sea, and backed by a wall of mountain. It is compact enough to be explored in a couple of hours, but to savour the maze of Cycladic architecture and alleys, built as much to confound pirates as to save space, to discover the island's story in its streets and museums, merits a good day's outing. And that's apart from lingering in shops, a harbour-view taverna, or on a beach. At the time of writing (autumn 2019) renovation works on the archaeological and Byzantine museums were expected, but they're otherwise open 8am–3.30pm (closed Tuesdays).

From the **bus station**, go along the causeway leading to the islet of **Palatia**, looking R at the start to a section of paved street from the prehistoric town. Go up the stepped path to the **Portara** (temple entrance), then circuit the islet clockwise. ▶

> The sacred island of Delos, mythical birthplace of and foundation shrine to Apollo, is visible to the northwest on a clear day.

The marble Portara (entrance) is the only significant part left standing of the 530BC **temple of Apollo**. It was commissioned by the 'tyrant' Lygdamis, who seized power from the unpopular aristocratic regime but was supported by the merchant classes and improved life for the island people. When he fell from power, building works came to a halt and portable parts were removed to embellish the town's buildings. The sheer mass and weight of the Portara's four 6m-long marble blocks, each weighing 20 tonnes, have ensured its survival in situ.

Walking on the Greek Islands – the Cyclades

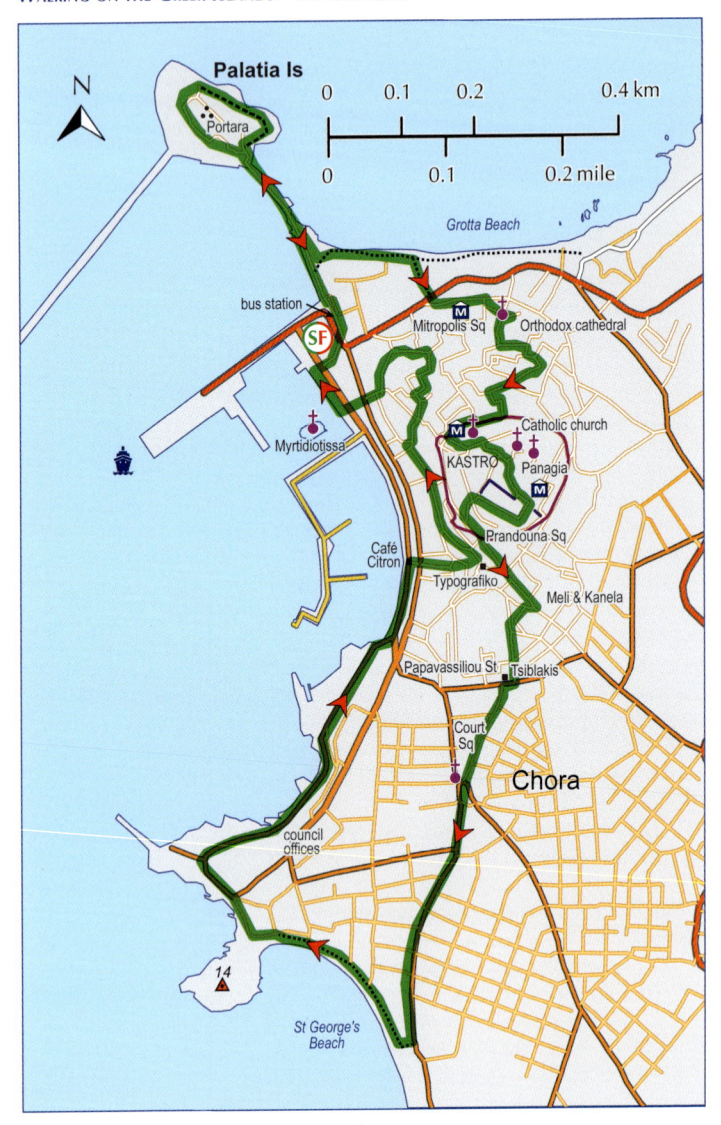

Return along the causeway and turn L before the first taverna, to **Grotta Beach** – so called for the caves beneath the far headland, not for the junk that's hurled there by wind and waves from the N. Turn R off the beach about halfway along, to a dusty triangle of land. Cross the main road to a memorial to Michael Damiralis, translator of Shakespeare into Greek. Turn sharp L past ground scattered with remnants of the Hellenistic and Roman marketplace. The cobbled path leads to a ramp down to the **Mitropolis Museum**, which may be open Easter–October, 8.30am–4pm, closed Tuesdays.

Temple portal, Naxos town, and Mount Zas, centre

In the Early Bronze Age, one of the oldest towns in Greece lay between this museum and the sea. The settlement of 2700–2300BC was such a distinctive landmark in Early Cycladic development that it was labelled the **Grotta-Pelos Culture**. The early town was lost to subsidence and rising sea-level, but on a calm day building blocks can be seen underwater offshore. The Mitropolis excavations unearthed part of the Mycenean town that peaked in 1600–1100BC. There were shrines for ancestor worship later covered by a tumulus. In the second and first centuries BC the Romans built their agora over the earlier town but preserved the tumulus as a monument to the city's founders.

Cross **Mitropolis Square**, passing a cluster of **chapels** dedicated to Panagia Chrysopolitissa (Our Lady of the Golden City), which honour the Virgin as protector of Naxos from the 16th century, to reach the 18th-century **Orthodox cathedral**. Set into the floor at the entrance is

Space-saving Cycladic-style thoroughfare, Naxos town

WALK 10 – NAXOS TOWN TOUR

the tomb of a Venetian nobleman with a carved skull and crossbones. From the cathedral, turn into the town up a broad flight of steps, then go L beneath an archway with a room above – a typical Cycladic architectural solution to creating extra living space. Fork L at a house with a collapsing balcony. ▶

Turn R under the arched way, and R again almost immediately (signed 'KASTRO'). Go L under another archway, up a wide-stepped path alongside a wall with an Anoixis Hotel sign. Go round L past the hotel entrance and turn R up steps, passing the side of a chapel (R). At the junction, turn R, then kink L–R with the main path that leads beneath high fortified houses delineating the outer boundaries of the Venetian citadel. ▶

Turn L, through the original wooden gate with an incised vertical mark on its R post that served as a yard measure for cloth. You are now in the Catholic enclave of the **Venetian Kastro**. The home of the Della Rocca-Barozzi family is immediately R. Turn up opposite, past steps L to the **Byzantine Museum** (closed). Farther on, bear R, signed 'Catholic Church'. A high wall of assorted stones rises ahead – part of the central complex of the *kastro* built in 1207 by the first Venetian ruler, Marco Sanudo. It housed a giant water cistern that could supply the *kastro* for a year.

> The **Catholic church** on the left has shiny white, 20th-century marble cladding but was founded by the Venetians in the early 13th century. Inside, though, is a double-sided icon depicting Virgin Mary and John the Baptist dating from the 12th century. Set into the floor is a procession of memorials to the island's most prominent Catholic families of the 16th–18th centuries. In an alley right behind the cathedral is the only Orthodox church in the *kastro*, Panagia Theoskepasti (veiled by God), with 13th-century, double-sided, portable icons, and double aisles dedicated to the Virgin Mary and Ag Anastasia Pharmakolytria (deliverer from poisons).

This lower town is the Bourgos, where Greek merchants and fishermen lived from 1450. In the 16th century a Jewish governor was appointed and the influx of Jews set up a leatherworking industry.

The mighty fortification wall incorporates the only tower left standing of an original 12.

WALKING ON THE GREEK ISLANDS – THE CYCLADES

Nikos Kazantzakis, author of Zorba the Greek *and the controversial* The Last Temptation of Christ, *was a star pupil at the School for a year or so in the late 1800s.*

Bear R at the cathedral and go past the former **Ursuline School**, a convent for Catholic girls founded in the 17th century, now a cultural centre. Farther on to the L is the **archaeological museum**, and at the back of its alley, the School of Commerce. ◄ From the museum continue clockwise, via an arch with a statue of the Virgin in an overhead niche. Continue down under the arch and turn L down through the SE gate to **Prandouna Square**.

Go straight ahead through residential Chora until just past the **Meli & Kanela café**, then turn sharp back R. Go down steps and L to **Papavassiliou Street**, emerging at the cavernous **Tsiblakis shop**, piled with herbs, cheeses, oil, pottery and baskets. Cross to the narrow road opposite, leading to **'Court Square'**, head for the corner and chapel diagonally opposite and go down this road, all the way down to **St George's Beach**.

In the sea are piled concrete blocks from an abandoned attempt to build a harbour for cruise ships.

Turn R along boardwalk and beach and continue to a pimple of headland scarred by an ungainly building. Go to the far L of car park and R along the seafront road, below **council offices** fronted by replicas of the Naxian Sphinx made for the Delian Sanctuary of Apollo in the Archaic period. ◄

Past the boatyard, reach the town's harbour-front, known as the *paraleia*, and go L alongside the shops and tavernas. Turn R at **Café Citron** towards **Typografiko taverna**, then L. When faced with a wall and pictorial map, go through another temple-remnant portico to do the circuit as shown on the map. After Labyrinth taverna, take L turns until you reach an opening back down to the harbour-front.

In 1922 he and five others were executed by firing squad in the final months of the Greek-Turkish War, a period known as The Catastrophe.

Turn R along the waterside, past the tiny chapel on the islet of **Myrtidiotissa**. Cross to a small park to reach a stern statue of Petros Protopapadakis, a national government minister from the village of Apeiranthos. ◄ The **bus station** is to the L.

WALK 11
Potamia villages and marble hills

Start/Finish	Bus stop, Kato Potamia
Distance	10km
Ascent/Descent	420m
Time	3¼hr
Terrain	Inland hills, villages and green valleys, with mostly easy walking on paved paths and dirt roads
Refreshments	Melanes, Ano Potamia
Transport	Bus service Chora–Potamia–Chalki, June–August only, leaving Kato Potamia 1.30pm!

Add on at least a couple of hours to this walk through 2500 years of island history, as there are distractions and detours to sites steeped in atmosphere. A former Jesuit retreat, now a romantic ruin in a valley oasis; an ancient aqueduct in use for 1200 years; a marble-workers' sanctuary; and monumental statues – all set among Mediterranean hills and surprisingly verdant valleys.

From the **bus stop** in **Kato Potamia**, turn off the bend and go down a paved alley between houses. Turn R at the bottom, past the **church**. Continue along the lane above orchard terraces, keeping L at a R-hand bend at a stream crossing towards a line-up of dark cypresses, looking for a wooden gate (L) with a latticed upper, and turn R, then R again before an entrance gate, onto a walled *monopati*.

Beyond ruins, turn R onto a narrow path to reach the main road. Turn L down to a sharp bend, and R off it, through a fence-gate. Follow the track through olive groves diagonally up L, with a sightline of terrace wall with square holes, and, up L, a cube of ruin. The earth track veers R, but you go to the L of it, along the start of a blocked and broken *monopati*, towards a cairn on a wall and up to the terrace wall.

WALKING ON THE GREEK ISLANDS – THE CYCLADES

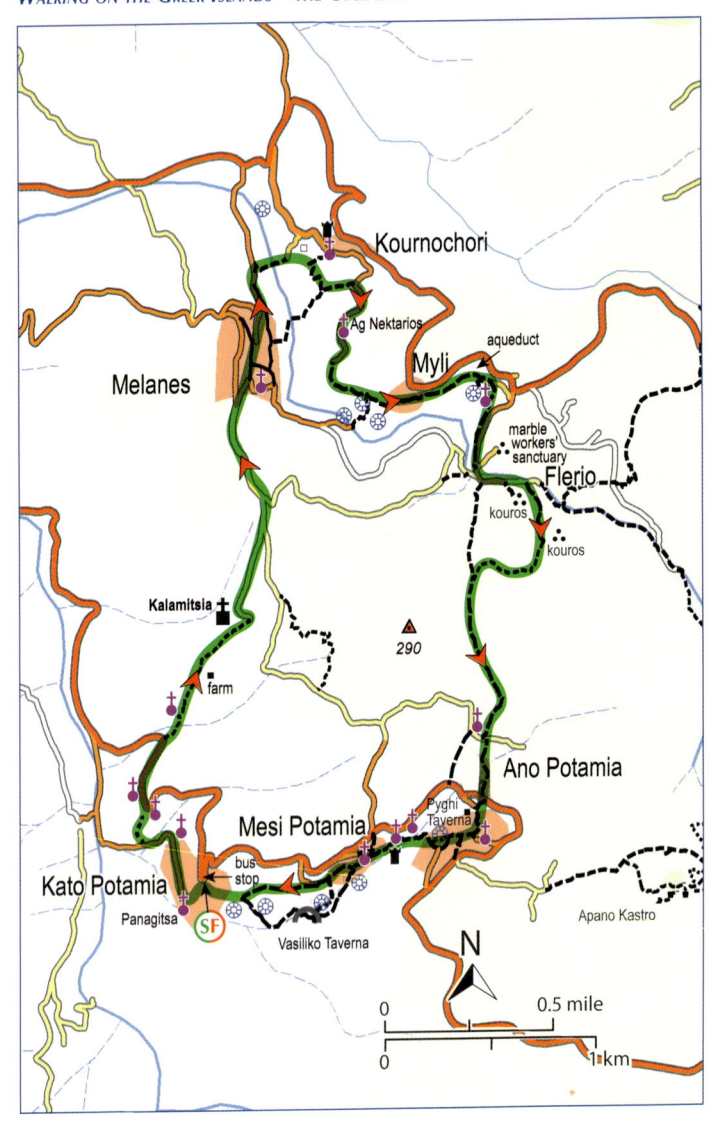

94

Follow above the *monopati*, past a goose and guinea-fowl **farm**. At a facing wall go R through a gap in the wall and then R again through a rock gap along a trail through aromatic and prickly shrubs. Pass bull-horn-style gateposts – the old entrance to **Kalamitsia**, an 18th-century Jesuit monastic foundation that proceeded to acquire a significant amount of property on the island.

Creating **monastic foundations** was one way in which the Venetians maintained a Catholic presence after the Turks took control. This rambling ruin straddles a narrow watered valley, where monks incurred the envy of the locals for their productive, tightly terraced gardens, and grew the first oranges on Naxos. Impressive interior spaces are open to the sky, and on the lowest level are a running spring and a mill, but beware: the floors are broken and the masonry unstable.

The route goes above the curved roof of the monks' cells onto a dirt road that bends beneath what looks like

18th-century Kalamitsia retreat for Jesuit monks

Crossing from the Melanes valley to Ano Potamia (high river)

a high-rise chapel but is actually a multi-storey pigeon-house. Follow the dirt road generally N, onto the concrete lane just before **Melanes village**. Fork R, then take the lower of two lanes off the hairpin bend for the three-taverna route through the village.

> The **village** name comes from *melas*, meaning green and shady. It was an economic hub of the island in the centuries BC due to the nearby marble and the well-watered, fertile valley that is still is one of the island's main areas of fruit and vegetable production.

Pass Βασιλης Taverna (small general store down steps R), then Aykyra (anchor), and finally Yiorgos, above the end-village car park and bus stop, where you fork R down a stepped shortcut back to the road and turn L. Beyond a trio of tubular metal barriers go sharp R down a concrete path, across the river and along a cypress-lined avenue.

At the end, turn R up the lane, L at the large **ruin** and onto a dirt path past water cisterns. Keep R at the first

Walk 11 – Potamia villages and marble hills

junction, beside a concrete water channel, and go L at the next. ▶ In spring you may have to push through thick growths of benign vegetation. At the top, turn R along a lane that winds above garden terraces, beneath the twin church of **Ag Nektarios**. Continue to the two-part hamlet of **Myli** (mill), where a leat trips merrily by the path, and whose springs have supplied Naxos town with water from the fifth century BC. In the valley is a stone buttress that once supported a mill-race.

At a R bend with a giant *platanos* (plane tree), turn L up a stepped path where water gushes from rock dribbled with lime deposits and laced with maiden-fern. At the top, cross a paved area with benches, and at the end of the village go straight ahead to a narrow dirt track bordered by a stone wall, which soon becomes a mule track overhung by prickly pear. At a marble-stepped fork go up L, and a few metres farther on look for a detour to the L to an excavated section of a late sixth-century BC **aqueduct**.

> Up L is Kournochori, named for the kouros statue you will meet later on the walk, and a Venetian tower.

> The **aqueduct** carried water 11km to Naxos town for some 1300 years, and was commissioned by the 'tyrant' Lygdamis, who was also responsible for the temple to Apollo at Naxos port. This entrance to the aqueduct's 220-metre tunnel doubled as a water-filtering basin.

The marble path leads up to a concrete road, where you take the paved path R. Beyond a small house, fork R towards a white chapel and information centre, which has useful maps and panels outside. At the asphalt road the route goes R, but first go L up to the peaceful and evocative **marble workers' sanctuary**.

> It's not hard to imagine why a goddess of fertility and a pair of giants – the guardians of quarry workers – were worshipped in this haven at the head of the watered valley called **Flerio**, beside an accessible seam of high-quality marble. The quarry was worked between the eighth and sixth centuries

97

BC, producing some of the most iconic statuary of ancient Greece and placing the Naxos marble industry at its creative and economic peak. Among the old olive trees are scattered half-finished pieces or 'seconds' of worked marble.

From the sanctuary, go down the lane and turn L along a shaded, stream-side avenue. Look R for the signed path to a giant marble statue **(kouros)** that lies abandoned at the spot where it was being sculpted some 2500 years ago.

The **kouros** statues depict idealised youths, and are among the earliest of the large-scale sculptures made in the Cyclades from about the seventh century BC. The statues were sculpted to formulaic proportions and design, with dreadlocks, a cryptic smile and one foot forward. The style became redundant from 500–480BC, replaced by sculptures with greater anatomical detail, more fluidity and asymmetrical movement.

Abandoned kouros statue on the hillside above Flerio

WALK 11 – POTAMIA VILLAGES AND MARBLE HILLS

Return to the shady lane and turn R to an opening over the stream course. Bear L up the path to **kouros** no. 2 – prostate, naked and open to the elements. From here, go back down a level and turn L above a ruined building, along a trail over a fallen wall. Follow it round to a junction with a small building and turn R, then L at next junction, and L again along the signed path to Ano Potamia.

The path drops in a perfection of marble paving, often slippery with the leathery leaf-fall of kermes oak, to a junction with a vehicle track. Turn L and immediately R, down a continuation of path to a main road. Cross obliquely L to go down the footpath L of the church to the **Pyghi Taverna** and the eponymous spring, where you can refill water bottles (you may have to switch on the flow in the wall, R).

Turn L at the taverna and go through the village of **Ano Potamia**, keeping straight ahead where the way levels at a small *plateia* (square) overlooking the luxuriant valley, then descend to a junction opposite a metal door. Turn R, then L at the stream. Bear R at the fork at the beginning of **Mesi Potamia village**, L at the major fork beneath Ag Yiorgos **church** down to a junction, and turn R. Follow this path until it joins a concrete lane, where you keep straight ahead at the fork, soon joining onto a country path that rounds the top of the valley. At the junction turn R to **Kato Potamia**, and take the second alley R back to the road and **bus stop**.

WALKING ON THE GREEK ISLANDS – THE CYCLADES

WALK 12
South coast to Demeter's Temple

Start	Bus stop, Kastraki (Apolafsi Taverna)
Finish	Bus stop, Sangri
Distance	8.5km
Ascent	335m
Descent	155m
Time	2½hr
Terrain	Dirt tracks and country paths over rolling countryside of phrygana and maquis
Refreshments	At beginning and end
Transport	Bus service Chora–Kastraki; Sangri is on the Chora–Chalki bus route

Throughout this walk there are big views of coast and rural heartland as you climb over a surge of brown hills rising from the broad coastal plain. The completely different world of the island's mountainous interior suddenly opens up, enclosing a wide fertile vale that has been farmed for 6000 years. Set off in time to visit the museum at the pre-classical Temple of Demeter (open Easter 8.30am–3pm, closed Tuesdays).

From the bus stop named for Manolis Makaris, late owner of Apolafsi Taverna, now run by his widow and sons, turn R inland up a sandy lane. ◄ Continue past a large white **house** (R) to the crest of the hill and an exposed **farm**, from where you can look back to the long strands of the SW coast between the wild Aliko and conical Mikri Vigla headlands, and the islands of Ios and Paros. Zas, highest peak of the Cyclades, dominates the mountainous horizon.

Go down and take the first fork L off the main dirt road onto a sandy track, and keep to this main track heading mainly NE, passing low white farm buildings up on a ridge. Carry on through a wire gate, swinging

On the hillside to the L is the restored 18th-century Oskelos Tower that gives Kastraki (small castle) its name – one of several residential strongholds built by the Venetians.

100

Walk 12 – South coast to Demeter's Temple

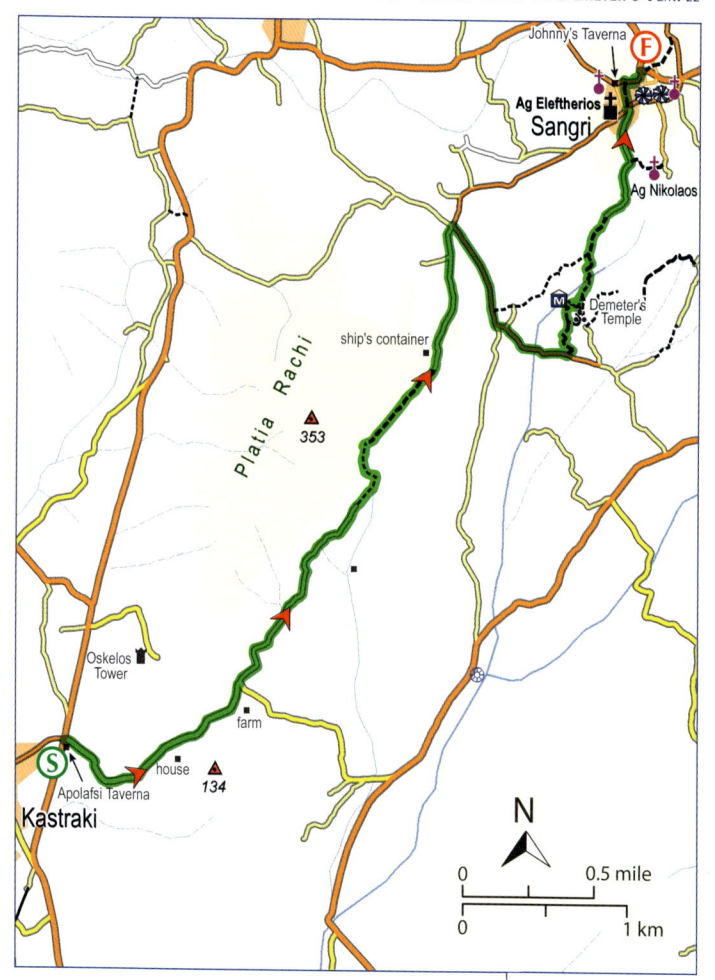

L along the flank of **Platia Rachi hill**. At a dusty junction, keep L and up. Go through a fence-gate where a farm track goes down R, and soon after, where the track widens and ends, go straight ahead through the wire gate

Walking on the Greek Islands – the Cyclades

The juniper hill dips to a new vista of fertile plain defined by abruptly rising mountains, and the little white temple of Demeter on a low rise.

at the corner, along a track between a fenced field and drystone wall, then through another fence-gate. There's dwarf juniper forest on the R and a very tempting path into it at a wooden pallet gate. Do not take this, but step up into the stony field and follow its perimeter fence, curving L, then R and up. ◀

Leave the field at a rocky path and go through the gap in a fence, then immediately turn diagonally up L and look R for the well-defined trail winding along a contour NNE, among dwarf junipers, spring-flowering sage-like *Phlomis*, strap-leaved asphodel, and in autumn, checkered purple *Colchicum*. Through a wooden gate the trail becomes less defined, but follow the line of a stone wall below R until you see a rusty fence ahead, and drop down before you reach it, to a clear mule track and turn L. At a cross-tracks by a red **ship's container** go straight ahead, where another farmed highland opens to the W.

Turn R down the asphalt road signed 'Demeter's Temple' and continue for 1.2km (past tempting paths off L), then go L up the paved path to the site. At the stone ticket office for **Demeter's Temple** go straight ahead to the **museum**, which helps you understand the site's various

Demeter's Temple, honouring the goddess of agriculture

WALK 12 – SOUTH COAST TO DEMETER'S TEMPLE

reincarnations. Go behind the museum, where there's a section of temple pediment, and up the wide path to the L of it. Pass a double metal gate (L) to tour the temple site, but return to this point to continue the walk.

> On this low hill, commanding land that has been farmed since Neolithic times, offerings were made to gods of fertility and harvest – you can see pits and channels where ritual juices were poured. The part-reconstructed **marble temple** dates from 530BC. Features such as the Ionic columns anticipated the order of architecture developed in classical Athens. The temple was roofed with translucent marble tiles, suffusing the interior with soft light, its exterior painted in rich colours. Ornamental fragments in the museum still carry faint traces of pigment. There's also a reconstruction of the Christian basilica that was built over the temple as fashions changed.

Go through the double metal gate to follow a worn trail along the terrace and over the broken wall R of a square stone building at the end. Just 12 metres farther on, drop down over another broken wall to the terrace below, follow it to the remains of a stone hut (R), then go obliquely across the olive grove to a line of shrubs. Cut down to cross the stream-bed and follow the clear stone path around a field boundary, up to a T-junction, and turn R on the route to Sangri.

The *monopati* emerges onto a ridged concrete lane and goes L and uphill. ▸ At the first houses of **Sangri**, turn L up steps beneath pine trees. Turn R at the top and almost immediately fork L along a paved lane, past **Ag Eleftherios monastery** and on to a junction. Turn R and then L down an alleyway to reach **Johnny's Taverna**. From the courtyard turn L to the main road and bus stop.

Down a path to the R is the small but perfectly formed Ag Nikolaos chapel in undressed stone, which has impressive 13th-century frescos. It is only open in August, 10am–2.30pm Monday–Friday).

WALKING ON THE GREEK ISLANDS – THE CYCLADES

WALK 13
Rural byways below Profitis Ilias

Start/Finish	Bus stop, Sangri
Distance	11.5km
Ascent/Descent	280m
Time	3½hr
Terrain	Easy going on clear rocky paths and tracks through farmland and meadows and between mountains
Refreshments	Johnny's Taverna, Sangri; water at Mersinos Spring
Transport	Bus service Chora–Sangri–Chalki

This walk gives a sense of rural Naxos life before roads, when paths connected villages and cultivated land. There are perfect picnic spots in meadows and groves thick with marguerites and wild lupins in spring and soft-gold grasses in summer. A hidden valley cuts between the sheer walls of two marble mountains, where eagles patrol, and just off-piste on the lower slopes are miniature wild rock gardens.

Go E along the road from the bus stop and over crossroads to a dirt track leading off the corner of a wide gravel area. Follow it down, right-angling around field boundaries until you reach a L turn with a pair of telegraph poles. Take this through fields. Soon the cuboid Bazeos Tower is seen ahead.

At an open field, follow its R edge then kink R along the bottom of the next field where the bulk of Profitis Ilias looms before you. Turn R at the farm track and L at the road. Opposite is a signpost to the mini-monastery of **Kaloritsa**, which straddles a cleft high on the mountain. ◄ Just beyond is **Bazeos Tower**, where you turn R up a brown rocky track.

Climbing the rough trail and back takes about 50 minutes; worthwhile for the ruins on a rocky shelf that evoke a remote monastic life in an extraordinary setting.

The **tower** was built in 1671 as a manor in the feudal system introduced by the Venetians, and which

WALK 13 – RURAL BYWAYS BELOW PROFITIS ILIAS

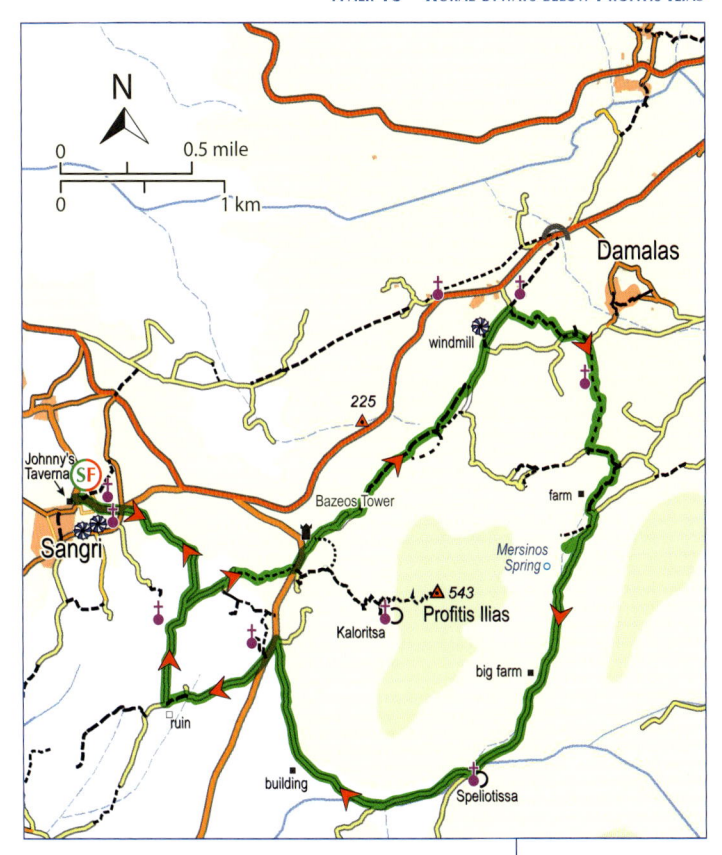

persisted as a Catholic enclave under Turkish rule. Enclosed within it is a monastery, which was abandoned in the early 19th century and taken over by the newborn Greek state. It was used for a time as a base for potters, then bought by the Bazeos family who now run a café and cultural events there June–September.

Farmlands of southern Naxos, seen from Bazeos Tower

Turn R beside the tower along a rocky track, which rounds up to the R past a tubular metal gate, and keep straight along the main track at a cluster of paths and walls until you reach a junction where a track comes in from the R. Fork L here and immediately L through a fence-gate on to the remnants of a wide, paved way, which you follow through meadows until it disappears under vegetation and a bulldozed track invades, then drop down R to rejoin the dirt track.

Turn L and continue to a junction, then bear L to pass beneath a **windmill** and heaps of slate. In the dip, turn R onto a *monopati* between walls and bear L at a fork between human-high walls, going around right-angle field boundaries through picnic meadows and following a bend to the R where a rival route goes off L. ◀ Reach the dirt lane again and turn L. You could continue along this lane to the village of Damalas, which has a delightful restored olive press and a working pottery.

See ahead the central villages arrayed around the vale of the Trageia. L–R: Tsikalario, Moni, Chalki, Damalas.

To continue on the circular walk, bear R up a wide rocky path through a blissfully bucolic mix of meadows, groves and the central sea of silver olives, with its mountain rim. At the top, where a path goes straight ahead, turn L into a shady *monopati*, and very soon cut R down

WALK 13 – RURAL BYWAYS BELOW PROFITIS ILIAS

rocks into a deep-sunken path – a tree tunnel that you follow to its end at a farm track. Turn L, and R along the dirt road that leads through the valley between the E flank of Profitis Ilias and the outer lumps of the island's spine. Soon, at the end of a concrete section (just before a giant marble-block terrace high up to the L), a brief detour R down a rocky path leads to the oasis of **Mersinos Spring**.

Back on the main route (which leads all the way around Profitis Ilias back to Bazeos Tower) continue on beneath delightful dells among boulders and dark junipers on the slopes to the R. Pass a **big farm** (R), and some way beyond, in a dip, turn L over the stream-bed and L to a bank beneath a little cliff, with the **chapel of Speliotissa** in a cave carved by swirling water aeons ago into a band of soft sugar marble.

Continue along the main dirt road to the asphalt road and turn L, then R onto a sandy track a few metres down. Turn R at the junction with **ruined buildings**, after the dip, and follow the lane back to **Sangri**.

Vineyards, olive groves and villages linked by old paths

WALKING ON THE GREEK ISLANDS – THE CYCLADES

WALK 14
Wild lands around Apalirou

Start/Finish	Turnoff to Ag Ioannis Theologos Adisarou chapel, on the road to Agiassos
Distance	9km, or 11.5km including Apalirou
Ascent/Descent	250m, or 505m including Apalirou
Time	3½hr, or 4¾hr including Apalirou
Terrain	Country paths and a long, easy-walking stretch of dirt road through undulating, wide farmland and rough pasture, then trails through wild shrubs and a rough climb and descent of the lower mountain slopes
Refreshments	Adisarou Spring. No other options on the route.
Transport	No public transport. Area for parking at turnoff to Adisarou Spring.
Notes	Mobile network coverage is intermittent. Take a stick/pole for rarely seen but potentially aggressive sheepdogs.

A foray into really wild Naxos, the back country of Marathou, where population density is maybe one goatherd per 5 sq km and where few islanders and certainly no tourists venture. The craggy height of Apalirou is a constant as you hike through the main farmland of southern Naxos and hidden valleys from which pinnacles and ridges of marble rise. The silence is tangible – apart from the bells of a thousand goats. There are havens of wildflowers, with anemones, marguerites, campion and crocus, in spring and autumn. The optional route on Apalirou is unclear and hard-going, but difficulty of access was the point of the castle's defensive position!

The key to ninth-century chapel of **Ag Ioannis Theologos Adisarou** is with Kyria Stella, at the first **farm** building down the main road on the R.

> On the outside, this is just another simple, local stone, **island church**. Inside, however, is the best aniconic wall painting on the island, exceptional for its

Walk 14 – Wild lands around Apalirou

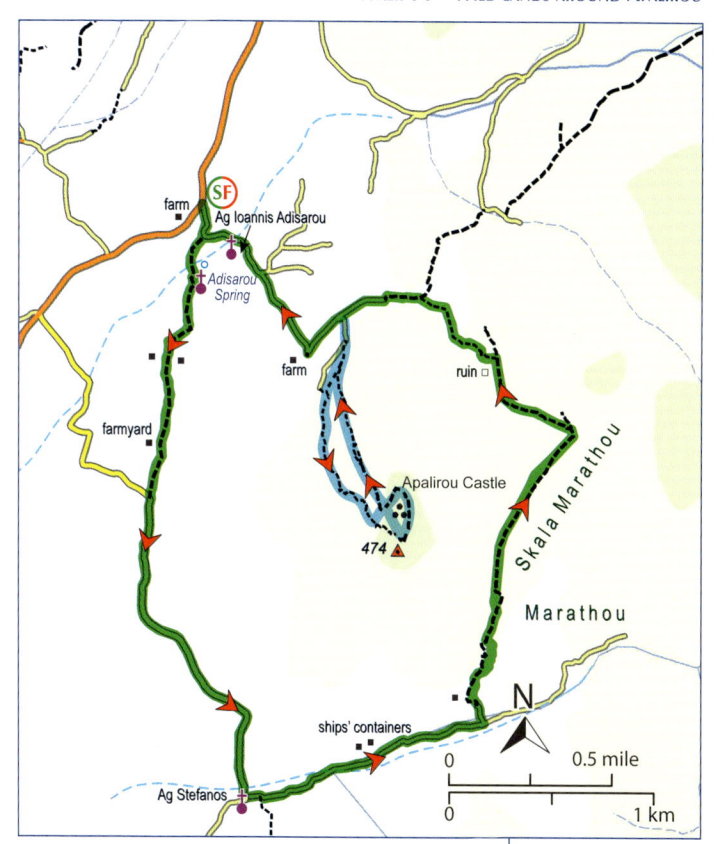

rich colours and skilful execution, with tessellated, coffered and interlacing geometric motifs, trefoils and rosettes. You can see traces of the base grid done by the master painter before itinerant painters came with their pattern books to finish the job.

From the road, follow the stony vehicle track to an open space with a house, and turn R along the broad, walled, rock avenue, which turns into a narrow path

In the olive grove meadow behind the spring, a ring of skeletal olive trunks around an empty core is said to be the island's oldest olive tree.

through a fence-gate to reach the dappled shade of **Adisarou Spring**. ◄ Go up to the **chapel** and turn R along the *monopati*, which you follow past pigsty containers, then through a **farmyard** and across an open space to join a track. Turn L, and L again at the wide dirt road.

Keep to the main track among the main farming region of southern Naxos as it swings SE along the S of Apalirou. There's a curve of battlements high on the NW edge, while S is the shore at Agiassos, where the Venetians landed and, they say, burnt their boats before invading.

The track dips to a stream-bed and goes up to a junction. In the field opposite is the stone-roofed miniature **chapel of Ag Stefanos** with a guardian gnarled olive tree. Turn L, following a stream course of marble boulders. Pass **ships' containers** (L) and then at a staggered cross-paths turn L. Just before an entrance gate, turn R through a fence-gate into the scrub and bear obliquely up through rocks and junipers. Here starts the tricky section, so look out for red paint marks.

Population of wild Naxos

Where the trail levels, head towards a low building and keep to the L of the wall below it until it veers R for the second time, then go up L past a large triangular rock and follow the trail roughly N until you reach a facing broken wall. Turn up L, and shortly after go R down a trail through the juniper wood and over a hump to a surprise patch of tilled land (which begs the question of where the access point for machinery could be). Look immediately L for a rock wall, step up it and turn R onto very stony open ground, which you cross up and L, to go through a gap in the shrubs that mark the rise to the next open terrace.

Go up another level, and the top, turn R. At a fork of cultivated strips, take the lower one and go along the top of the field, which ends at a trail through junipers. Go up and L, initially towards the E side of the mountain, then up to a facing, loose stone wall. Go up to the L of it and there is the identifiable but broken beginning of **Skala Marathou** bordered by a rusty fence atop a wall that slices up the mountainside. You may occasionally have to divert around vegetation or minor collapse, but generally follow a straight diagonal to a rocky col – gateway to a hidden world, an inland sea of hazy scrub with island peaks.

Turn L to descend a loose stone animal trail down the apex of the valley, crossing over two low rock

The marble steps at Marathou

WALKING ON THE GREEK ISLANDS – THE CYCLADES

You can hear 1000 goats, but try spotting them!

walls as it levels towards the bottom. An almost proper path leads you to the R and passes a copse of hardy junipers. ◀ Continue to the next stand of juniper and turn L at its start, going over a wall and down between a **ruin** and an unusually sturdy tree. Turn R just below, along the bottom edge of the wood, and then head L towards the flat gap between twin peaks. Watch for red paint spots, but any trail NW will do, heading to a gap in the next copse and passage over a low W–E wall.

Now keep to the L of a N-running wall and head to the NW of the wild land, then go through a fence-opening at the corner of the wall. Turn L along the *monopati* to its end at a goatyard, then L again through a fence-gate. Follow the dirt road R.

Optional ascent of Apalirou (1¼hr return)

The easiest ascent of Apalirou starts where the track widens about 200 metres beyond the goatyard, via another dirt road that goes obliquely up L. Turn L steeply up the mountain just before the **farm**, following the clearest trails through shrubs then heading E over increasingly

From Apalirou Castle towards Profitis Ilias (far L)

WALK 14 – WILD LANDS AROUND APALIROU

bare rock, to go round the base of the main defensive wall. A trail on the N side leads to the summit.

> During the serious Arab pirate raids of the eighth century, locals and their livestock retreated to the summit of **Apalirou** and built fortified walls, cisterns, houses and chapels. The coast is visible but far enough away to give defenders time to prepare. In 1207 the Venetians under Marco Sanudo landed at Agiassos Bay, besieged the castle and began the 300-year Venetian rule of the island. Apalirou was abandoned after Sanudo built the *kastro* in Naxos port.

To descend, find a way steeply just S of the defensive wall, then head NW for the R side of a barren ridge, which you cross over L before dropping through shrubs and back to the farm. From there return to the main route.

Continue to a junction with farm buildings where the concrete lane hairpins steeply down, and follow this all the way back to the starting point. Just before the first house on the L, a brown sign directs you to **Ag Ioannis Adisarou chapel**, and just beyond is the R turn back to the main road.

Walking on the Greek Islands – the Cyclades

WALK 15
Central villages and Fanari foothills

Start/Finish	Bus stop, Chalki
Distance	9.5km
Ascent/Descent	415m
Time	3½hr
Terrain	Deep-cut lanes shaded by olive trees and evergreens; rough climb up a bouldered stream-bed; rough trails through high, open country; traditional paths through and linking villages
Refreshments	Chalki, Moni
Transport	Bus service between Chora, Chalki and Moni

This magical route climbs into foothills of Mount Fanari and courses around the upper tiers of a natural amphitheatre. There are glimpses through the trees of limestone heights sharp against the sky, white triangles of villages perched on the hillsides, gems of early Christian chapels, and a fabulous diversity of spring flowers. Breathtaking views fall to the southwest, where isolated peaks rise from a sea of inland vales. The route starts and finishes in the arty and charming village of Chalki ('ch' as in loch).

From the bus stop, go up the lane beside **Protothronos church** and its sentinel Norfolk Island pine. ◄ Follow the lane past the 1742 *pyrghos* (fortified manor), built by the Venetian Catholic Barozzi, and turn R. At the main road go R, then cross to turn L at a white-washed wall. The lane bends R to an abandoned olive pressing building. Turn L at its corner to **Kaloxilos** (good wood), past the church with early Byzantine and Archaic temple fragments embedded in its walls.

Follow the lane R past the **folklore museum** (tel +30 69740 26967), then bear L and L again to a little square and turn R. Kink L–R, and go L where steps go straight up, then follow this lane through the village. Cross a small

Protothronos (first throne), seat of the Orthodox Bishop of Naxos in Byzantine times, is only open for services but the Pappas may show you around, especially if you attend Sunday morning liturgy.

114

square with a picturesquely crumbling former *kafenion* and balconied houses, some with bridges to valley-view gardens.

    Leaving the village, keep straight ahead, wind over a stream-bed and turn L at an old community wash-house, heading towards the hamlet of **Pighi** (spring). Where a concrete road joins L, keep straight on past a chapel (L), and turn R where a concrete lane signed 'MONH' goes straight ahead. Keep L at a bend where a path drops R, and go straight up at a L turn opposite a breezeblock building. At the next junction go L past neat walls and metal gates. Keep R where a track goes down L, past spiky agaves (ignoring the *monopati* to the R), to reach a distinctive curve of wall where the lane bends L. Here turn R up a steep rock path. ▶

    Beyond the chapel turnoff, reach a stream course beneath plane trees and turn R to follow it, guided by red spots. Go L of a fallen tree, up the L bank for a bit, and back to the stream-bed, then through a fence-gate waymarked '8' and along a terrace. Return into the

Neoclassical style kafenion, Kaloxilos village

After a wire gate, look for little path R to the immaculate miniature chapel of Ag Spiridon in a hobbit land of rock-garden terraces spilling down to the SW vales.

Looking southwest from Ag Spiridon chapel

At a break in the trees, look down to a marble wine press on the terraced foreground and beyond to a marvellous perspective of characteristic Naxos landscape.

stream-bed, then thread up and around boulders and banks, and go through a sheep-height fence-gate. Ahead is a vertical rock-face cleft by a sometime waterfall, which you climb to the R of, up rock-cut steps.

At the top, follow the wall R, turn L through a gate-less gap to see a plane of sloping grey rock, and go straight up to a wall with a red arrow at the top. Turn L onto a walled *monopati*. ◂

Where the *monopati* starts to crumble, bypass it via the terrace R (red paint), and drop back down L opposite a sturdy but roofless building. Look out for and follow red paint spots, swinging R where there are a couple of prominent solitary rocks. Go N then E along the mountainside, dipping through stands of kermes oak, beneath surprise areas of bracken where the bedrock changes to schist. After descending through a tree tunnel, pass a two-tier wine press and shelter, then drop to a stream-bed. Follow this down to a marble-cobbled section, where you go round a blocked section, up to the R bank and follow the trail L to a gulley with marbled *monopati*.

WALK 15 – CENTRAL VILLAGES AND FANARI FOOTHILLS

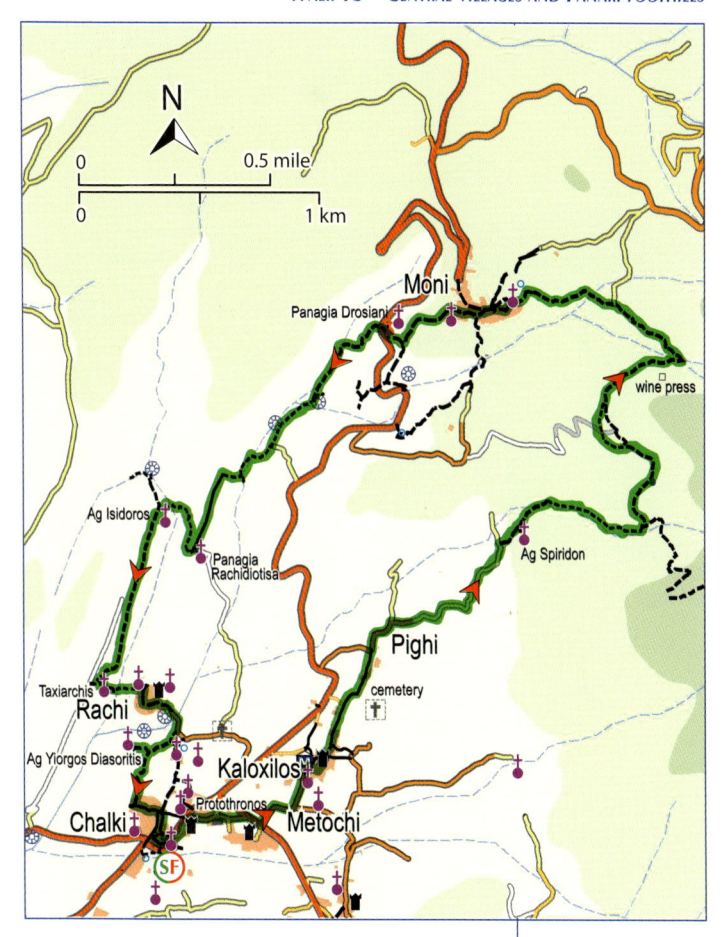

Climb down and turn R, then follow the clear old working route all the way to the village of **Moni**. Disregard a signed path '8' that descends L, and brush through wild fennel, beneath quince, fig and mulberry trees, to the vegetable garden terraces on the village outskirts. At the wash-house, bear R and follow the main

Down steps L is Eleftheria's workshop. She is one of around 20 women who weave sometimes intricately patterned, rectangular shapes dictated by the hand-loom for covers and cloths.

alley as it turns L and R, then generally W, to reach a *plateia* with a mulberry tree. ◄

Go below the tree and R (for tavernas and cafés, take the stepped path R at the top of the square then go down to a parking area and R), along a path looking S. Do not be tempted down the path waymarked '4' to the L; instead keep R, gradually winding down L and out of the village on another part of *monopati* 4. At the junction turn R along the path below **Panagia Drosiani**.

> **Panagia Drosiani** (open 11am–6pm, 1 May–mid October) is one of the most important Christian churches in the Cyclades for its sixth-century foundation and paintings remarkable for their beauty and realism, compared with later, stylised Byzantine iconography. There are rosy-cheeked women, ruddy-complexioned men, and rare depictions of Christ as young and beardless. The church is an agglomeration of memorial chapels that were once surrounded by the monastery for which the village of Moni is named. The original east-end chapel probably housed the tomb of a holy person, then others were added, as people hoped some of the holiness might be transferred to their own bodies.

Cross the asphalt road to reach path 4 opposite and go steeply down, keeping L. Cross a stream-bed (there's a bridged remnant of mill up to the L) and bear L immediately afterwards. At a concrete lane, cross obliquely to go down steps, then keep L and follow the path until it crosses the stream-bed and turns R up a walled path. Near the top, turn L through a fence-gate onto a dirt track along the open hillside.

The major turn L at the end of the track goes past the chapel of **Panagia Rachidiotisa**, charming in form and stunning in location, but you take the walled *monopati* that leads sharp R down off the turn before it. At the junction shortly after, turn R and see the ruined triple-aisled basilica of Ag Isidoros chapel across the valley. Keep L

WALK 15 – CENTRAL VILLAGES AND FANARI FOOTHILLS

down the cobbled, curvy path to reach a stream-bed, which you cross and immediately squeeze between oleanders to go up steps set into the wall, then turn R along the edge of an olive grove and continue to its end. ▶ Turn L up marble slab steps to reach the sixth or seventh-century **Ag Isidoros**, whose original timber roof was replaced by the stone, barrel-vaulted structure in the 10th–11th centuries.

Go below the chapel then up R. Climb over the broken wall to a narrow dirt path and turn L. At a fork leading down to stream-bed, keep R and up, continuing along the path until you pass above the restored **church of Ag Taxiarchis** (Archangel Michael; open daily 11am–2.30pm July and August) before turning L through a fence-gate to wind down to it.

Below Taxiarchis, take the path across the valley bottom and up to the tumbledown outskirts of **Rachi**. Turn R, then L at the telegraph pole, cross a paved area and wend R through the hamlet to a stream-bed with a giant eucalyptus. Follow the lane R to a right-angle L bend and take the narrow dirt path off it. Bear R at the junction and R again for **Ag Yiorgos Diasoritis** (George the Saviour).

A 10-minute detour straight ahead goes past stone beehives set into the opposite hillside, to a ruined mill-race.

The church is all natural stone and undulating tiles, sturdy, barrel-vaulted and domed, with a high-rise bell-tower. It's only open July and August 10am–2pm, but inside is the greatest collection of **11th-century frescos** in the Aegean. They were painted at a time of peak creativity on Naxos, when money and skills were plentiful. The high-quality work demonstrates that the local master painters were up to speed with the latest colours, subjects and styles.

Return to the chapel turnoff and go R, then L at the next junction with a wire gate. Turn R and follow the path to cross over staggered crossroads, reaching a junction opposite the Kitron Distillery in the heart of **Chalki village**. Turn R, then L above the *plateia* and L again to reach the main road and bus stop.

Walking on the Greek Islands – the Cyclades

WALK 16
Filoti village and Mount Zas

Start/Finish	Bus stop, Gefyra square, Filoti
Distance	9.5km
Ascent/Descent	730m
Time	4hr
Terrain	Steep climb up village lanes and the mountain itself. The descent is an acute gradient of loose soil and stones; then a narrow, bouldered stream-bed.
Refreshments	Filoti, spring water from fountains at Aria Spring
Transport	Bus service Chora–Chalki–Filoti

If visitors do just one hike on Naxos, it's usually up Mount Zas, the highest peak in the Cyclades – so be prepared for company. Signs recommend you do it at dawn, which isn't a bad idea in summer, and it is exciting. The views, down precipitous crags and cliffs to glorious perspectives of land, sea… and the rest of the Cyclades, are worth every effort.

Go along the Gefyra terrace, shaded by big plane trees (there's a water fountain to fill bottles in front of them), and turn L opposite Baboulas Taverna. Keep R at the fork signed 'Ιατρειο' (doctor), past a communal washing facility. At the bend with an arched well tunnel (L), whose spring has long since been diverted, go steeply up the lane all the way to a **car park** at the apex of the village.

Turn sharp L over a concrete patch onto a *monopati*. At a junction with sloping marble slabs, curve R up steps to the asphalt road, and cross obliquely to fork R, signposted 'Monastery of Fotodotis'. On the first bend, take a shortcut up to the next bit of road and cross to another path that slices off a bend. Back on the road, turn R and walk along to **Ag Marina chapel** in a little courtyard.

Turn R up a dirt path in front of the chapel and follow it up, L, then to the R of a **house** and join the single-track

WALK 16 – FILOTI VILLAGE AND MOUNT ZAS

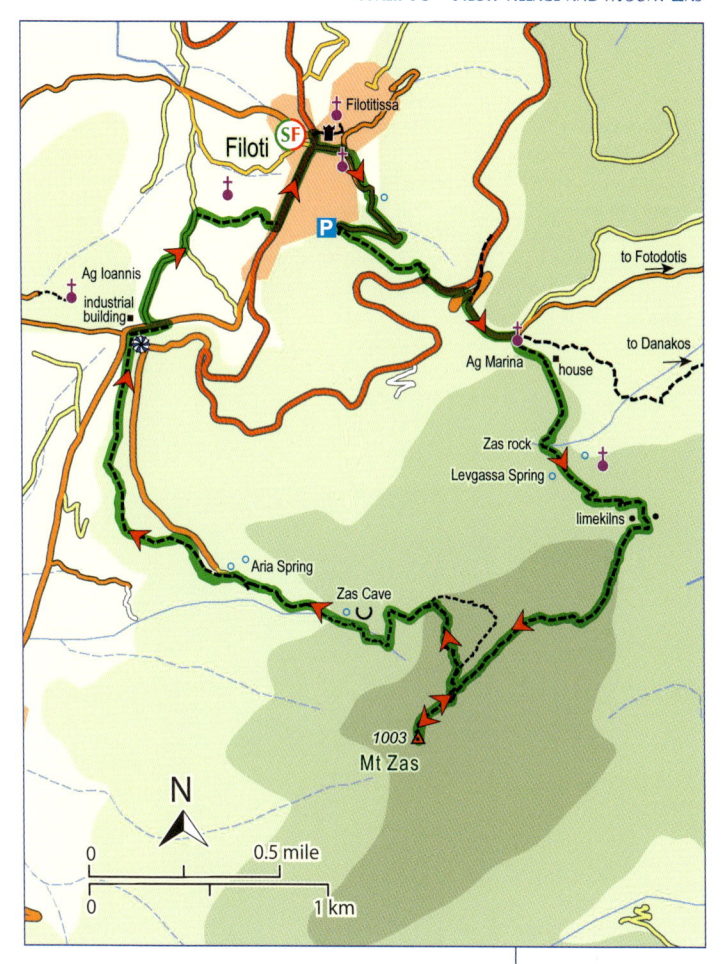

path along the mountainside, with views to the sea and islands of Donousa and Makares. Go through a wooden pallet gate, around the valley head and past a bulldozed track slashing in from the L. Look R for a large **rock** engraved on its upper surface with the inscription (age

121

WALKING ON THE GREEK ISLANDS – THE CYCLADES

unknown) 'ΌΡΟΣ ΔΗΟΣΜΗΛΟ ΣΙΟΨ' (mountain of Zeus, protector of herds). Shortly after, reach the water troughs of **Levgassa Spring**.

The stone pits L and R are limekilns, where the calceous rock was broken down to produce cement and whitewash – you can see the vitrified rock beneath the fig tree in the second.

As the path ascends steeply, beware of going off-piste at the z-bends, and when it becomes less distinct as it levels and rounds a small spur, follow cairns and waymark '2' up R past a signpost. ◀ At a wall ahead, signed 'το κοροφη' (summit), turn R uphill, and then L at the corner. A vista opens SE to the islands of Amorgos (the biggest and most distant), Ano and Kato Koufonisi, and the uninhabited mound of Keros. The path among the deceptively soft-looking cushions of wickedly spiny bushes is clear-cut at first, but later, take your choice, guided by cairns and red dots.

Where the hillside levels into a saddle, head L. You can see the W side of the island, with Chora (Naxos

Spiny broom and Mount Zas in June

122

town) far below NW and Paros island beyond. Continue SW, cairn to cairn, towards the **1003m summit**, where Zeus, head Olympian god, is said to have received his signature thunderbolt.

Dawn ascent of Zas, highest point in the Cyclades

> Pairs of Bonelli's eagles or spaced-out groups of griffon vultures may be patrolling the crags on **Mount Zas**, and sometimes swifts slice through the air with audible speed and handbrake turns. There are days, too, when just one species of insect completely takes over: black or red beetles swarm over every surface, or, if you're lucky, it may be the turn of red admiral butterflies.

Retrace your steps from the summit, keeping to the NW edge of the ridge, for around 350 metres, to a break in the solid rock cover at a gravelly stretch. A pair of cairns and waymark '2' indicate the downward route obliquely L to a broad shelf of hillside. Turn R, and towards the end of the shelf go steeply down, following cairns, red spots and red-earth-stained tracks. Where the hillside becomes even steeper, head towards a stone threshing circle among walled enclosures until you are almost at a facing wall, then turn L along a briefly level path.

Follow the wire fence R and climb over a rock ledge, then follow the wall around to the R. Just before the wall leads uphill R, turn L down to a prominent tilted rock, then head slightly L facing the scree slope. Go down an inclined plane of rock, past a cairn and a blue arrow. Below an overhanging rock, turn R to pick your way down the gulley that falls precipitously from the peak. Look for a couple of bushy evergreen trees clinging to the rocks; up to the R of them is the concrete-framed entrance to **Zas Cave** in an arch of rock-face.

> The accessible interior of the **cave** reaches back some 100 metres, but it is very dark, the surface uneven and slippery. There's a pothole R, and above it a fretwork of limestone deposits. According to some, the god Zeus was secretly brought here in secret as a baby, after his mother Rhea rescued him from being devoured by his father Chronos. Zeus was nursed by nymphs, and a pair of warriors had mock fights outside the cave to drown his gurgles and cries. More solid evidence of ancient life has been found in the cave – Neolithic vessels, more than 5500 years old.

Continue, mostly to the R of the gulley, soon seeing a paved path that winds down to **Aria Spring**, whose water is apparently rich in potassium. At the far corner L of the water cistern, take the mule track down and then straight ahead alongside a wall at the bottom of steep rough land beneath sentinel cypresses. At the corner with a bushy kermes oak, continue between walls overhung with trees.

The path descends, going through a wire gate, then levels, rounds to the N and emerges into open hillside. ◄ The path swings below a **windmill** then leads down to the road, where you turn back L and go R beneath **industrial buildings**. Take the second turn R up a rather uncomfortable *monopati* of loose stones, to a junction at the foot of **Filoti**. Turn R then L up to the main street, and L back to the bus stop.

The pimple of Ag Ioannis chapel atop a giant knuckle of rock is seen opposite, and far ahead the village of Moni perched in the mountains.

WALK 17
Apiranthos to emery mines and port

Start	Bus stop, Apiranthos
Finish	Moutsouna
Distance	11.5km
Ascent	315m
Descent	905m
Time	4½hr
Terrain	Mostly downhill on uneven working paths in woodland, then exposed mountains with a 20-minute climb, broken rock trails, then pleasant tracks in coastal lowlands
Refreshments	Apiranthos, Moutsouna
Transport	No practical bus service. Take two vehicles to finish and return with one of them to the start, or hitchhike back to Apiranthos.
Accommodation	Anatoli Studios, Moutsouna, tel +30 22850 68288 or +30 69721 71303

The walk starts from a village that hugs the side of a marble mountain and has distinctive dialect and traditions, a marble terrace of cafés, and small but fascinating museums. You follow steep, wooded paths where farmed terraces are crammed into a narrow valley floor, climb to a tiny chapel on an isolated knoll, then cross a rocky shoulder to a severe, magnificent limestone landscape with the rusting remains of emery mining. Country paths drop to an ever-opening coastline with a richly coloured, sea-bitten headland and a string of beaches, two of which are at the tiny port of Moutsouna.

APIRANTHOS

The village, also called Aperathou, was regarded by the rest of Naxos as a nest of robbers and lawlessness, according to Victorian traveller Theodore Bent. Even today the villagers are known for striking a hard bargain. Cretans are believed to have settled there from the 10th century and their influence is evident in rhyming couplet poetry, local weavings, and festive customs and costumes. The marble village of today dates from Venetian times, and

Walking on the Greek Islands – the Cyclades

the tower mansion rising from the rock on the main alley bears the Lion of St Mark, emblem of Venice. World War II hero Manolis Glezos is the village's most famous son. He founded its museums of archaeology, natural history and geology. In 1941, aged 19, Glezos scaled the Athens Acropolis and tore down the swastika of the occupying Germans, and at 91 became the European Parliament's oldest member. The population of Apiranthos is about 300 but was much bigger when the emery mines were active. Now villagers use leftover dynamite for Easter fireworks.

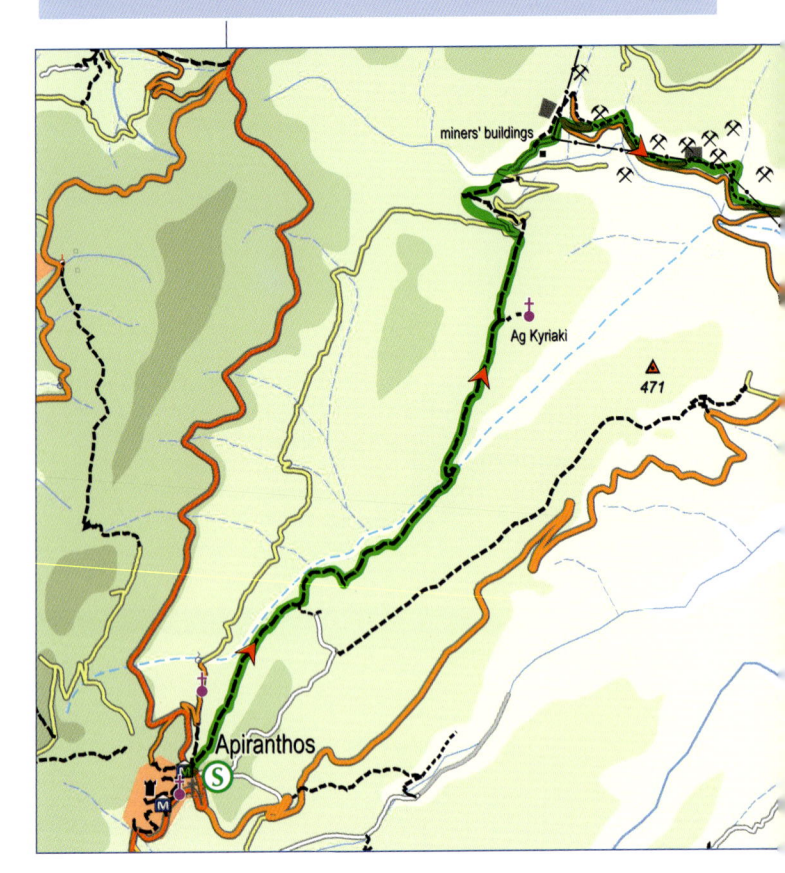

WALK 17 – APIRANTHOS TO EMERY MINES AND PORT

From the bus stop, go into the village opposite the church, turn sharp R under the main road and follow the often paved path for about 1.5km along the valley-side, shaded by small-leaved kermes oak, Oriental plane trees and sections of overhanging cliff. Keep R at a fork where our path is supported by a high retaining wall, and again at a path to a farm building L, and up broad steps to a two-mule path that sweeps around a valley-head on a high wall.

From metamorphic mountain to sedimentary headland

Look NNE for the chapel of Ag Kyriaki on a rise in the middle of interlocking spurs, camouflaged against the rock from which it was built.

The path levels and emerges into phrygana, and beyond a wooden railing or two it bisects a threshing circle. ◄ Wind down the start of a marble-paved avenue that crosses a stream-gulley then plods uphill. Near the top, where you see the **Ag Kyriaki chapel** beyond a smallholding, turn L (waymarked '1') through a wire gate, to continue the main route.

For a 15-minute round-trip to **Ag Kyriaki** (open Wednesdays and Saturdays 8.30am–2.30pm July and August), go straight ahead. The sun-bleached storyboard is a poor substitute for the experience of entering the chill dark where ninth-century frescos depicting pomegranates and birds slowly appear like magic paintings as your eyes adjust to the light. Here, birds and fishes have replaced Mary, Christ and apostles in the most sacred position of the semi-circular apse.

Offshore are the Small Cyclades islands of uninhabited Makares, and beyond it Donousa, population around 180.

The path rolls over to the next valley, beneath slanting slabs of marble and above a saddle of high fields. ◄ Beyond a smallholding, go through a gate,

WALK 17 – APIRANTHOS TO EMERY MINES AND PORT

and at the junction with a dirt track, turn L and almost immediately R down paved steps onto a rough trail that soon descends into the valley. Keep R at the (signed) fork above the stream and follow the paved path to a dirt road. Turn L, cross the stream-bed and go up past roofless former **miners' buildings**, to reach the stone towers and rusting mechanisms of the emery industry.

> Giant pulleys redirected bucketloads of emery on overhead cableways from the valley above to the Moutsouna line down to the port, where the rock was weighed and transferred to ships. **Naxos emery** was among the world's finest, the main source for the western world for centuries. Extracted through open-cast and underground mining from the Cycladic period, it was crushed and used to smooth and shape marble artefacts, and from the 19th-century, as an industrial abrasive. Feel the weight and density of the dark, scintillating rock, which comes from the molten bowels of the Earth, a mix of corundum, magnetite, hematite and quartz, and on the geological hardness scale is only one point less

Major junction on emery cable way

than diamond. Demand for Naxos emery reached its modern-day peaks in the 1920s and 1960s. It was replaced by synthetic abrasives, and the mines closed apart from minimal work by a few miners in order to qualify for pensions.

From the rusty cable junction, fork L up the stone-macadam lane to the corner and turn at the sign onto a broken rock trail. Follow the lower red spots down to the wall and L along a paved way leading to gaping holes in the cliff. ◄ Pass in front of the mines, and after the last, round a small spur, climb down loose rocks to another shelf of marble path and continue seawards.

The island of Amorgos is spread along the horizon.

Step over or under stout, rusty cable and soon after head for a streak of red paint that marks a fall to the road and turn L towards fortress-like buildings and a battlement of wall climbing the mountain. At the bend, climb R, over a pile of rocks (red paint and '1'), and go beneath mine buildings and pulley wheels, then follow the clear but rough path beneath cliffs. Leave the marble way down a red-paint-marked trail falling to the road and turn L.

At the first hairpin, turn L onto a rocky path that drops to round a little valley then climbs and levels. The way ahead is clear for a couple of kilometres, but rarely smooth-going, sometimes passing beneath the cable with buckets still loaded in a state of suspended, down-tools animation. ◄ The path gradually descends, in its ankle-turning way, to the coastal lowlands.

There's a rare spot of shade above a fall of bouldered stream-bed by a concrete pump house.

After winding down over exposed grey marble slabs, look R to a break in the wall with a horizontal '1' directing you R across a small field with a **hut**, and go obliquely L to cross the white-pebbled stream-bed. Go straight on, through the mesh gate onto a wide and pleasant track through dark maquis shrubs.

The track turns R towards a **ship's container** and then L just before it. There are '1' waymarks on the gates of the official *monopati* (R), but until Naxos Municipality has persuaded the local farmer to open a way through his animal enclosures, you may have to go straight along the track at the top of the field and turn R at the end to the walled path, then R through a fence-gate to the wooden sign.

Go in the Moutsouna direction down a dirt track past a **solar farm**, then turn L onto a *monopati* down to a stream-bed. Cross to go up the track opposite, continue to a cross-tracks and go straight ahead. Wind down the Spanish broom way, and keep L at fork below buildings, ending up going along a valley littered with industrial leftovers in the little emery port of **Moutsouna**, to sea and tavernas.

Arriving at the emery port of Moutsouna

WALK 18
Koronos, mountain and east-coast bay

Start	Bus stop, N end of Koronos village
Finish	Lyonas
Distance	7km
Ascent	250m
Descent	810m
Time	2½hr
Terrain	Steep, uneven descent, initially along shaded valley, then open rocky country, with one exposed marble path climb
Refreshments	Koronos, Lyonas
Transport	Bus service Chora–Koronos. Both Lyonas tavernas offer free lifts back to Koronos for customers.

The old route to the cut-out bay at Lyonas is short and dramatic, with plunging and ungainly marbled paths, at first thickly bordered by green, then between naked marble crags punctured and scarred by emery mines. At a pass between two rocks, at the summit of the only climb, there's a magnificent coastal panorama. Lyonas Bay, at the foot of a sheer cliff and with a beach of wave-smoothed pebbles, is lovely for swimming.

From the **bus stop**, go down the oblique asphalt road to the parking area and turn sharp L down a long flight of wide steps, then go straight down a paved, stepped lane and keep R to the old well on the corner, which served this neighbourhood of Livadaki (little valley). ◄ Turn R alongside a high wall, bear R up steps past a grey metal door, then go straight ahead at a cross-paths. Curve L then R, then go straight on to steps and bear L at the fork down to the **Platsa**, the main village square.

Turn L down the signed path and follow its white-edged stepped way to the next waymark sign and turn R in the direction of Lyonas. Cross a deep-cut cobbled

Until mains water arrived in the 1960s, each of the village's neighbourhoods had its own well and plateia.

WALK 18 – KORONOS, MOUNTAIN AND EAST-COAST BAY

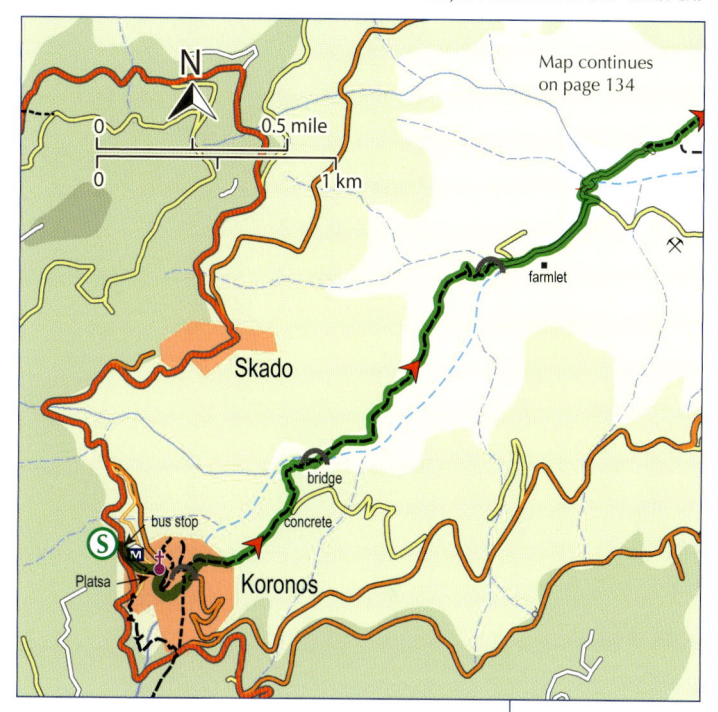

underpass and follow a '10' waymark ahead to the L, until you reach the abrupt end of the village and a country path.

Keep R along the main path down-valley, reaching a brief **concrete** section, after which take the second footpath L ('10'). Steep and stony, this leads to an arched **bridge** over a white-bouldered stream-bed. Enjoy while you can the level path and dappled shade beneath a row of Oriental plane trees, before going through a fence-gate into open mountain country.

You're now walking an intermittently uneven and marble-paved path, which descends via red mud-stained trails to a stream-bed over another bridge. Go R and uphill to walk through a **farmlet** and goat enclosure

WALKING ON THE GREEK ISLANDS – THE CYCLADES

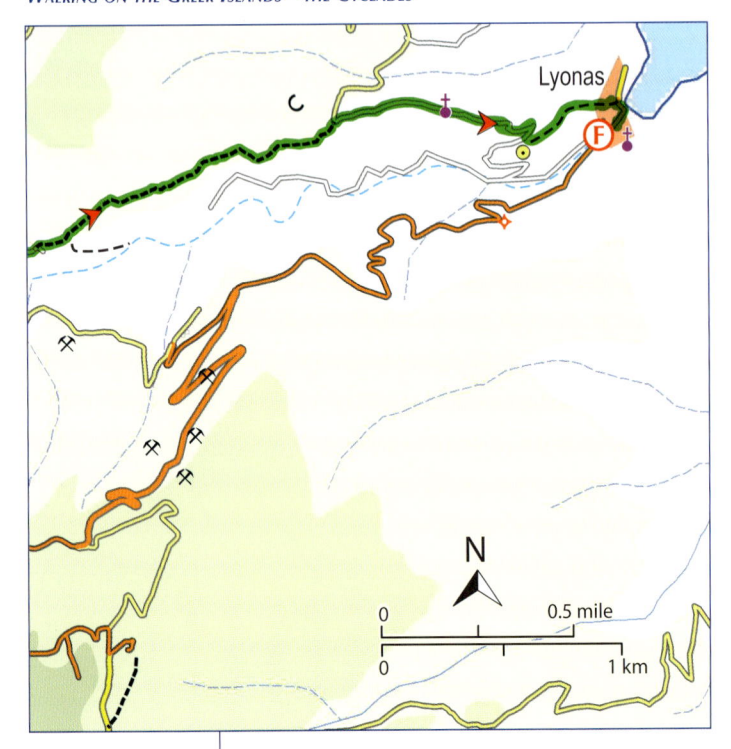

The farmer might invite you into his run-down place for a raki, and to sell you a kilo of home-made kefalotyri cheese.

The harsh mountainside across the valley bears black holes and scree slides, the scars of emery mining.

astride the track. ◀ Some 150 metres beyond the farmlet, fork L ('10') to go back into the valley and up the opposite side. Look for a big olive tree on its own earthy platform (R) at a sharp bend in the track and turn off opposite, L, marked by a cairn, onto a trail that becomes an ascending path of marble that leads over a rock-framed pass at the top.

You are now following a contour above a deep ravine far below, sometimes descending gently. ◀ Reach a concreted road and follow it down past stands of *Euphorbia dendroides*, acid-green in early spring, turning hot-pink and gold. After a R–L hairpin, and the next bend to the R, look for a small entrance to a trail on the L, marked by a

WALK 18 – KORONOS, MOUNTAIN AND EAST-COAST BAY

cairn and '10'. Almost opposite, a wall snakes vertically down a mountainside; below is a **threshing circle**. From here, the steep, narrow path leads all the way to sea and tavernas at **Lyonas**.

Tavli the dog at the monopati marble pass to Lyonas

Walking on the Greek Islands – the Cyclades

WALK 19
Kynidaros, downriver to Engares

Start	Bus stop, Kynidaros
Finish	Bus stop, Engares
Distance	8km
Ascent	195m
Descent	570m
Time	3hr
Terrain	Steep descent through exposed, bouldered land to a shaded stream valley on dirt tracks and traditional paths, some of which are steep and uneven
Refreshments	Kynidaros, Engares
Transport	Bus services: Chora–Kynidaros, Chora–Engares

A walk of great contrasts, plunging from the marble-quarrying village of Kynidaros through wind-sculpted metamorphic rocks, into a valley of cool, dense green. Perspectives down-valley to the west coast are spectacular, framed by giant boulders streaked and stained with many-coloured minerals. From a lost village and ruined monastery you follow the course of one of the island's few year-round streams, domain of riverine birds, turtles, freshwater crabs and dragonflies, while far above bleached peaks pierce the Mediterranean sky.

Kynidaros is the only Naxos village whose population is increasing, now around 400. The original settlement was in the valley of Chalandra below, but after persistent and bloodthirsty pirate attacks in the 15th century, surviving villagers moved to the mountain. It's a village of music and dancing, and some of its musicians are nationally renowned.

From the **bus stop** on the R-angle bend in the village take the path L of white steps, signed with a polished marble monolith, up into the village. Turn R and go sharply uphill

WALK 19 – KYNIDAROS, DOWNRIVER TO ENGARES

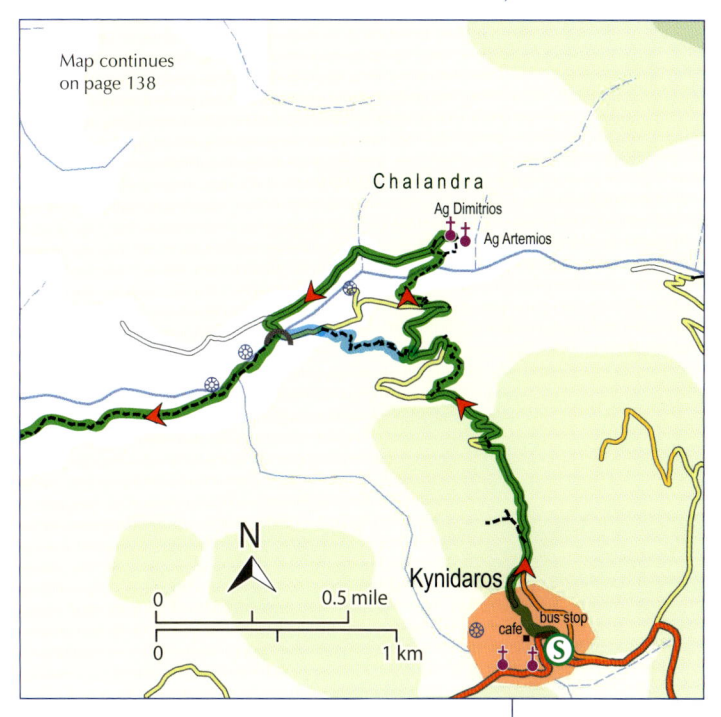

above the wall with '11', at a corner **café**. Go through the arched alleyway, past a paved platform. ▶ Turn L, and at a concrete road take the higher fork.

At the top, where you see a quarry ahead, go L and continue along the dirt road, over the brow of the hill. A marble monolith to the R marks a shortcut *monopati* that rejoins the dirt road, where you keep R and downhill until the next '11' waymark for the next shortcut. After a few winds of dirt road, the next path off-piste to the R starts with a neatly paved section.

Soon, deep in the valley, you see the triple-arched roofs of Ag Artemios. Rejoin the dirt road and continue down, past a *monopati* on the L beyond the second bend.

Deep channels border the path to carry deluges of winter rain, then there's a fountain where you can fill water bottles.

WALKING ON THE GREEK ISLANDS – THE CYCLADES

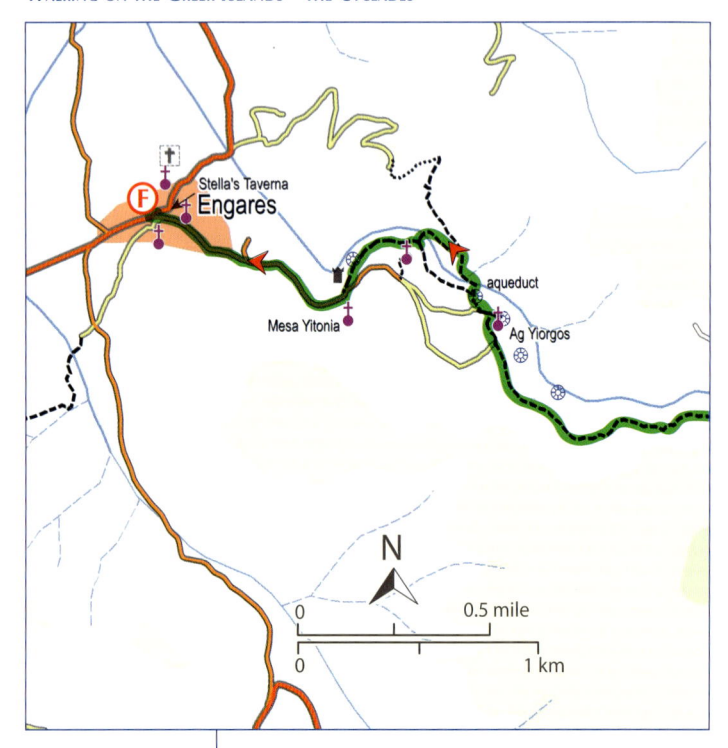

This *monopati* is a **short and lovely cut** to the bridge, but it misses out interesting monastery and church ruins. It follows a contour on the valley-side and after entering the trees it winds down R, passes above a house and continues to the dirt road, where you turn L. Turn R on the far side of the bridge and go under it to join the downstream route.

For the monastery in the valley, continue for another two bends to a large boulder and adjacent rock with red spot, and turn R. Keep straight down steps at the fork, going through a fence-gate to a sandy terrace, and turn R below the buttress of an old mill-race. Continue upstream over water-smoothed pebbles and boulders for some 200 metres, to a sandy clearing and cross where a red spot marks a bridging point over four large stepping boulders. Push through the tangle of oleanders and roots and go R along a mule path.

Follow the path L uphill to a sandy road at the top. Turn R to visit the evocative ruins of Ag Dimitrios and Ag Artemios in the verdant setting of Chalandra (hazelnut) where the people of Kynidaros lived before they moved to the safety of the mountain top. You'll reach the curved stone roofs of **Ag Dimitrios** first. ▶ Go through the gate L of the main building and follow the path obliquely down R to the triple basilica of **Ag Artemios**, one of the largest churches on the island.

Ag Artemios was jointly founded, together with a school, in the late 1700s by the then Bishop of Paros and Naxos, a naval officer from Paros serving in the Turkish fleet, a leader of the island's Orthodox community, and the local people. The Turks, who governed Naxos at the time, supported Orthodox monasteries in founding schools.

Metamorphic boulder country above the green, watered Chalandra valley

This was a complex of chapels but is now animal quarters and a fodder store.

WALKING ON THE GREEK ISLANDS – THE CYCLADES

This is where the shortcut rejoins the main route.

Head W along the sandy road until it drops steeply to a **bridge**. ◀ Turn L just before the bridge and under it to go downstream, along a pebble and bouldered path. The path crosses the stream to reach a sandy terrace, then climbs to a *monopati* along the valley far above the watercourse, and ends at a fence-gate to a dirt track.

Pass above beehives, turn R to the tiny **Ag Yiorgos chapel**, then go L below it. Beyond a brown metal gate, turn R towards the arches of an **aqueduct** and follow the path L to the stream. Cross the stream and turn L along a sandy track, which ends at a fence-gate (R). Keep straight ahead over boulders. ◀ Shortly after, cross the stream over a rickety plank, then go R and L to stone buildings. Turn L through them via a fence-gate and follow the trail high above the stream.

Look L for a deep, dark swimming and turtle pool.

After passing a 1787 tower house, emerge on a lane at a mixture of ruined and restored buildings – the hamlet of **Mesa Yitonia** – and turn R. Look L for a water spout set in the rock-face, keep L at the fork in the road and walk above well-tended gardens and groves, through the village of **Engares**, to the main road. The bus stop is opposite – but **Stella's Taverna**, up on the R, may be a priority port of call.

The bridge over one of the island's rare year-round streams

THE NAXOS STRADA

Tavli the local dog surveys western Naxos from Fanari heights (Walk 23)

You'll be among the first to walk the new, improved and officially mapped, long-distance Naxos Strada – as this is the first book to publish it. The 52km route from southwest to northeast coast takes in a brilliant cross-section of the island's landscape and history. The Strada is not waymarked as such, but incorporates many waymarked sections of the island's paths.

The route's name is Latin, from the Venetians who conquered Naxos in the early 13th century and dubbed the island's pathways *communes stradas* – although some of the paths date way back to the earliest settlements.

The first Naxos long-distance path for hikers was officially opened in 2008 in the presence of various island dignitaries and the vice-president of the European Ramblers Association. Lack of follow-through and publication meant it never became known, used or maintained. Ten years later it was revived and re-routed (twice), renamed the Naxos Strada, and published on local maps, even though some sections remain impassable. It may be that these have been fixed at the 11th hour before publication but in case they haven't, I have offered diversions. The Strada route published on the Anavasi Naxos map, and on boards in some villages, may differ slightly from the route described here due to the diversions, to reduce road walking or to avoid conflict with other walks in the book.

The route is in five day-walk sections, each starting and finishing on a bus route (although services are seasonal). Some Chora hotels offer transfer services to and from start and finish points, and Naxos Bus Tours (email naxostransfer@hotmail.gr) may be economical for groups of five or more.

Walking on the Greek Islands – the Cyclades

WALK 20
Strada 1: Plaka to Kato Potamia

Start	Bus stop, Plaka Beach, or bus stop at Ag Anna
Finish	Bus stop, Kato Potamia
Distance	10km
Ascent	265m
Descent	370m
Time	4½hr
Terrain	Dirt tracks threading through the coastal plain become waterlogged after heavy rain in spring. A sharp ascent on bouldered hillside, maybe thick with fairly benign vegetation. Many traditional paths through hilly interior country.
Refreshments	Ag Anna, seasonal along coast, Vivlos, Kato Potamia
Transport	Seasonal bus service Chora–Ag Anna and Plaka Beach, and Kato Potamia–Chora (June–August)
Accommodation	None in Kato Potamia; hotels in Chora offer transfers

As you climb through tumbles of bald, sculpted fine-grained granite, you look back to the carpet of coastal fields below, and along the strands of the west coast. Over the ridge, an immense interior landscape opens up. Tumultuous valleys converge from a mountainous rim, hiding ruins of historical interest. After all the ups, and a few downs, you'll reach Kato Potamia (down river), the lowest of the three steep-stacked stream-fed villages.

◀ From the **bus stop** at Plaka Beach, bins and bend inland, go straight ahead, SSE along the coast road. After 500 metres pass a wooden sign that is the alternative, signed Strada route, but this involves quite a long stretch of asphalt and concrete road. Instead, continue to the end of the dirt road and go along a boardwalk, then walk along the beach for another 500 metres.

After the beach decking of a seasonal bar, turn L inland alongside a white wall and follow the main track

You can start this walk at Ag Anna, a resort that retains some fishing-village charm: circuit its bay and bouldered headland and go along the coast for 2km.

142

WALK 20 – STRADA 1: PLAKA TO KATO POTAMIA

inland, kinking L–R a couple of times to reach a **junction** with sign 'Παραλια/Beach', and turn R. Follow the dirt road to the third bend and turn L off it where there's a small **building** with a red iron door, and bear R at the fork to go along a bamboo avenue for quite a way.

Keep L at a fork with a breezeblock wall curving R, and follow the main track, heading past a couple of concrete cube buildings and another turnoff R, then leaving the bamboo for open coastal plain. Follow the route as it kinks around lots of potato-field boundaries, and at a little **building with a vine-ridden pergola**, bend R.

At a junction with a facing wall, turn R, soon bordered again by bamboo. After heading E for some 700 metres, bend L at a blue metal gate ahead. About 30 metres later, turn R into a rough, terraced field and go up the R of it. Go R of the second terrace then bear L up a (possibly overgrown) path whose route can be clearly traced ahead along the hillside through wild country knobbled with rocks.

When you see a **chapel** embedded high in a boulder, turn R to pass beneath it. Switchback to the R of the next **chapel** and towards the next, beside the remains of a **tower**. The village of Vivlos (aka Tripodes) is in sight, and you follow the lane towards it, past farms and above a narrow valley of boulders, prickly pear and escaped bougainvillea. At a crossing of gulley and triangle of cross-lanes turn R up the widest of the lanes, then go L–R through the houses to the main road and turn L.

Opposite a small **car park** on the corner, turn up the lane heading NE beside the bakery (sandwiches, cakes, pies). Right on the corner is a tap with fresh spring water to replenish bottles. At the fork go R and bear L/straight (waymark '6'), keeping on the main lane where farm tracks go off. ▶ Keep L where a steep lane goes up R, and at a concrete section fork L up to a T-junction.

Turn R – see a curve of hill with a single building ahead, and keep straight ahead at a R bend (to a field). At the next R bend, on a concreted section, turn off L onto a country path. At the top, join the main road, turn R and cross to a dirt road L a few metres on, then immediately

In the banks are leathery leaved Pistacia lentiscus (mastic, whose resin has been used for chewing gum, varnish and liqueur), and the palmate-leaved chaste tree, said to subdue sexual appetite.

Walking on the Greek Islands – the Cyclades

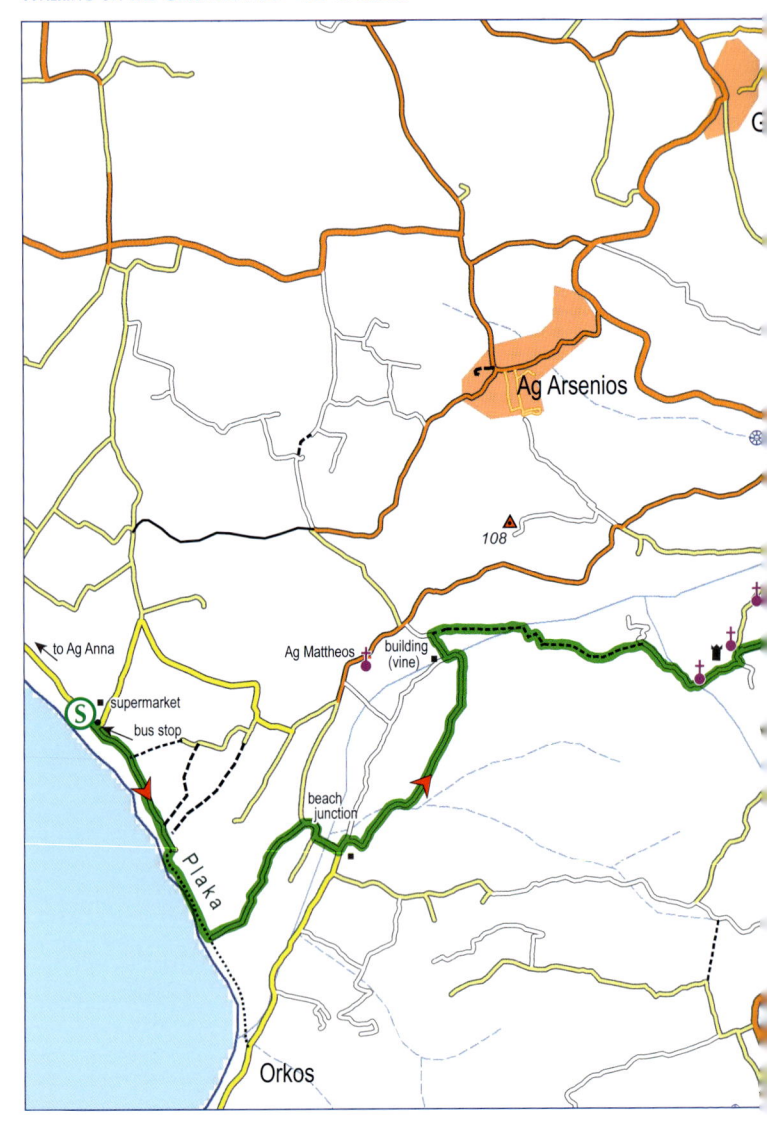

WALK 20 – STRADA 1: PLAKA TO KATO POTAMIA

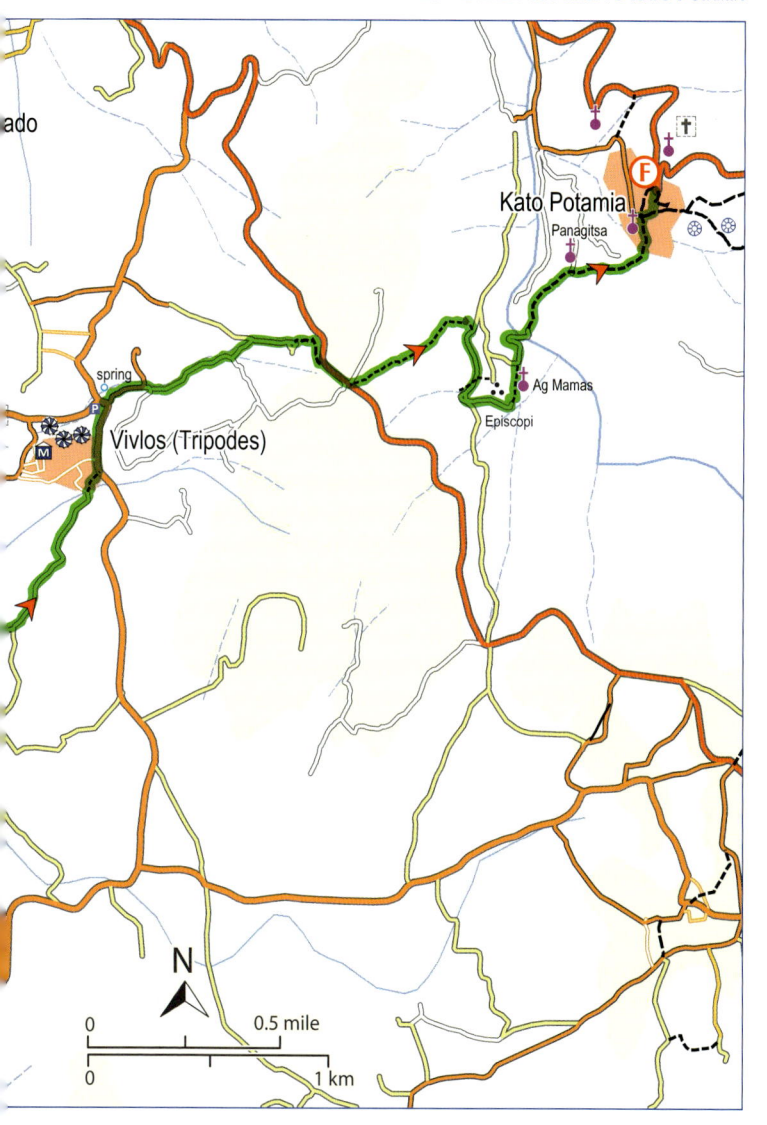

turn R off it onto a *monopati* dropping into the valley. Look back over the high agricultural valley falling abruptly to the coastal plain, the pointed cone of Stelida, neighbouring Paros, and Naxos town with its hilltop *kastro* clearly defined.

Cross to a dirt road, immediately turning R off it onto a *monopati* that drops into the valley. Keep to the main path, winding down to a junction opposite a once-impressive gateway. Turn R and follow the dirt track for about 375 metres, passing below L a large water cistern and the sad remains of **Episcopi**. ◄ After a dip, take a sharp L turn on the rise, with a brown sign to Ag Mamas. Go through the fence-gate onto the old path, watching out for spider webs slung across at head height. Pass a new vehicle track and building, then go through the gap in the wall L to reach **Ag Mamas**.

When the **Byzantine church** was first built in the 10th century it was one of the biggest and most important on the island. It is locked, but the exterior

This was built as a bishop's summer residence in 1707.

Spring glory with Phlomis, on the path down to Ag Mamas

Local spin on Constantinople architecture at Ag Mamas

is a fine example of how architectural ideas from Constantinople, such as the domed cruciform structure and arcaded windows, were adapted by island craftsman using local stone. Recycled materials such as the fifth-century BC marble egg-and-dart *spolia* above the north entrance, suggest it was the site of a sanctuary, and there are also remnants of an early Christian building. After the 13th-century Venetian occupation it became the seat of the first Catholic bishop. Ag Mamas was a third-century AD teenage martyr and friend of wild animals, including his signature lion companion, and became the patron saint of shepherds.

Leaving the church, head N through a field, over a broken wall and along terraces to a dirt track. Turn R downhill, going through a fence-gate to reach a junction. Turn L over the stream then up R onto a mule track curving up between walls. At the top, where a new track leads L to **Panagitsa chapel**, go straight on to a continuation of the old footpath beneath a new building. It leads around the valley, turning L at a junction, going down to a bridge over a stream choked with brambles and then up to the village of **Kato Potamia**. Turn R at the **church** and L up an alley to the main road and bus stop.

WALK 21
Strada 2: Kato Potamia to Filoti

Start	Bus stop, Kato Potamia
Finish	Bus stop, Filoti
Distance	10.5km
Ascent	590m
Descent	330m
Time	4hr
Terrain	Village alleys, which flood with stream overflow after heavy rainfall. Trails, some rough and steep, over bouldered hills, and country lanes through olive groves. The Apano Kastro alternative route is steep and unclear.
Refreshments	Chalki, Filoti
Transport	Bus service Chalki–Filoti–Apiranthos
Accommodation	Filoti: neoclassical guest house, ztzannini@gmail.com, tel +30 69722 78420; and Baboulas Taverna, tel +30 22850 31426

The walk moves from stream-fed, shaded villages to a bald and bouldered upland with a tor-top castle and mysterious grave circles. There are sweeping views of the sea of olives – the vale of the Trageia – and surrounding mountains. You walk among olive groves that conceal cute Byzantine chapels, then climb via a secret wild part of the island to lively Filoti, largest village in the Cyclades and centre of production for the area's 60,000 sheep.

From the apex of the hairpin bend below the **bus stop**, go straight down the pavement into **Kato Potamia** and turn L at the bottom. Keep straight on, past a sign for Kokkos Tower, past a ruin, orchards and a *sterna* (cistern) to **Vasiliko Taverna**, where you turn L up the lane then R alongside a high wall. At the end go sharp R down a *monopati* and follow the stream. Pass (R) the derelict 1686 **tower**, former family home, mill and granary of the Kokkos family.

WALK 21 – STRADA 2: KATO POTAMIA TO FILOTI

Mr **Kokkos**, a middle-class lawyer, was implicated in an uprising by local Orthodox islanders against Venetian Catholic landowners, during which one of the Venetians was killed. Mr Kokkos was in turn 'murdered', but his widow lived on in the tower. Daughter Anoussa, however, married young Jabati Barozzi, the son of her father's assassin!

Beyond the tower, turn L and climb steeply past a former cobbler's house at a kink in the path (R), its turquoise door marked by a matching shoe last. At the top, at a pair of telegraph poles, bear up R past a water fountain. Where a rock bursts out of a house wall go sharp R, then go L down steps with green wooden railings and along a trail that rejoins the stream.

Turn R at the **mill house**, and opposite a metal door go L through **Ano Potamia** (high river), past zig-zag wooden railings to reach a terrace with a Persian lilac tree, paved seating and a valley view. Turn R up steps, keeping L at house no. 36, to reach the main road. Cross obliquely L to a steep concrete track, which soon becomes dirt road bordered by aromatic shrubs, where *Serapia* orchids hide in spring.

Pass an offshoot to farm buildings (R), and where the main track swerves L go straight ahead over brown rocks glinting with mica. Bear R towards a '5' waymark on a rock. ▶ Ahead is the tor topped by Apano Kastro, and just before it a gap in the wall on the R leads to **Ag Andreas chapel**, which houses fresco fragments dating from the 10th and 13th centuries, including unusual aniconic designs.

Alternative route via Apano Kastro and Geometric graves

Go beyond **Ag Andreas** to where the main path bends L, and go straight ahead through the wire gate in the wall. Follow rough trails roughly along the line of the wall R. Where the wall bends R, go straight up (literally) towards a rectangular-blocked Hellenistic wall, and turn R above it, above a ruined chapel R. Continue to another chapel ruin and turn L just before it to scramble up to the summit.

Underfoot is the paved 'Potter's Way', built under the Venetians for transporting pottery from the Chalki area to Naxos town.

WALKING ON THE GREEK ISLANDS – THE CYCLADES

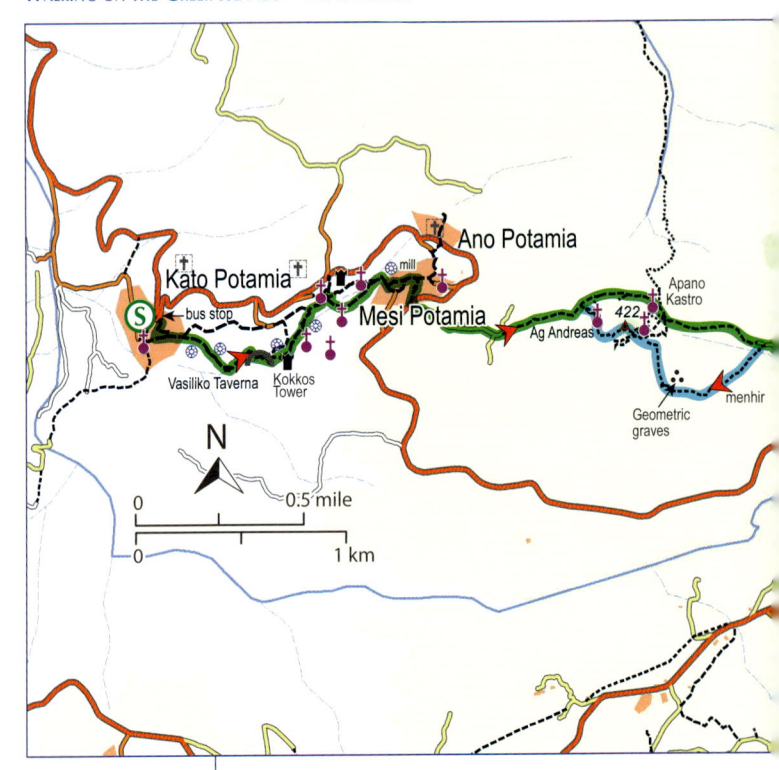

Ruined cisterns, chapels and fortifications are all that remain of the **Apano Kastro** (high castle), which was built by the Venetian Marco Sanudo II in the 13th century but probably used as a defensive position from early civilisations. From its summit are 365-degree views over two of the island's richest valleys and down to Naxos port.

Return to the last **chapel** and go L to the E side of the tor and a ruined bastion. Wind down beyond the tower then go R beneath it, generally S, over sloping rocks and through a gulley, to a wall. Turn L, then R through a gate

WALK 21 – STRADA 2: KATO POTAMIA TO FILOTI

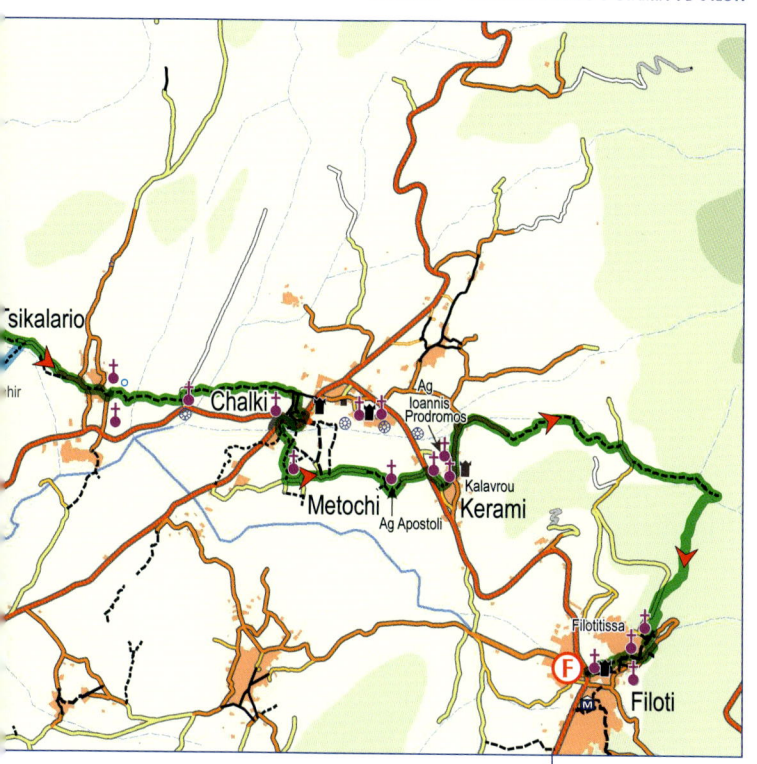

and go across a meadow to a wall topped by a fence with openable bits. Go straight ahead and start looking for **stone grave circles** of various diameters up to 12m – these are the family graves of immigrants who settled in remote and defensive situations such as this during the Geometric Period. Turn towards the peak of Mount Zas and follow trails until a path drops L down a small valley, looking up R to a wedge-like menhir – the Geometric cemetery entrance. Follow the valley path down to a dirt track and turn R to rejoin the main route and continue to **Tsikalario**.

WALKING ON THE GREEK ISLANDS – THE CYCLADES

Just before a low building with a goat-hanger for stripping carcases, a wooden sign R directs you along an alternative, 20-minute return route to the Geometric Period cemetery: follow the cairns.

To stay on the main route from **Ag Andreas**, follow the path up and L to circuit the N side of the tor, passing above a broad, secret valley. At a facing outcrop of rock, go R, beside a wall with a chapel behind, and continue over rocks whorled by a seasonal watercourse. Go beneath a smallholding on an outcrop, beside the wall and through a wire gate to a vehicle track. ◄

Continue to **Tsikalario** and along its main lane to a parking area with a chapel, laundry block, and a spring said to supply the island's best drinking water. Go down the mule track at the far upper corner and continue through olive groves to reach a wide dirt road with a **chapel** opposite and road below. Turn L then R onto a *monopati*. Below an enclosure with a wooden pallet shed, cross the riverbed to more *monopati*, eventually reaching a fork with a tall wire gate. Turn R along the paved path into **Chalki** – once the island's inland capital.

At the junction, turn R then immediately L, then R again, and walk to a junction opposite the Valindras Kitron Distillery (liqueur made from leaves of the lemon-like *Citrus medica* tree; open 1 April–end October,

Geometric-period grave circle, and Mount Zas

152

WALK 21 – STRADA 2: KATO POTAMIA TO FILOTI

10am–4pm, tel +30 69425 51161). Turn R, then L into the *plateia*, and R to the road. Turn L and across the main road to a white-walled lane, past a square washing place, and cross the open space to the path opposite, then fork L. At the junction turn R on a path between olive groves to a concrete lane, then turn L.

At the next junction turn L, then bend R and continue E, ignoring turnoffs, for some 500 metres and then bend R to pass below the 11th-century **Ag Apostoli**.

The **church** is closed, but art historian Nigel Gilchrist says the exterior carries most interest, a sophisticated and unusual design with a tiered west frontage. Stone steps lead up from the narthex to a small, domed oratory for private prayer, and on the south side is a blind arcade of five arches with decorative ceramic air vents called *phialostomia*.

Beyond the church go L, and L again at the junction in **Metochi**, along the concrete lane to the main road. Cross to a paved fork and go R, signed Markopolitis. Turn

Unusual three-tier architecture of Ag Apostoli chapel, Metochi

WALKING ON THE GREEK ISLANDS – THE CYCLADES

> This was built by the wealthy Greek Markus Politis, a leader of the Orthodox islanders in an uprising against Venetian Catholic overlords.

L into **Kerami** up a steep path and go L at a fork to reach the giant pink **Kalavrou tower-house**. ◄ Beyond the last house of the village, in an olive grove on the L, is the small, simple **Ag Ioannis Prodromos** with ancient marbles framing its entrance.

Continue down the lane, and at the fork go straight up R alongside a high wall with massive marble offcuts. The lane levels with the tops of plane trees, turns to earth, and ends at a rusty iron gate (L), where you go R, up a narrow path. Keep L at a fork and go through fence-gate, past more companion plane trees, and curve R into the stream-bed. Where a concrete road joins from the L, continue along the stream-bed boulevard.

At the fence-gate, turn R up a rocky path slippery with kermes oak leaves, which opens to a scenic, tumbledown path. Immediately beyond another fence-gate, turn L up a brief, stony cut to a dirt road and turn R. At the bend, turn L onto a wide rough track through a gate to a trail that winds up through open scrub. When you meet the stream-bed, look up R for a wooden sign, and a bit farther on, turn sharp R to it, up a distinct section of supporting wall.

Through a fence-gate, head straight up a slope of naked rock in private pocket of wild Naxos. At facing wall, turn L. The path drops then levels above a road, goes R towards a wall and zig-zags into a dip and becomes clear again up the opposite side. At the road, go L briefly, but before the fork below the big church, go upslope to the wall and turn R behind the church and down to a village pavement. Turn R at the car park L and go down steps to the main lane. Turn R, then R at the bend, along an alley to a chapel, which you go below and then R to reach a big square with a plane tree, and go R along the S side of the big church of **Panagia Filotitissa**. Wind down L to the main road and bus stop.

WALK 22
Strada 3: Filoti to Apiranthos

Start	Bus stop, Gefyra square, Filoti
Finish	Bus stop, Apiranthos
Distance	8.5km
Ascent	695m
Descent	465m
Time	3hr
Terrain	Steep climb through village alleys and on traditional paths, descent via a valley of woodland and terraces, then descent on old paths through wooded hillsides
Refreshments	Filoti, Apiranthos
Transport	Bus service Chora–Chalki–Filoti–Apiranthos
Accommodation	Apiranthos: Anastasiou's Rooms, tel +30 22850 61312, +30 69865 17333 (call in at first café on R at start of village, opposite church)

A lovely stretch of the Strada, connecting Filoti to the first village of the northern mountains. From the top of Filoti you look over the wooded slopes, the olive groves of the Trageia and much of the island you have explored so far. Nightingales have been heard in the wooded valley to Danakos, and the poet Byron is said to have wanted to be brought to die at Fotodotis Monastery. Although there is no evidence of his visiting the island, the building and its view are certainly to die for.

From Gefyra square, with its plane trees and water fountain, go up the paved alley by the corner shop and curve R to go along the S side of the huge **Panagia Filotitissa church**. Beyond the big plane, and the acacia tree at the end of the courtyard, turn up L, and at chapel, go up behind it and R. Continue to the road and turn L, then go R onto a signed *monopati*.

Follow the *monopati* up and around the valley, ending beside the retaining wall of the Filoti–Apiranthos

Walking on the Greek Islands – the Cyclades

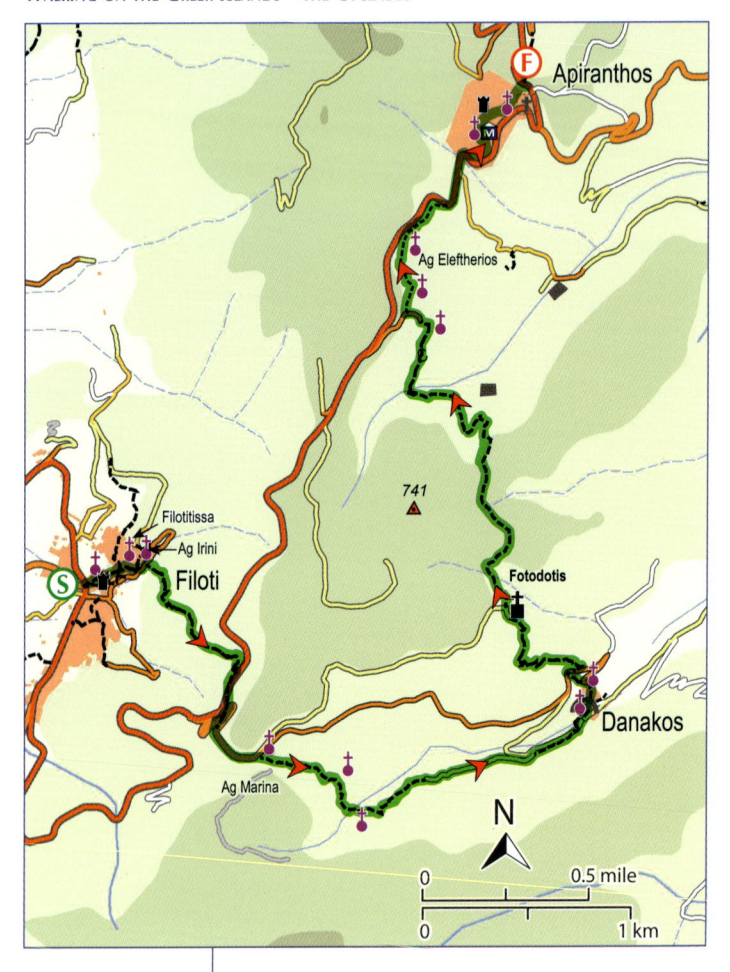

road. Cross the road to a path that leads over a rockfall and beneath a copse to the next road section. Go R and cross to steps marked '2', up a rock shortcut to the road barrier, then turn R along the road to the **chapel of Ag Marina**.

WALK 22 – STRADA 3: FILOTI TO APIRANTHOS

Take the *monopati* at the corner of the courtyard and road, going down through a fence-gate. Keep R where the path levels and follows a contour midway up the valley-side. Negotiate a fence-gate or two, then drop beneath a hanging bramble tunnel to cross a stream-bed. Turn L then R to a path invaded by Spanish broom, and then, at a small ruin up R, scramble L down a schist slope. Go R at the bottom and through a fence-gate, and later another, before dropping to a stretch bordered by evergreen acers.

Beyond a brash stone building backed by a stack of impressive terrace walls, and an open cross-track area, follow the dirt road through rocky phrygana hillside. At the sharp L bend where the track continues down, go straight on to an uneven rock path that ends at steps down to a concrete road. Turn R and look L for '2', marking the way down to a giant plane tree centrepiece in a square with a spring source. Turn R up past the chapel into **Danakos village**, and another square.

Take the blue-railed steps in the far R corner up to the car park and a taverna, go L to fork up the lane and then go up the wide concrete steps leading off the bend. At the road, cross obliquely R and turn L up a marble path that weaves up to **Fotodotis Monastery** (open July–August, daily except Sundays, 11am–2pm).

The fortified monastery of Fotodotis encloses a chapel

This mighty tower of **Fotodotis Monastery** envelops a complete church, referred to by a Catholic traveller called Venier in 1182, the first record of its name as Fotodotis (giver of light). Archaeologists found traces of a seventh-century chapel and a pre-Christian temple. There's a written record of conquering Venetian Marco Sanudo handing over the church to a Catholic order of monks in the 13th century, but the fortifying tower wasn't built until the 16th century, when it was one of the Orthodox monastic foundations encouraged by governing Turks. The church has a carved iconostasis for the Orthodox liturgy and a side chapel for Catholics. If you go up the exterior stairway you can see the top of its dome embedded in the first floor, surrounded by cell-like living quarters, and in the courtyard the remains of monastic self-sufficiency. It was last occupied by monks in the 17th century.

Take the dirt track that leads up from the monastery, and where the concrete begins, bear R to go along trail '3', to the L of a fence above a house. Push past invading Spanish broom and other vigorous but harmless vegetation, negotiate a slanting rock, then swing R around the head of a little valley and join a traditional path in a gulley. Go through a fence-gate at the top, and cross the track to the satellite station to go through another. Follow the rough path that bridges a col to the next valley. ◂

The village of Apiranthos sparkles white to the R, and the peak of Mount Fanari is ahead.

As the trail begins to descend, it forks and you go up R, with Apiranthos in your sightline, up wide rock steps and through an oak copse. At a L bend down a steep rock path running above a deep-walled gulley, go down and around a giant boulder with a topknot of trees. At the junction with '3' on the facing wall, turn L, dipping over a stream-bed and passing beneath a rock overhang. Continue around a big view down-valley, and at a vague junction, bear up R and continue to a stream with a covered spring on the L.

Go up the dirt track opposite, through a fence-gate and past tethered dogs. Bear R at a fork and go along a narrow, sometimes overgrown, concrete path behind a low house. Turn L to the dirt road, then turn R, and R again at the next junction past the dinky **church of Ag Eleftherios**. The *monopati* eventually turns to concrete path and lane, and you fork L to emerge on the main road at a traditional products shop.

Go L to the next hairpin bend at the foot of **Apiranthos village**, and just beyond it turn L up marble steps. Bear L at green metal doors, then go up and turn R. Keep L and up at options, and then turn R before a café. Keep L again and emerge at a row of balconied houses in various states of repair, then reach a small square. Go along the path R of the arched alley. Look L for the grey-doored **archaeological museum** (open daily excluding Tuesdays, 8.30am–3pm, possibly Easter to September). ▶ Pass beneath a **Venetian tower** 'growing' from the rock, and come to a wide terrace. Sharp down R are the folklore (+30 22850 61361), geological (+30 22850 61725) and visual arts (+30 22850 22725) museums, closed Tuesdays, variable opening times according to season. Note the finely carved marble gateposts on the **church**, and arrive at the main road and bus stop.

Over the col, the village of Apiranthos is in sight

The collection includes fishing and hunting scenes carved onto rocks dating from the fifth millennium BC.

Walking on the Greek Islands – the Cyclades

WALK 23
Strada 4: Apiranthos to Koronos

Start	Bus stop, Apiranthos
Finish	Main square (*platsa*), Koronos
Distance	11.5km
Ascent	760m
Descent	785m
Time	4½hr
Terrain	Steep, exposed climbs up and down dirt tracks and marble mountain paths; crumbling schist trails through scrub. A few shaded paths around Sifones and Keramoti.
Refreshments	Apiranthos, Keramoti, Koronos
Transport	Bus service Chora–Chalki–Filoti–Apiranthos–Koronos
Accommodation	Koronos: Stavros Traditional Houses, tel +30 69465 80777; Marilena Palaiologou, tel +30 69720 06176

Classic sections of the island's paved byways crest the limestone massif commanded by Mount Fanari. From the heights there's a huge, eagle-eye view of Naxos' west side, as you pass through small, lost worlds of high pastures and ruined farmsteads. There are shaded paths through a deserted hamlet and a drop into a deep-cut green valley where Keramoti village is perched on a little spur.

From the **bus stop**, enter the village by the **church** L, and opposite, beside the weaving co-operative, turn R up broad white steps. At the first junction keep R, then go up through the village as straight ahead as you can, with a kink L, to reach the road at the top. Cross to go up the lane, and just beyond a **waterworks building** turn sharp L onto a signed path. Kink down L–R at the fence-gate, then follow a zig-zag course up the mountainside. The path becomes a clear earthen trail leading to a dirt road, where you turn R. ◄

After 250 metres along the dirt road there's a clear 25-minute return detour to the summit of Mt Fanari (beacon), from where there's an aerial view of Naxos and its neighbours.

WALK 23 – STRADA 4: APIRANTHOS TO KORONOS

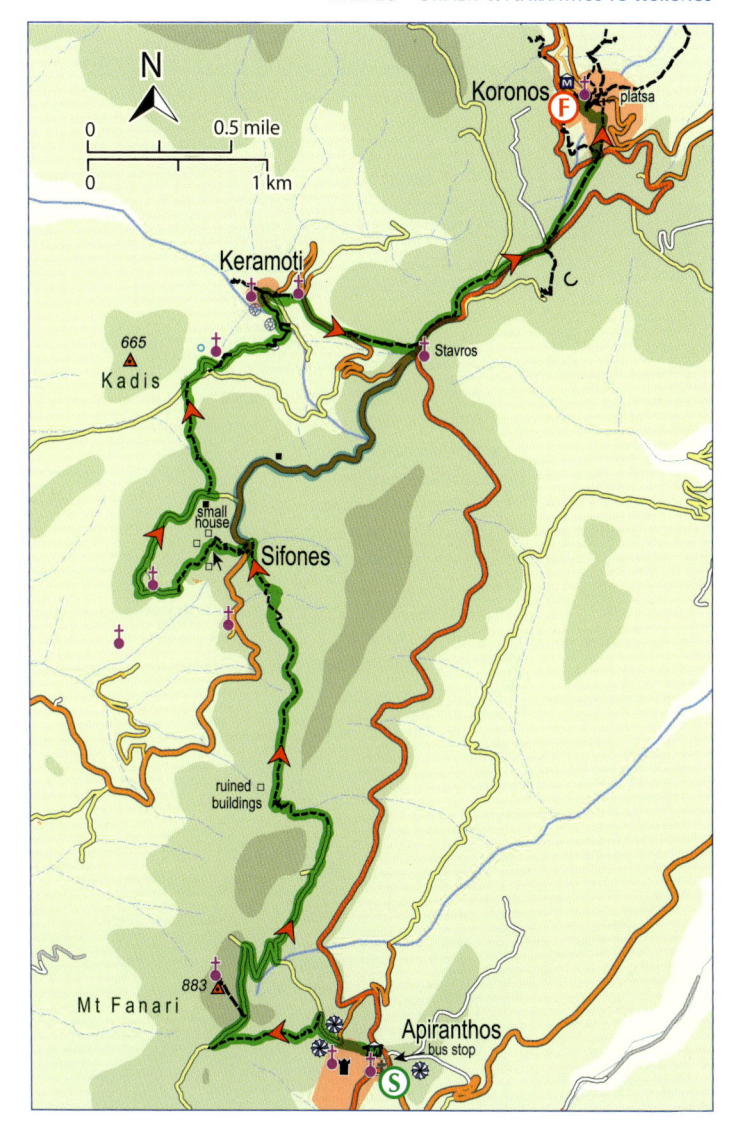

Continue to the end of the dirt road and turn R downhill. At the third bend, turn L along a waymarked stony track, past a concrete building with an awesome panorama of deep-cut spurs and ridges, snaking walls, sea, and the islands of Makares and Donousa. At a wall with a red spot, keep L up the stepped mule track. This becomes a broad, naked marble thoroughfare that surfs the brow of the hill to a sudden fall of land and a wide westerly view. The path descends like a collapsible ruler, then levels to roughly follow a contour beneath a Mohican fringe of marble ridge.

Pass above **stone buildings** that are part of the terraces. Watch out where marble gives way to schist, and sections of path crumble. Through one fence-gate, the path turns to trail through low scrub, and beyond the second it heads down to a valley. Turn L at the streambed, with '8' on the facing wall, and follow its course, a favoured spot for dragon arum. ◄

This dark purple-crimson plant smells of carrion to attract flies, which fly into the spathe and are trapped there overnight to wallow in the pollen, and released the next day.

At a triangular clearing bear R onto a dirt trail that leads down to a glade with a large tree just above the road. Turn L down steps under the road and follow a grassy path. At the junction turn L, through a fence-gate, to go through the ghost hamlet of **Sifones**.

Crazy marble path down the Fanari mountainside

At the next fork keep R, soon turning L where you see a **church** ahead. Keep straight on through another

WALK 23 – STRADA 4: APIRANTHOS TO KORONOS

fence-gate and at a tiny farmstead bear R up a randomly unsurfaced/concrete road. Follow this round to the R and up for some time until it swerves R above terraces of vines and reaches a **small house** on the R. Opposite, there should be waymarked steps up to a traditional path between broken walls.

> The following section, the link to Keramoti, may still not have been opened. If there are neither steps, sign nor access through the fence, and the path appears blocked, continue to the end of the dirt track at the main road, turn L and walk along it for 1.5km to pick up the Strada at Stavros.

The official, hopefully newly opened path bears L through dense maquis then along the R of a small steep valley above vine terraces, and goes down to a dirt road at Kadis, where there's a water source by the buildings. Turn R and fork L past the **chapel** to go along the valley opposite Keramoti. Descend until a clear, narrow *monopati* goes down L, follow it to a ruined building and turn R. Turn L to cross the stream and go up via blue railings at the start of **Keramoti village**.

Turn R to a small square, then R again. ▶ At the car park at the top of the village, go straight ahead up a concrete lane, soon branching L on a marble path to reach the road. Turn R along the road, and around the bend, follow a wooden sign L, up a rocky path. At the top, go L through the fence-gate and along the road for a few metres to **Stavros** – a vantage point with an unobstructed view to both the east and west coasts of the island.

Go L off-road at the wooden sign. Keep R at the forks, rejoin the asphalt road and turn L. After some 200 metres look L for a marble path L, to the R of a broader track, and follow it to rejoin the road. Cross to go down steps into **Koronos**. Turn R at the junction, go straight at crossways, then L at next junction. Go all the way down to blue-posted wooden railings, then L and on to the main square (*platsa*) and its cluster of tavernas.

A *kafenion*, open all year, is down to the L.

WALKING ON THE GREEK ISLANDS – THE CYCLADES

WALK 24
Strada 5: Koronos to Apollonas

Start	Main square (*platsa*), Koronos
Finish	Bus terminus, Apollonas
Distance	11km
Ascent	495m
Descent	1035m
Time	4hr
Terrain	Deeply shaded paths between mountain villages, with thickly vegetated sections before and after Skado. Long, exposed and rocky descent through scrub and rocks to a wide bay.
Refreshments	Koronos, Skado, Komiaki (seasonal), Apollonas
Transport	Bus service Chora–Koronas–Apollonas
Accommodation	Apollonas: Kouros Hotel, tel +30 22850 67000

The northern villages teeter on steep mountainsides mantled in deciduous trees and fed by streams and mill-races, where wildflowers bloom later than in the south of the island. The long descent to Apollonas is in complete contrast, over exposed and open Mediterranean scrub, with an assortment of richly coloured rocks, walls of brown schist and quartz glittering with varicoloured minerals. You are on a level with the meeting of sea and sky, heading down to the miniature port and bay that seem scooped out of marble cliffs.

From the SE corner of the main square (*platsa*) with its cluster of tavernas – Koronos is the liveliest of the north villages – follow the waymarked 9/10, white-edged stepped path down. At the next sign, turn L towards Komiaki and continue along path 9 into the open hillside.

Head towards an isolated **church** (R) and keep L at the fork below it. At the next fork go steeply straight down, possibly pushing through high but relatively soft vegetation, to cross a narrow stream. Turn R through

Walk 24 – Strada 5: Koronos to Apollonas

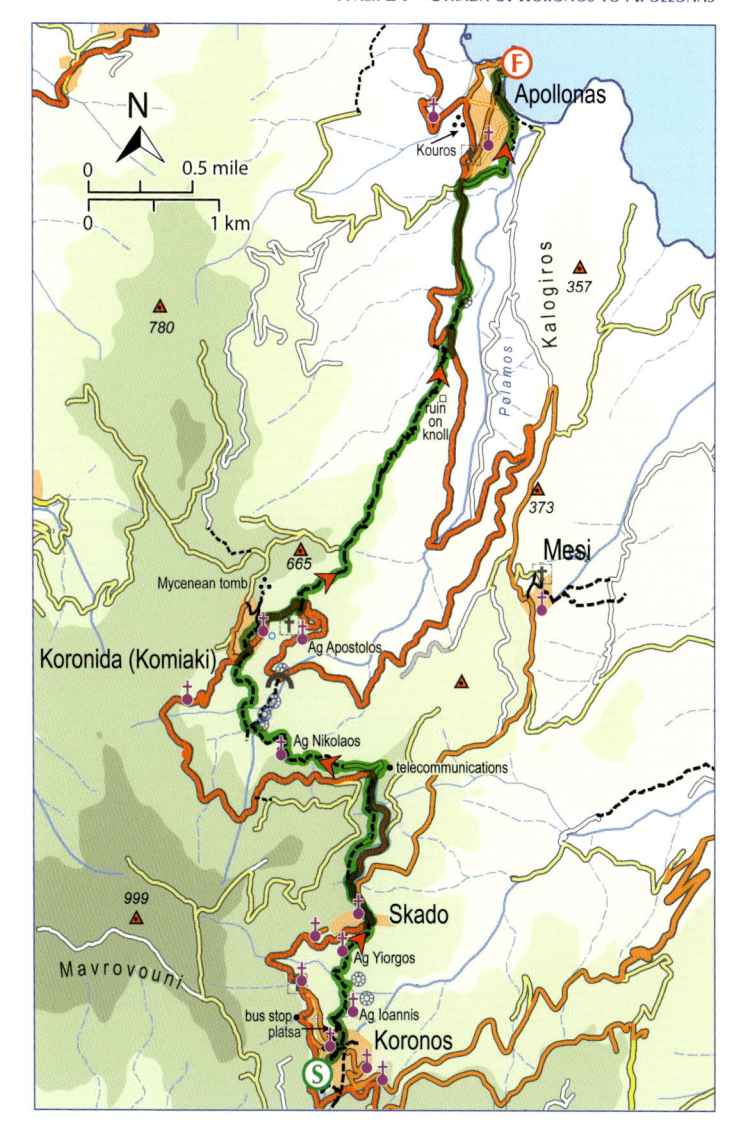

more enthusiastic greenery to reach a ruined mill, go up its L side and turn L at the junction above it. Continue along a narrow, cobbled path above the narrow valley, and turn R at the next junction below **Ag Yiorgos**, which you see above to the L. Finally on a proper rock path, continue under a road bridge into **Skado** and turn L.

Until World War II, **Skado villagers** depended on emery mining for their livelihood and left farmland to waste, so when, under German occupation, the mines were closed, many starved to death. The population is now about 120.

Take the L fork along the road past the war memorial, and just off the bend R, follow a waymarked sign L up promising schist-slab steps.

This is the next long-neglected section of the official Strada route. If it becomes impassable within 50 metres, return to the road and follow it for about 1.4km. You'll pick up the Strada again at a hilltop telecommunications site, just after the elaborate wooden sign L.

The long descent to Apollonas

WALK 24 – STRADA 5: KORONOS TO APOLLONAS

All being well, follow red spots on rocks, with occasional glimpses of stone path below, winding up and then R to a gulley which you scramble up to reach a copse of evergreen oak. Turn R onto a path that turns to dirt track. Where the track veers L, turn off it at a freestanding rock on the R with a '9' waymark. The trail roughly follows the line of the road below, heading obliquely down towards **telecommunications** antennae. It drops to the road, marked by a wooden waymarked sign, just before the site.

Cross the road to go along the lane immediately L of the antennae and down to a concrete bordered terrace. Go straight across to the entrance of a *monopati*. At a wire fence-gate (R) keep L uphill, then follow the path around the densely shaded valley head, past a *sterna* (cistern) with a walnut tree (rub a leaf to release scent). Fork L immediately after this and keep L, dropping steeply then crossing a water channel. Reach the outskirts of **Komiaki** village, where the path runs beneath houses and meets the road at Panorama Taverna.

> Komiaki's alternative, newer name of **Koronida** is either from Princess Koronis of Thessaly, loved by Apollo, or Koronis the nymph, who fed the young Zeus goat milk and Naxos honey at the cave on Mount Zas. Komiaki is derived from the possibly Mycenean settlement of Komi. Farming and the highly rated local wine are the main preoccupations, plus the Easter *kounia* (swing) festival when boys set up swings for girls and recite improvised poems as they push them.

Cross to go up steps and keep R to the *plateia* with a water fountain, then L towards the church and immediately R at the post office. Go R at the next turning, and down to the road. Steps up L lead to the **Mycenean Tomb**.

> A round trip of 20 minutes is worthwhile for the intact **beehive tomb** tucked into the hillside. Said to be the tomb of a local Bronze Age 'king', it's

one of only three of its kind – the other two are on Mykonos and Tinos – is in perfect condition and you can go inside.

To continue on the Strada, go L along main road, round the bend and then L down the waymarked '9' path. Pass a stone shelter with living roof and soon see Apollonas in its bay far below.

On meeting a wide dirt road, go R to the bend, then cut down the signed path L. The long route down is generally straightforward and visible, with a zig-zag section down to a knoll with a building that showcases the range of local stone. The path widens beside a wall of schist blocks like petrified logs towards a more distinctive knoll. Just before it, cut down to a walled path at the end of a long, **ruined building** (R). ◄

The islets floating in the sky-sea are Xtapodia (octopus) and Tragonisi (billy goat island).

Weave down to a dirt track and turn R through a fence-gate, then go around the bend past a house and roofless building to reach the road. Go L, and at the first bend turn R down the waymarked '9' path, which steps down to a vegetated path bordered by the walls of a **mill-race** and leads to an enchanting stream with waterfalls and pools, bordered by horsetail (*Equisetum*).

Cross the stream, follow the path to the road and turn R. Continue to a bridge, and just after this, turn R down a track to the riverbed. Turn L and continue to the beach beside Hotel Kouros. Walk along the curve of beach to **Apollonas harbour**, which in classical times was the main port from which Naxian marble was exported. The bus terminus is at the far end of the quay.

> Make time to visit the village's most famous resident, a **statue** which at 10.7m tall and 130 tonnes would have been the classical world's largest monolithic figure. The beard indicates that this is not a *kouros* (idealised youth), nor Apollo as suggested by the village name, but the god Dionysos, patron of this region.

AMORGOS

Northwest coast of Amorgos and the 'Big Blue' of Aegean Sea (Walk 30)

WALKING ON THE GREEK ISLANDS – THE CYCLADES

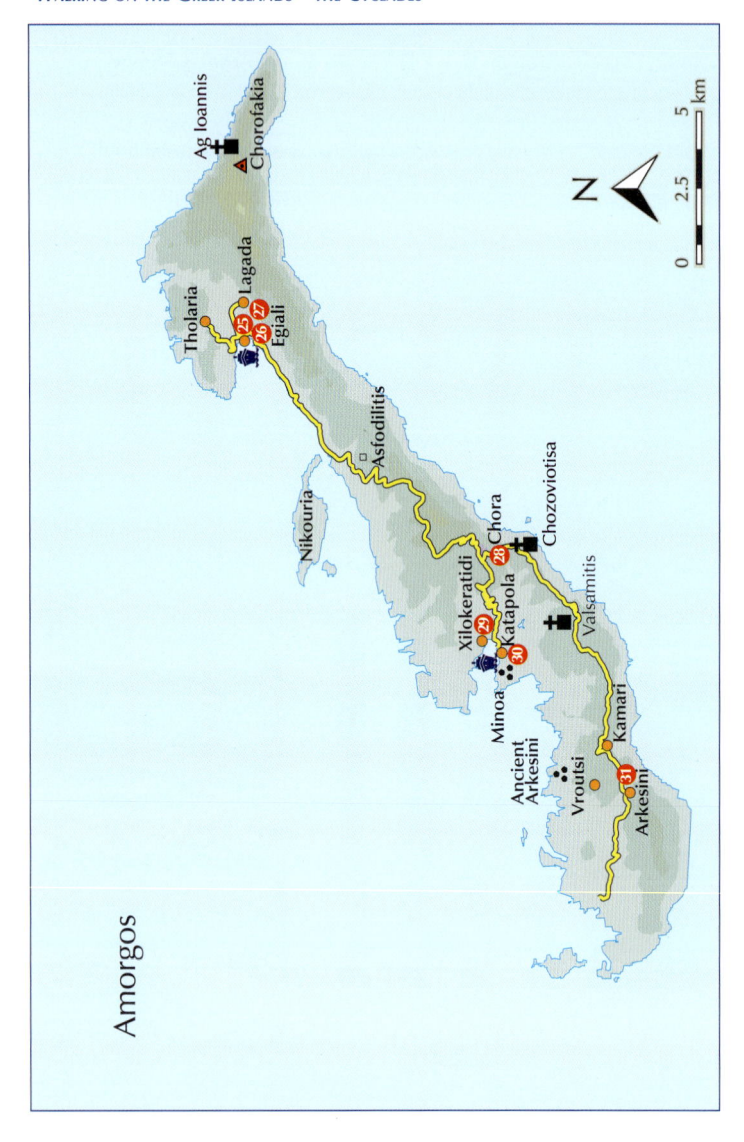

Amorgos

Amorgos is the most remote, insular, unspoilt and sensual of the four islands, giving an experience of Greece as it used to be before the advent of package tourism. There are villages where the curvaceous cubic forms of Cycladic architecture hug the profile of the land they are built on, taverna tables set at the edge of fishing-boat-bobbing harbours, and vestiges of tough-terrain farming settlements that haven't changed much in 5000 years. Electric power wasn't installed until the 1980s, and the road linking the main ports of Egiali and Katapola was surfaced in 1991. Many fine, cobbled paths are still in working use. Amorgos is a favourite resort of the French, partly due to Luc Besson's 1960s classic film *Le Grand Bleu*, which captures the island's iconic dizzying cliffs and coastal blues (you can watch the long, depressing story of obsession and free-diving in some harbourside bars).

The island is said to lie at a convergence of energy fields, which, together with a particular geomorphology, gives extra potency to the aromatic shrubs. According to phytotherapist Birgitte Roth, these yield essential oils of up to 97% proof compared with a Greek average of 67%.

This long, thin, remote, rugged and ancient island is like a last bastion of defence at the southeast edge of the Aegean. It emerges from the ocean like a leviathan with a giant rounded snout at one end, petering out in a tail of lowland on the other. On its inward curve, snub-nosed headlands with deep-cut bays provide the only sheltered harbours. The outer, southeast coast just over the mountain spine is almost continuous, sheer cliff. The island is about 30km long, barely 2km at its narrowest, and soars from sea level to 800m. Water is scarce, with only two seasonal streams, as the main country rock is porous limestone or marble. Many springs were lost to fissures following a 1956 earthquake (the one with severe repercussions in Santorini).

The island's remoteness has made it a popular place of exile, from Romans dissenters to 20th-century communists. Under the Venetians, Amorgiots maintained their independent spirit, and in the 18th century, in the late Ottoman period, there was a surplus of oil and cereals, a democratic local government, and the island's population rose to 4000. Today it is about 1800, centred in the ports of Egiali and Katapola and the inland capital of Chora, which are linked by the island's only bus service, have the widest choice of accommodation, and all-season shops and services.

WALKING ON THE GREEK ISLANDS – THE CYCLADES

WALK 25
Egiali and mountain villages

Start/Finish	Egiali port car park
Distance	11km
Ascent/Descent	585m
Time	4hr
Terrain	Mostly stone or earth paths through exposed, open scrub, with a short, steep cliff scramble and indistinct trails, and some prickly overgrown sections
Refreshments	Egiali, Tholaria, Lagada
Transport	Bus service Katapola–Egiali–Lagada (terminus at Egiali port)

Cliff-hugging trails on the island's northwest headland run above sandy coves and crystal-clear Aegean blues; and to the southwest, blunt headlands buttress into the sea. You walk the upper tiers of a craggy amphitheatre above the wide *kambos* (plain) that opens to Egiali Bay. The island's earliest settlers landed here, and a city-state occupied a knobbly height. The living villages of Tholaria and Lagada, built high inland to be safe from pirates, are gems of Cycladic style.

Head N along the shore of **Egiali Bay**, over a tumbledown ruin with Roman bricks where traces of clay and ceramic shards indicate it was once a pottery. ◄ At the end of the beach, called **Fokiotripa** (seal hole) for a some-time seal shelter behind the large rock beneath the cliff, turn R up the cobbled path, then go sharp L opposite a flat-roofed building. The path circuits above the hamlet of **Levrosos**, and perched on the cliff below the last building is Café Levroso, with its 1970s island-hopping vibe.

Fork R up to the cliff-top path, keep R at a pair of stone pillars with no gate, then go round the top of a valley. Keep seaward at the next fork, stepping through a wall, and continue round and down to **Psili Ammos**

Other remains on the shore are said to be of a former bathhouse that perhaps provided some home comfort for political exiles of the Roman Empire from 133BC.

WALK 25 – EGIALI AND MOUNTAIN VILLAGES

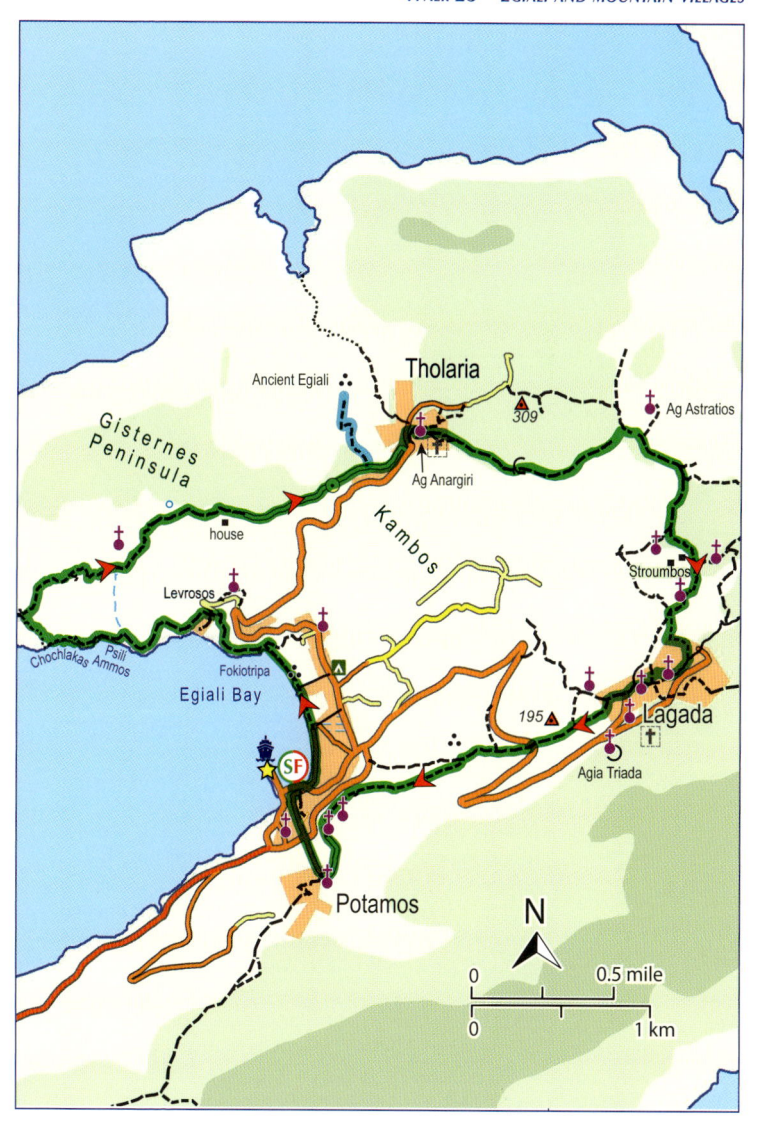

Path-clearing above Egiali Bay

(high sand) beach at a feathery tamarisk tree. Go to the far R corner of the beach, to the start of a trail that climbs up and around to **Chochlakas**. Clamber over giant pebbles to the far R corner, past a precious wedge of flat land, neatly cultivated beneath uncompromisingly stark hillsides.

Look for a white spot painted on a rock just beyond where a wall terminates brokenly onto the beach, and head steeply up, generally NW, on indistinct trails with occasional cairns and white paint spots. Climb R of a broken terrace wall then aim for a gap in the L end of a wall that runs across the hillside above. Turn R through the gap and follow a level, sometimes clear path on the upside of the wall. Round a couple of narrow valleys, and when faced with a rusty coloured stone wall and fence, go below R then L, following a hosepipe across a dry cranny of valley and to the R of the wall ahead.

Follow the most beaten trails along a terrace, then above beehives and a couple of cypresses. Soon cross another dry stream-bed and go L up the stepped path, which levels then climbs through a shade of chaste tree and oleander, before more winding steps. Pass a watering hole for animals, wasps and dragonflies, then a breeze-block poultry and dove condominium, and join a vehicle track past a smart **house**. At the junction opposite a circular corrugated iron enclosure (a sort of dew pond for animals), go straight on.

> Just over 200 metres later, on the L, is the start of an optional 50-minute there-and-back detour to the acropolis of **Ancient Egiali**. Pick your way around the remains of the citadel – some statue bases and scraps of defensive wall, with no explanatory signs. But look from the summit down a cleft to the sea for a sense of the location favoured by early Cycladic settlers: an isolated but easily defended hill with access to the sea. There would have been, 5000 years ago, low stone buildings, domestic goats and sheep, and mean patches of land for cultivating wheat, barley and pulses. Around the seventh century BC Ionian islanders established Egiali as the third city-state of Amorgos. The Romans buried their dead nearby, in arched tombs known as *tholoi*, from which today's village gets its name. The hilltop settlement was abandoned in favour of the more hospitable coast below, probably in medieval times, during the Venetian occupation.

To continue on the main route, keep going along the concrete road to a junction, bear L into **Tholaria** (population about 150) and take the wide steps R into the village. Turn L at the end of the first flight beneath the churchtowards a café, then R and up to the L of the big **church**, and go R behind it. At the bottom of steep steps with a column fragment and font, turn L then L again up steps at fork. Turn R 30 metres on and continue to the end of the village. ▶

The calcareous rocks are studded with the rounded *Euphorbia dendroides* that moves through a startling range of colours from spring to late summer: acid-green to flaming gold, orange, crimson and purple.

Cycladic house at Stroumbos hamlet

Where the path levels and swings R, a sign points L to the **chapel of Ag Astratios** on a knoll. ◄ Continue around the valley head, passing the shell of a chapel (L), then keep R. At a group of stunted cypresses above a fork, keep L. Pass a stone arch over a miniature ravine, and shortly after, a well that used to provide pure mountain water to Lagada. At the fork where path '4' leads uphill, go R, down to the protected hamlet of **Stroumbos**.

A detour passes the fallen remains, and the big, rectangular blocks of a former watchtower dating from unstable Hellenistic times.

Long abandoned by native islanders, many of the **Stroumbos** dwellings have been restored by foreigners. Planning laws dictate that only renovation to the original layout is allowed. There is no mains water or electricity: 'We'll only accept power lines if they are channelled underground,' say the residents who want to preserve the perfect 'natural Mediterranean garden' environment.

At a ruin and wooden sign 'LANGHADA' on a wall, fork R downhill, then go L below another ruin to reach the stream-bed. ◄ Keep L at a fork, then L again at concrete steps. Just beyond a two-mule stone shelter, turn

From here the climb to the village is arduous on a hot day, and in heavy rain becomes a torrent.

WALK 25 – EGIALI AND MOUNTAIN VILLAGES

sharp L up steps. (Peep inside the rounded corner house to see a typical interior.) Keep L at a little two-door house with a front yard, L at a junction towards a smart wall and then go R at the top of **Lagada** to the *Loza*, the village's equivalent of a high street.

Go to the L of a general store then follow the main lane down until you reach Niko's Taverna (L) and a herbalist opposite with potions distilled from potent Amorgos plants. Take the lane R downhill. At concrete tanks go L to cross the asphalt road to a continuation of the mule path. ▶ At a concrete building like a lost bus shelter, turn L up a *monopati* thick with oregano. Follow this above the town to a dirt road, which leads to a car park, and then go R down to the port at **Egiali**.

Wedged into cliff-face high L is Ag Triada (Holy Trinity), built in eighth century AD to be safe from pirates.

Spring flowers on the monopati *from Lagada to Egiali*

WALK 26
Remote north: monastery and mountains

Start/Finish	Egiali port car park
Distance	16km
Ascent/Descent	975m
Time	6½hr, with 3hr and 4½hr options
Terrain	Dirt roads and paved paths through farmland then scrub and rock. Precipitous unmarked trails in the mountains. Very little shade throughout; set out by 8am in hot weather.
Refreshments	Egiali and Lagada only. Take plenty of water.
Transport	Bus service between Egiali and Lagada

The full circuit visits the island's highest and starkest outposts. You can do the steady climb along paved paths to a pearl of island monastery and then return, or continue to the defined but vertiginous trail with sheer cliffs above and below to Stavros. Only the fit and confident wayfinder should continue over Kroukelos, where the route is unmarked over barren rock and sometimes narrow outcrops for about 2km (although sightlines and direction are clear). The reward is an awe-inspiring perspective of this isolated bulwark of island in an immensity of ocean.

From the port, stroll along the seafront until you reach a dirt parking area, then turn inland to the road and turn L. Take the first R along the main lane through the cultivated plain of the *kambos*, keeping R after an open patch of land and R at the next two forks. At the right-angle bend, turn L, over the stream-bed and take the stony lane R. At the first fork, go R, then L at the next, joining a mule track between walls.

Keep L at the next junction, then R at the one after, negotiating loose stones and spider webs. Climb steeply to a T-junction and turn R, then immediately L. Keep L at the junction with three stunted cypress along the level path, then take a narrow R turn between a rock and a wall, waymarked '4'. The dome of **Panagia Epanochoriani** (Virgin above the village) comes into sight, and at the junction you turn L up steps towards it.

Panagia Epanochoriani was built on the foundations of a pre-Christian temple, whose materials were recycled (an Ionic anthemion above the entrance, a Doric column). The field below the front of the church has arched waterholes and is called *Embigi* (from the words for blood and source) for when the spring water ran red with blood from pilgrims massacred by pirates. There's a well behind the main church from which you can draw drinking water.

From the main church, take the concrete path SE towards a chapel and turn L just before it, onto a very stony mule track. Keep R at the junction, then L at the well-maintained Lagada–Theologos path. ▶ The route continues uphill, eventually levelling out to border high valley meadows dotted with Spanish broom and small-leaved kermes oak, indicator species of the Mediterranean. The

Chapel near the Epanochoriani monastery

If you decide to opt out of continuing on the mountain circuit after reaching Ag Ioannis Theologos, this is where you will return to for a more direct route to Lagada.

WALKING ON THE GREEK ISLANDS – THE CYCLADES

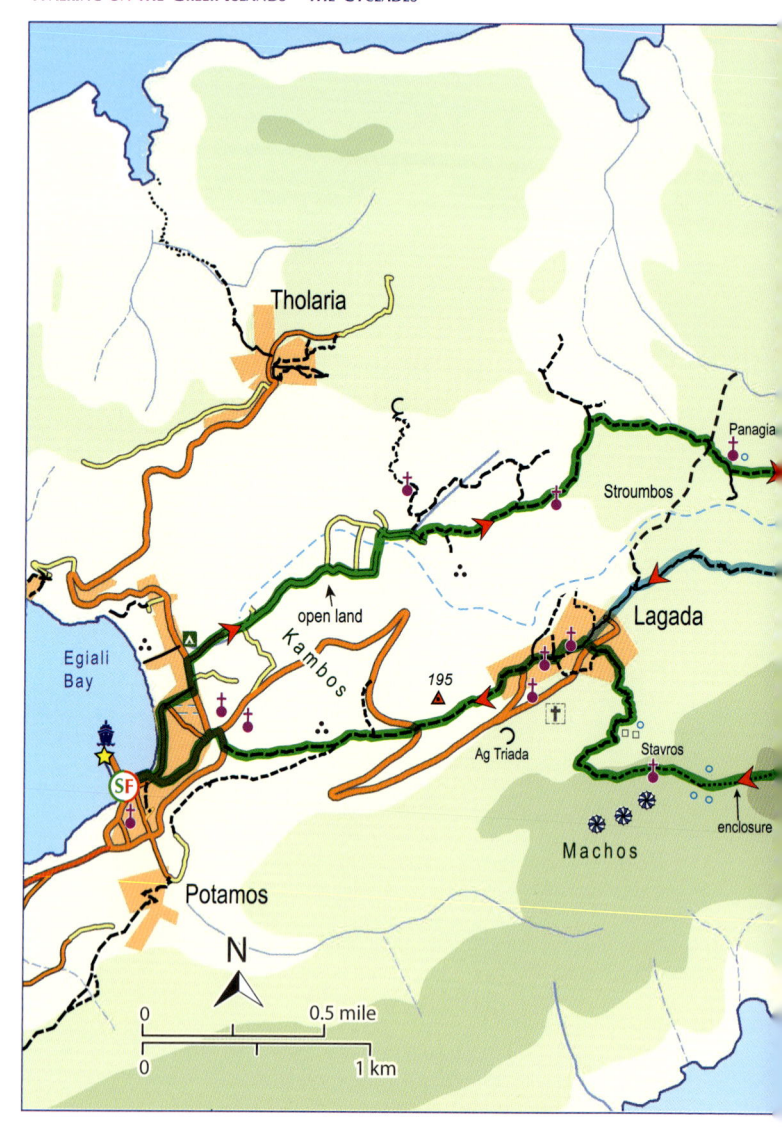

WALK 26 – REMOTE NORTH: MONASTERY AND MOUNTAINS

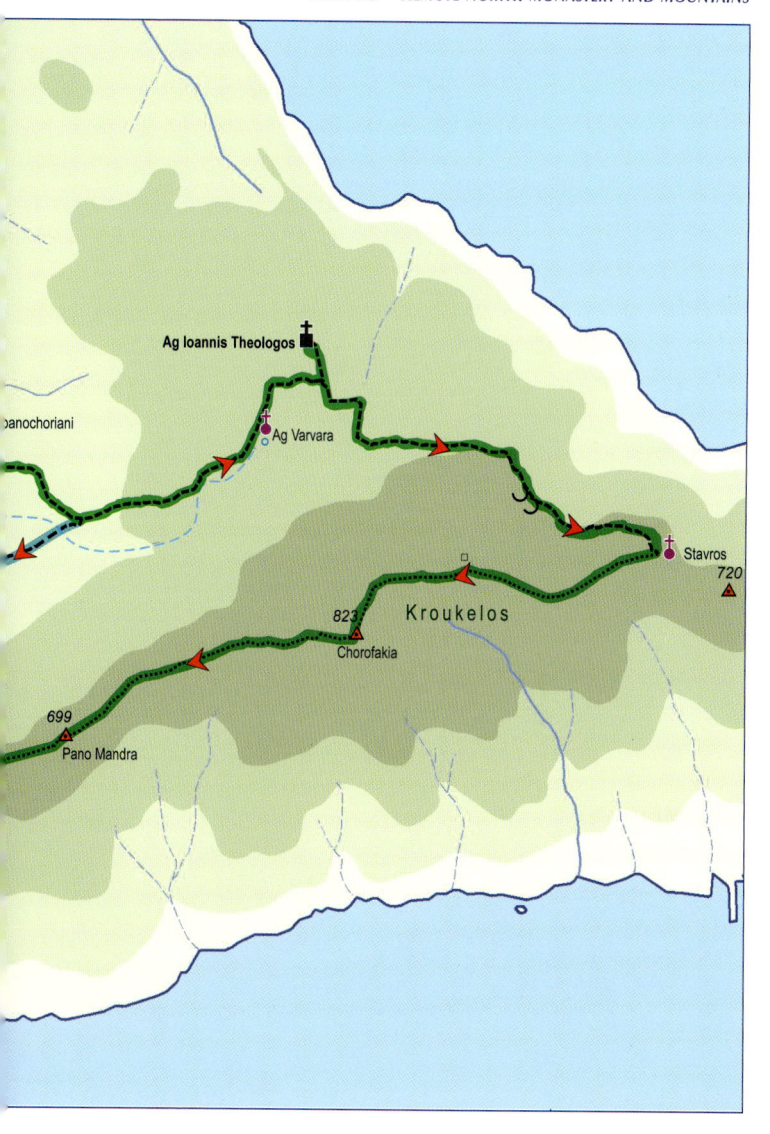

route circuits L of **Ag Varvara chapel** and a well with part of its arched stone roof still intact. Soon after, you'll see the white splash of **Ag Ioannis Theologos** ahead, and at a small white farm building, turn L up to the monastery.

> Ioannis Theologos is the apostle John, who laid his head on the bosom of Jesus at the Last Supper – from which we get the expression 'bosom pal' – and to whose care Jesus entrusted his mother. The **monastery** is believed to be the earliest founded on Amorgos, in the ninth century AD, although today's buildings date from the 1300s. *Spolia* (architectural salvage) set into the altars bear witness to a pre-Christian temple. Festivals are 8 May and 26 September.

If you don't want to continue to Stavros and Kroukelos after visiting the monastery, return to the junction with the Lagada–Theologos path and go straight on to Lagada and Egiali.

◀ To continue to Stavros (1½hr return) on its narrow waist of barren land at the end of Amorgos, go straight ahead at the building below Theologos, following a wall round to the L and not through the tempting gap in it. At the junction, follow the wall R and up. Around the tip of mountain, the land falls away in a great semi-circle,

Descent from the mountains via Stavros chapel

300m to the sea, and the path threads over scree slopes with **caves**, and jagged scars above, eventually climbing to **Stavros**.

Cliff fall to Big Blue, below Stavros

> A vertical drop south below Stavros are a **bauxite mine** and a tiny jetty, now only accessible by boat, to which ore was transported in overhead cables. Economic production of bauxite, a principal ingredient in aluminium, ended in the early 20th century, but some 70 years ago around 150 men were still working there. Miners would leave Lagada village at dawn on Monday and return the following Saturday.

You can retrace your steps to the Lagada–Theologos path from here, but to complete the full circuit, go past the renovated building SW of the chapel and follow the trail that worms up **Kroukelos**, initially red-earthed and marked with cairns. ▶ At a flat area of tan earth and broken buildings, cross to the end of the far R wall and round the L end of a long, low rock outcrop. Keep to the ridge, roughly W, towards a particularly large cairn on the rise ahead, and look for the trig point on **Chorofakia**, highest

The vegetation is too stunted to impede your way, and the only signs of animal life are snails hugging the sides of cairns in pendulous clusters to conserve moisture.

> It's hard to imagine that these northern slopes were clad in oak trees that were the island's top natural resource until consumed by a forest fire of 1835.

peak on Amorgos and your next sightline. You may lose sight of it over dead ground, but maintain the direction as there is no obvious route over the uneven but low-lying rocks.

From the summit, descend gently, to the R. The rest of Amorgos peels away and Naxos dominates the NW horizon. Head roughly in the direction of Tholaria village on the opposite side of the Egiali bowl, then towards the rock ridge up R. Brace your knees and follow the line of ridge-top rocks as closely as possible to the next summit of **Pano Mandra**. ◄

From the next trig point go to the R of an **enclosure**. Commanding the rise ahead are derelict windmills. Go into the dip to a scattering of **windmill bases**, rough-hewn water troughs and **wells** (with water a long plop down), and beyond to a defined trail, which you follow to a chapel (also **Stavros**) stuck onto a rock face.

Beyond it, continue to a large gap in the wall marked with cairns and a red spot, then on past **roofless buildings** and a **covered well**, and turn R at the junction, along a mule track. At the next junction go L past more old settlements and enclosures, then spiral down over loose stones, among a tapestry of faded greens, creams and rusty pink vegetation, to **Lagada**.

At the first signs of habitation, go R and R again at concrete steps, then L. Turn L at the next junction and R to the car park. Cross it and turn L, then follow the stepped, main alley past Niko's Taverna. At a concrete cistern junction, go L to the main road, cross it and take the cobbled mule track down to the road above **Egiali**. Turn R, then L to the port.

WALK 27

Along the island spine to Chora

Start	Egiali port car park
Finish	Bus stop, Chora
Distance	13.5km
Ascent	930m
Descent	645m
Time	5½hr
Terrain	Relentlessly exposed mountain, with steep climbs, so start early in hot weather. Mostly clear, rocky paths and earth trails.
Refreshments	To Steki café near Asfodilitis (seasonal)
Transport	Buses between Chora, Egiali and Katapola; and Chozoviotisa Monastery–Chora

This walk is starkly beautiful. From a high, narrow waist of land the coast falls away on both sides of the island spine. There are eerie ghost villages, strange rock drawings and the ruins of a medieval hostel, but most of all there's Amorgos: a lone battlement at the end of the Cyclades. The *Palia Strata* (old road) has been well worn through the ages by traders between Egiali port and the dinky hilltop capital of Chora, and by pilgrims on their way to the island's most important monastery, embedded in a vertical cliff. Chozoviotisa Monastery (open daily 8am–1pm and 5–7pm), is about 4½hr from Egiali.

Go to the W end of the terrace above the car park, up wide steps by Pension Apollon, and up the lane. Cross the road to a car park and turn R up steps, at a sign waymarked '1', to climb through **Potamos**. Just after a smart building with an imposing view of Egiali Bay, at the fork below the **church**, turn R. Beyond the war memorial at the top of the steps, go sharp L – not towards chimneys – then second R.

Walking on the Greek Islands – the Cyclades

WALK 27 – ALONG THE ISLAND SPINE TO CHORA

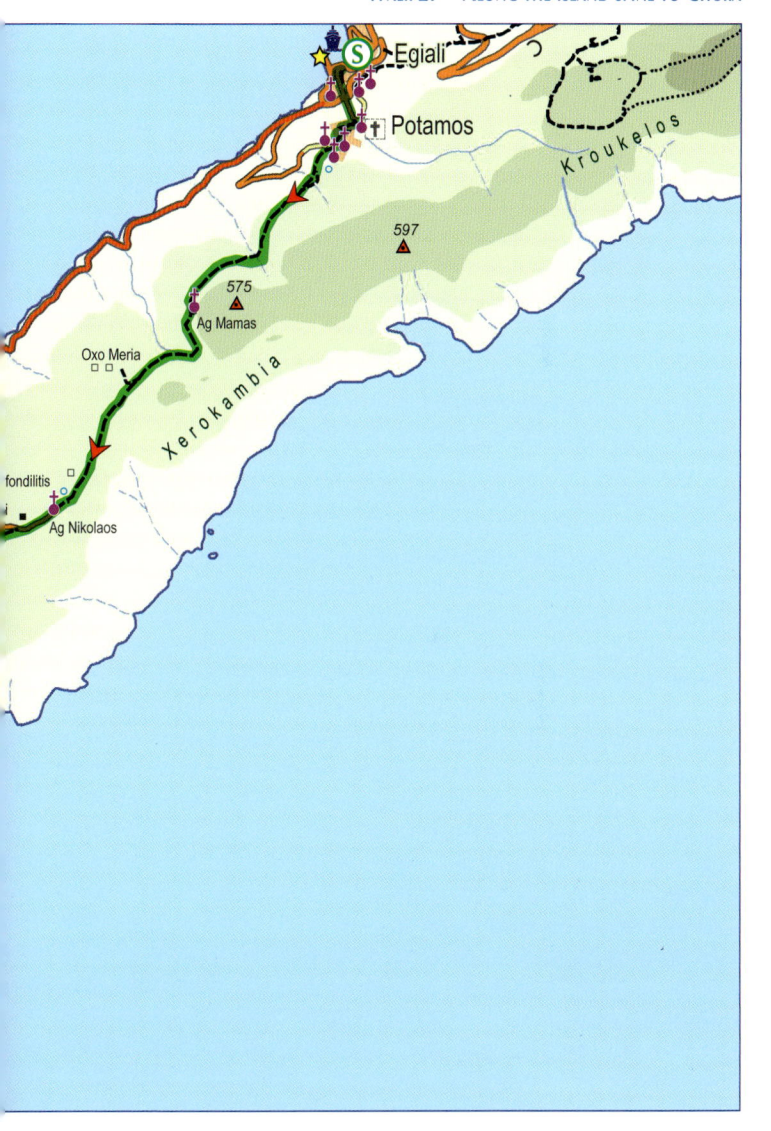

Egiali

Potamos

Kroukelos

597

575
Ag Mamas

Oxo Meria

Xerokambia

fondilitis
Ag Nikolaos

The way ahead over sloping slabs of naked rock favours high ground to avoid ravines.

Beyond a pale-blue gate with a sea view, follow the walled rim of cliff where the coast opens out and a chapel nestles in the steep scrubby hillside. At the end of a terrace go L, take the next turn R, and go through the next tier of houses. At the end of the village, go straight on where steps fork back uphill, and keep L where a concrete road comes up from the R. Look out for tap and standpipe R, then fork L and up, keeping R where steps lead L, and joining a path that crosses a concrete terrace with a shrine, a spring and a view. The sometimes stone-paved path levels along old terraces, although sheer cliffs are above and below.

Drop to a stream-bed, and immediately afterwards go L by a flourishing fig tree, up an initially wide-stepped path. At the crest of the hill, **Ag Mamas chapel** offers the last shelter for some time. ◄ From the chapel, descend and circuit the valley head. Distances between landmarks in this increasingly barren land are longer, and you trudge on until you see a curve of mountain ahead R, with a lone windmill and the skeletal remains of **Oxo Meria** (outer place) below. The area is called **Xerokambia** (dry fields)!

The path opens into a rocky triangle, with a walled track to the ghost village, which you go L of, through a wire gate, and keep L again at the next open area. Follow

Abandoned settlement of Oxo Meria on the dry spine of Amorgos

WALK 27 – ALONG THE ISLAND SPINE TO CHORA

a line of telegraph poles to the village of **Asfondilitis**, now little more than a huddle of animal shelters and wells.

> **Asfondilitis** had a life 4000 years ago, when it was an early Cycladic settlement, and in the late 19th century when it was a cheese-making centre. Then, the old men wore traditional costume incorporating a waistcoat and a red knitted cap called a *skoufia*, which hung to one side of the face. Today, rock-face drawings done by a disabled teenage girl in the early 1900s have become a tourist attraction. You can see the originals in a roofless stone building on the village outskirts to the right. The clearer images beyond and down a stony path to the left are copies.

Continue along the main lane past **Ag Nikolaos church** and past **To Steki** (the place) café. Where the concrete road bends R, break off L, up a slab-rocked path. After more than a kilometre of steady climbing, pass a low stone building down R and the beginning of a high vale of enclosures, from which the path heads between parallel walls then up to round the next spur. Pass a lichen-blanched outcrop and occasional cairns, then the trail rollercoasters on to a concreted cairn, cresting the hill and heading obliquely down.

> Seawards, the south side of **Nikouria island** falls into the triangle of Kalotiri Bay. The island is uninhabited, although it was a leper colony in the 19th century, and remains of a sanctuary and a defensive wall are evidence of a third millennium BC settlement. From the ninth century BC to the fourth century AD, when the three city-states of Amorgos were flourishing, it was the perfect location – offshore yet centrally placed between Egiali and Katapola – for minting the island's coins.

After the next spur, look L for man-made stone columns on the ridge above, which mark the site of

Xenodochio (hotel), a medieval hostel on the *Palia Strata*, now used by goats. Take a brief diversion to the site or go straight on – both well-trodden trails lead to a col crossed by dirt tracks. Take the lower dirt track half L, which edges along the SE of the island.

Beyond an old caravan, take the narrow track down L towards the trail that you can see snaking between high cliffs and a hard place, traversing the area known as **Kapsala** – another favourite location for 1800BC settlers. Beyond the remains of a settlement among a litter of white boulders expelled from the crags above, climb to a metal gate. ◄ Soon, round a corner to see the tip of **Chozoviotisa Monastery** wedged into the cliff.

> From the ninth century AD, monks carved simple cells (sketes) in the pitted cliffs.

A wooden icon of the Virgin Mary, miraculously discovered and intact at the foot of the Amorgos cliffs, inspired the founding of **Chozoviotisa** in 1088. It was from Khoziba Monastery in Jericho (also built into a cliff) but had been broken and lost when icons were banned. The icon is in a tiny ninth-century chapel at the top of the monastery, and brought out at Easter to be ceremoniously transported around the island's main churches. The monastery is eight storeys high and never more than 5m deep. The community was self-sufficient, with cisterns for collecting rain, olive and wine presses, ovens, chickens, and vegetables grown on cliff ledges. The monastery became very wealthy, owning several small islands. Today, it depends for its survival on visitors' donations, a box for which is in the room just below the top chapel. Visitor dress code: skirt length below the knees, top covering shoulders and torso for women; minimum ¾-length trousers and sleeved top for men. A tin chest inside the entrance contains sarongs and (very large) trousers.

Go downhill from the monastery to the car park. The bus stop (lift to Chora) is a small white shelter up the asphalt road at a junction. About 100 metres beyond, turn R up the stony path and wind up to a wire gate

WALK 27 – ALONG THE ISLAND SPINE TO CHORA

Chozoviotisa Monastery, embedded in the cliffs

through to a car park. Bear L into the charming Cycladic hilltop town of **Chora** and take as straight a course W as possible to reach the main bus stop.

Walking on the Greek Islands – the Cyclades

WALK 28
Inland capital to Katapola port

Start	Top-of-town bus and car park, Chora
Finish	Katapola
Distance	9.5km
Ascent	325m
Descent	660m
Time	3½hr
Terrain	Exposed phrygana hills with clear country paths, a stretch of asphalt road, and a steep, bushy scramble down from Minoa
Refreshments	Springs for refilling water on asphalt roadside, and at Valsamitis Monastery
Transport	Bus service Chora–Katapola

A gentle start through the island capital tumbling beneath its inland tor moves onto classic country paths that thread around deep spurs. There are distant glimpses of the deep wedge of Katapola Bay. Suddenly you switch to the east side of the island, to a road that runs above vertical cliffs and infinite sea, then return inland to a monastic oasis of peace and prophecy. Mountainside paths lead to the site of Ancient Minoa, towering theatrically above Katapola.

Go into the town, past **municipal wells**. ◄ Fork L at the tiny Fotodotis Café and go through the arched alley, reaching a miniature chapel at the entrance to a square with the triple chapel (dedicated to the Three Great Hierarchs) ahead.

Keep R and wiggle down to a *plateaki* (small square) and a café. Go down steps and R of the next chapel, past the **Byzantine Museum** (open 8.30am–3pm Tuesday–Saturday).

These were installed 1935, but underground water cisterns date from the area's earliest occupation, and there are medieval vaulted chambers and an aqueduct.

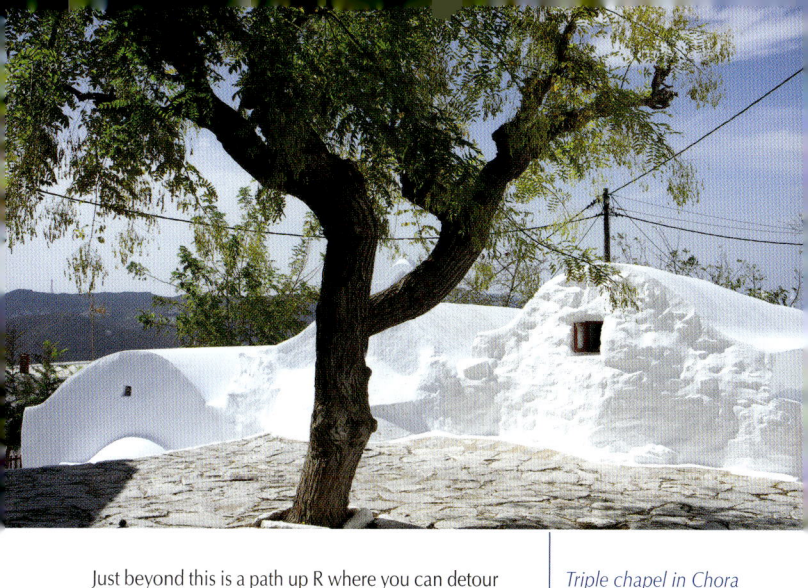

Just beyond this is a path up R where you can detour to the *Loza* (the main square and traditional trading centre), and the protuberance of rock topped by the **kastro** at its top L corner. The fortified houses and battlements were built during the Venetian occupation, although the little chapel at its base is early Christian. From the seventh century AD, Saracen pirate raids made life on the coast untenable, so islanders moved inland, and by the ninth century had established Chora as the island's capital. Chora's permanent population is about 400.

Continue to a right-angle turn L just before a general store, and go L again at the Jasmin café-bar down to a junction, where you go R towards a tunnel beneath the road, but go up steps R just before it. Turn L along the road for about 250 metres then leave it to go R, down a wide, slatey *monopati*, which you follow beneath low buildings up L and chapels neatly perched on rock outcrops down-valley. The way is clear, undulating along a generally midway contour of the hillside.

Path eventually turns to dirt track, joining a major dirt road coming up from the R, where you keep straight on to

Triple chapel in Chora

Walking on the Greek Islands – the Cyclades

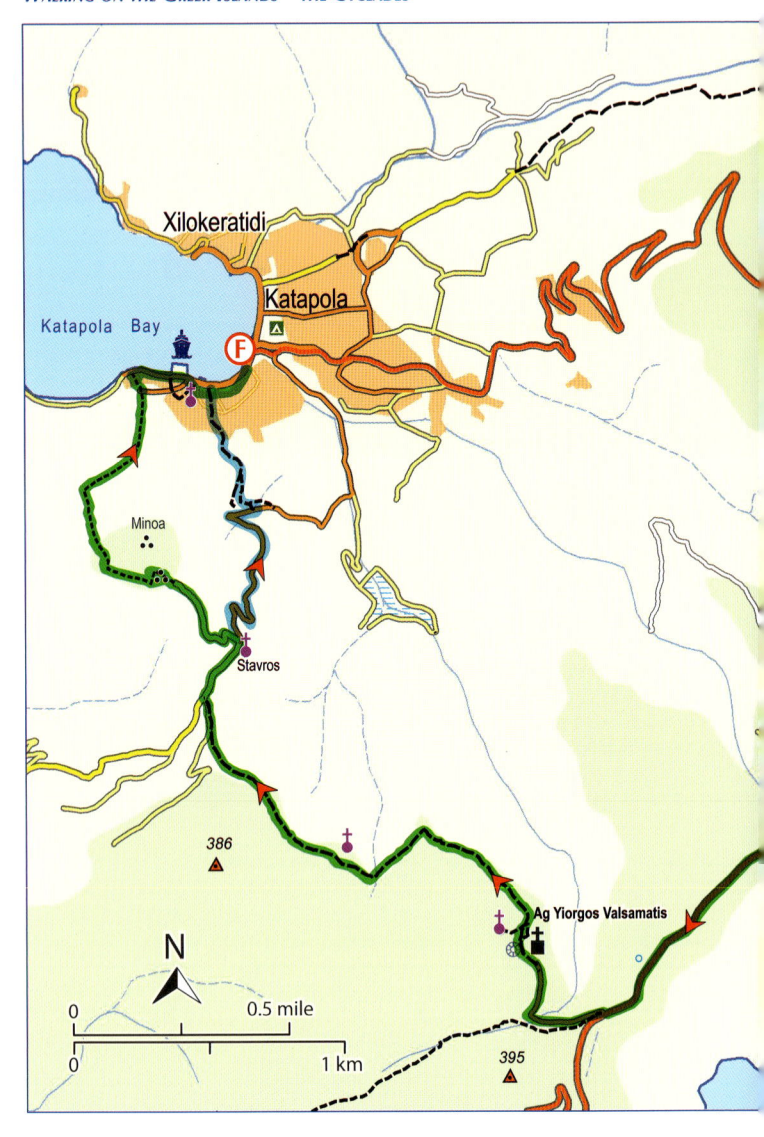

Walk 28 – Inland capital to Katapola port

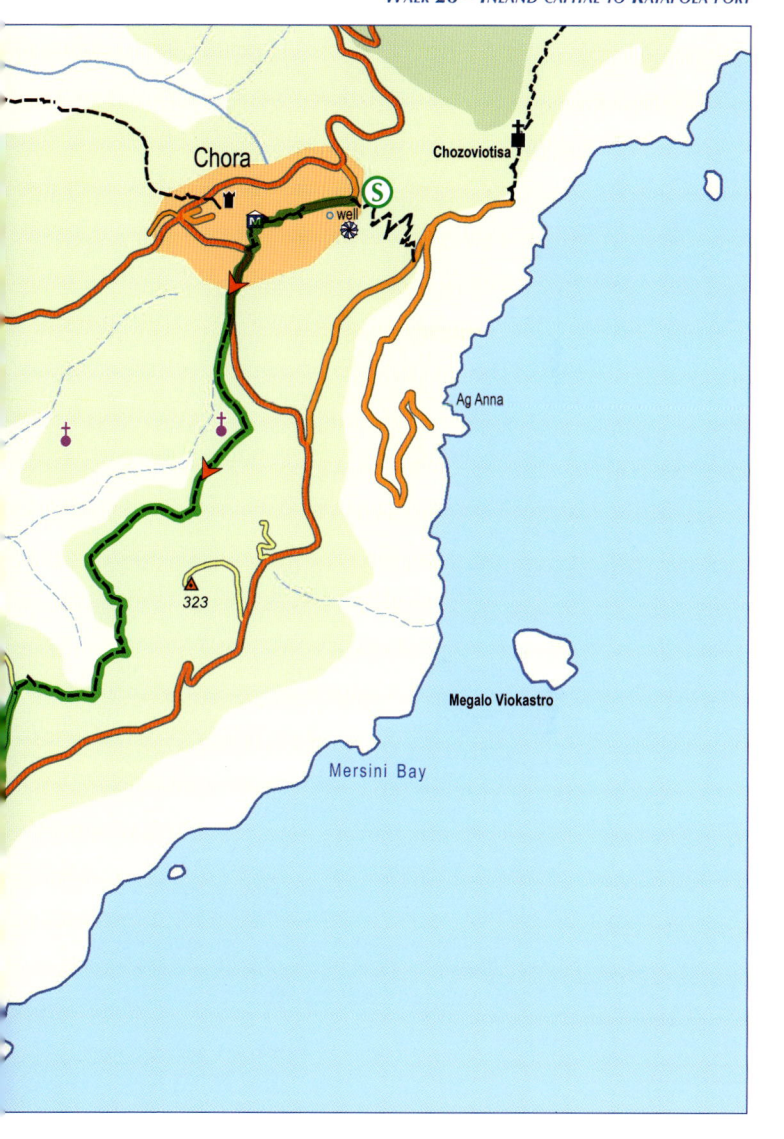

Chora
Chozoviotisa
well
S
Ag Anna
323
Megalo Viokastro
Mersini Bay

After some 900 metres look for a tap with spring water set into rock R to refill water bottles.

the main asphalt road and turn R. The abrupt fall of land to the infinity of Big Blue compensates for the 1.4km of exposed road-walking. ◄

Turn R at the signed road for **Ag Yiorgos Valsamitis** [sic: the saint's name is interchangeable with Varsamitis].

> The 16th-century **monastery** (may be open Easter–September 9am–1pm and 5–7pm) enjoyed peak popularity in the 18th and early 19th centuries, when mariners and others came in thousands to consult the oracle – a miraculous spring that flows in a rock-cut channel (inside the church). Its prophetic powers were activated by a priest who interpreted a tumbler of water and anything floating in it. Ag Yiorgos Varsamitis is the patron saint of Amorgos; his name comes from a mint-like plant with antiseptic properties, locally known as *Varsamos*.

Take the upper L fork directly above the monastery and go through the gate, passing beneath a water cistern and a former mill-race buttress. The path leaves monastery land through a gate into open country, rounds a spur and rises to a crest marked by a rock and a cairn, then follows a contour around spurs and valley-heads. Cross the verdant cut of a narrow stream-course, draped with maidenhair fern, with dark cypresses below, after which a vista of coast gradually opens. The path falls to a dirt road past a small farmhouse, where you turn R, then R again, to the chapel of **Stavros**. Go L through the gate opposite to reach the main entrance to the acropolis of **Minoa**.

The first impressive sight is the supporting wall of a late fourth-century BC gymnasium, with big, interlocking stone blocks. Pass to the L of this and step up R through the old city's S entrance to where the draped lower half of a guardian goddess statue stands.

> In the ninth century BC, **Minoa** became one of the island's three city-states, and over the next few centuries, temples, civic buildings, a gymnasium and

a stone drainage system were built. The hilltop city declined during the Roman rule, its citizens moving down to the harbour of Katapola (lower city) in the fourth century AD.

Late 4th-century BC latrine at the acropolis of Minoa

Go R above and behind the temple to the R of a fragment of rubble, stone and brick wall that was part of a vaulted Roman water cistern, then drop down to the R of the gymnasium wall. To check out the latrines, climb on and walk along the top of the wall to the L corner. Circle back to the S gate and round the SW slopes.

A sign for 'Acropolis' directs you to the summit, site of a **late Stone Age settlement**. Later there was a Cycladic settlement on the S slopes, but archaeologists say there is no evidence for the claim that King Minos, wealthy monarch of Knossos Palace on Crete and Ariadne's dad, spent his summer holidays here.

▶ To stay on the main route, continue around the hill seawards and NE and below a length of mighty fortification wall, in places nearly 1.5m thick. At the farthest

For an easy route back, return to Stavros and go down the concrete road and then the *monopati* beyond the overhanging rock bend to Katapola.

Katapola Bay from the acropolis of Minoa

NW point looking to the headland, go up R to the square remains of a tower, then L to follow the downward course of the 11th-century BC fortification. Continue until you see a clear trail R among the scrub, then follow goat paths NNE, heading for the spur where you can see the future path etched into the bare land, dropping to a large white-stepped building on the harbour front. Aim L of two little huts on the slope beneath. Immediately wind down steeply to the houses, through a gate bottom L, then turn R along the lane that leads to the far edge of **Katapola port**.

WALK 29
Old routes inland to the capital

Start/Finish	Xilokeratidi jetty
Distance	11km
Ascent/Descent	475m
Time	3¾hr
Terrain	Exposed outward journey. Paved lanes, dirt roads and rough traditional paths with some steep ascents and descents, and some indistinct cross-country trails.
Refreshments	Chora
Transport	Taxis and buses Chora–Katapola (Xilokeratidi is a 10-minute walk from Katapola on the opposite side of the bay)

This walk begins and ends at the Greece-as-it-used-to-be haven of Xilokeratidi with its fishing boats and waterside taverna tables, and in-between follows the old *strata* linking Katapola Bay and the inland capital of Chora. It's easy to imagine pirates anchoring along the nibbled coastline, which could be a template for Treasure Island. The shore is left far below as you climb into starkly handsome limestone country, where views of the island's rugged coast open out to the southwest.

From the jetty, continue NW beside harbour and beach to the village end, go R up the steps, then go L–R to the telegraph-pole junction. Turn L and continue along the paved coast road, above the cemetery, until you reach and take a L turn down steps to the narrow strip of **Treis Ierarches Beach**. ▶

Walk the length of the beach then go up a rocky path onto the low, wave-cut headland with the blue-domed chapel of **Ag Pantelemonas** (the man who blessed everyone). Continue round, leaving the headland at the corner of the next beach to go up to a facing wall and turn R alongside it. Go through a gap about halfway along and

> If the sea is high, continue along the lane to the hamlet of To Nero and pick up the route description from there.

WALKING ON THE GREEK ISLANDS – THE CYCLADES

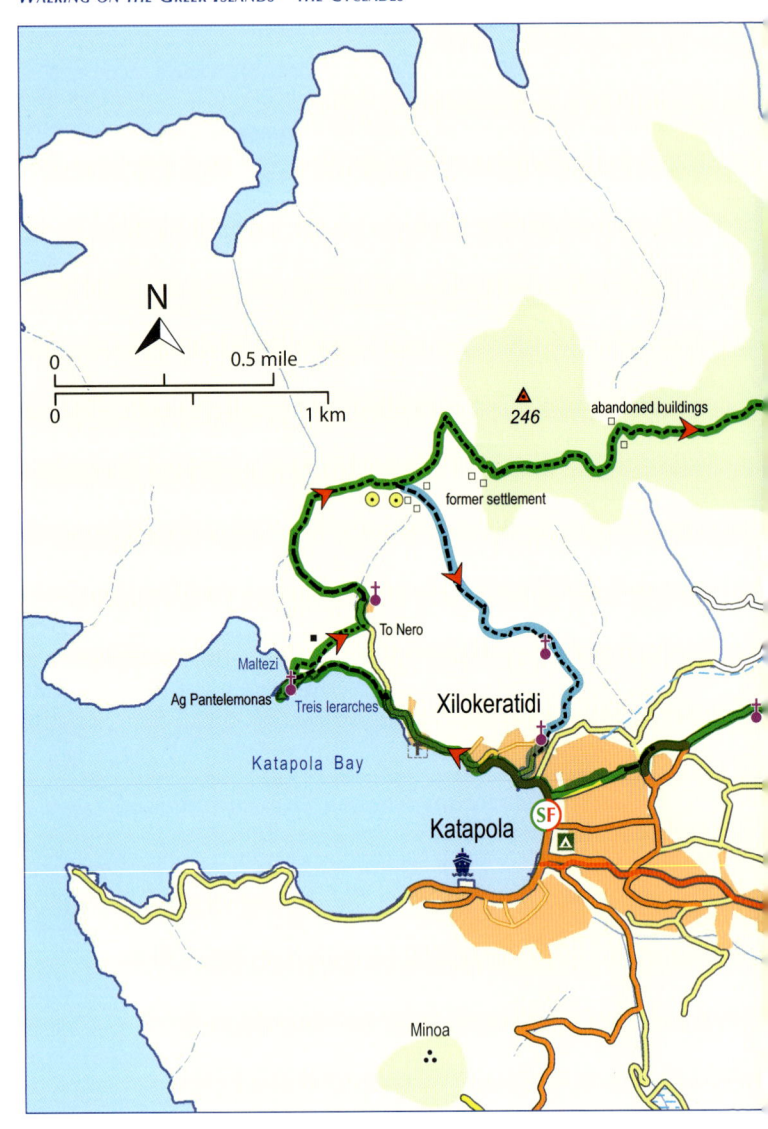

WALK 29 – OLD ROUTES INLAND TO THE CAPITAL

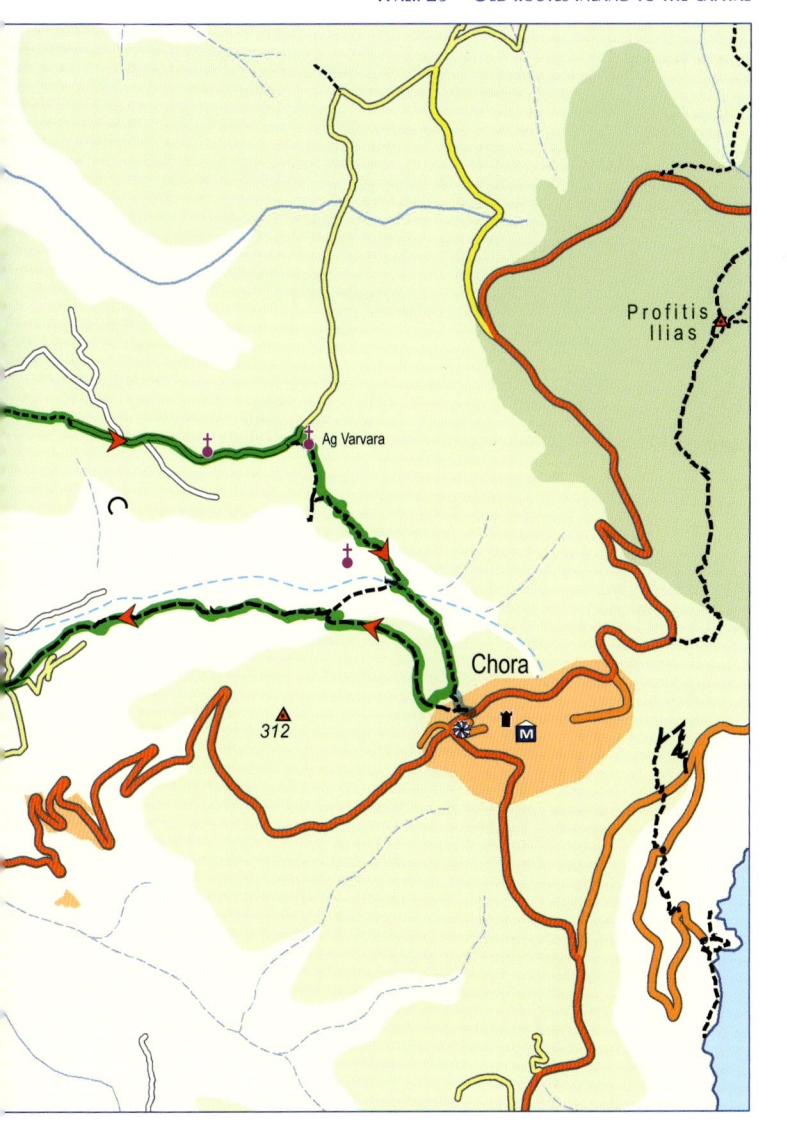

Profitis Ilias

Ag Varvara

Chora

312

Seaview cemetery before Tries Ierarches Beach

cut diagonally across to another wall coming from the jetty you passed earlier. The old path goes below the building ahead but is barred by a locked gate, so cross the wall some 50 metres before, then turn L to circuit skeletal buildings. Join the *monopati*, which leads to a steep concrete road, and turn L through the hamlet of **To Nero**. Go through the proper wooden gate at its end. ◄

> On the R are the wells that earned To Nero (water) its name.

Follow the wide, stepped country path uphill, turning inland, and at a junction marked by a rusty-faced boulder, keep straight ahead/R up rock steps. Pass a cluster of **ruins**, then go R and through a seven-bar gate. Beside the next ruin is a magnificent **threshing circle** with a view across Katapola Bay to the acropolis of Minoa and along the SW coast. Keep straight ahead just beyond, where a path heads down R through these crumbled remains of a settlement that speaks of more active farming in the past. ◄

> For a short circular walk you could return to Xilokeratidi down this path, keeping R at bottom.

From the junction, head uphill, waymarked '8', passing a small hut with a giant rock lintel. Turn sharp R, ascending steeply. Go through a fence-gate, then thread along trails stained earth-red on white limestone, bearing R and following cairns past another **former settlement**. At waymark '8' on a facing rock, go L. Keep L of a tall

WALK 29 – OLD ROUTES INLAND TO THE CAPITAL

wall alongside resin-scented juniper, and rise to a breezy brow of hill with an upright tooth of rock set in the L wall.

Descend to **abandoned buildings** and turn sharp R up a rocky gulley. About 15 metres after the end of the last building, where the forward path is overhung by wall, turn L at a cairn and towards waymark '8' on a rock above R. Follow a trail and cairns through the earth-stained rock, generally E. ▶ The limestone rocks peter out, the trail becomes clearer and you descend to a gravel vehicle track, which you follow straight ahead all the way to the **chapel of Ag Varvara**.

Turn R just before the chapel, and keep R where the path widens to descend steeply into the valley, going over an oleander-bordered stream-bed at the bottom. Climb the initially stone-paved path, going L at the fork after 55 metres. Keep R over exposed planes of rock, then sharp L, and where the route is unclear over another wide-sloping rock, head up R towards a concrete block building. Where the path splits, go R to continue the route, or L if you want to break the journey in **Chora**.

Profitis Ilias (Elijah) dominates the skyline, and soon you can see the inland capital of Chora to its R.

Sternbergia lutea brighten the limestone crevices off the track to Ag Varvara

Chora, the inland capital, around its central tor

For **Chora** go L and below a slope of scree and rubbish, past a concrete-covered cistern, to the main asphalt road. Cross the road and turn R to a bus stop and Bayoko mini-taverna.

The easy-to-follow footpath '2' rounds spurs and drops, sometimes steeply, for more than 2km, emerging at a wooden sign onto a dirt track. Go straight ahead at the cross-tracks to a concrete road, then fork R and continue to junction. Turn L to the first telegraph pole and sharp R down a narrow dirt path. Now head seawards, turning R–L past a luxuriant pine tree, to reach the harbour road and turn R to **Xilokeratidi**.

WALK 30
Rollercoaster route: Katapola to Vroutsi

Start	Bus/car park, Katapola
Finish	Vroutsi
Distance	8km
Ascent	595m
Descent	340m
Time	3hr
Terrain	Easy going over coastal hills, on dirt roads and traditional paths, but exposed, especially on long climb from Ag Saranda
Refreshments	Vroutsi
Transport	No public transport to Vroutsi. Taxi from Chora or Katapola, or hitchhike.

Follow in the steps of farmers and villagers from the acropolis of Minoa and its downtown port of Katapola, to rural Kato Meria. The way rolls high along the coast, with deep-creased headlands, the texture of worn upholstery, thrusting into the ocean. In the valleys crouch ancient places of worship, and avenues of paved paths wind towards the undulating farmland of Kato Meria.

From the car park, turn L along the harbour and fork L at the bakery. Turn L up a narrow lane with a telegraph pole. At the junction turn L up steps and go past the church onto a dirt, then paved, path and continue up to the concrete road, where you turn R beneath a rock overhang and wind up past the **acropolis of Minoa** and the **chapel of Stavros** on the crest.

> **Katapola** means low town, as opposed to the acropolis (high town) of Minoa that looms over it in the south. The first people to settle on Minoa and use Katapola as their port came in the fifth millennium

Walking on the Greek Islands – the Cyclades

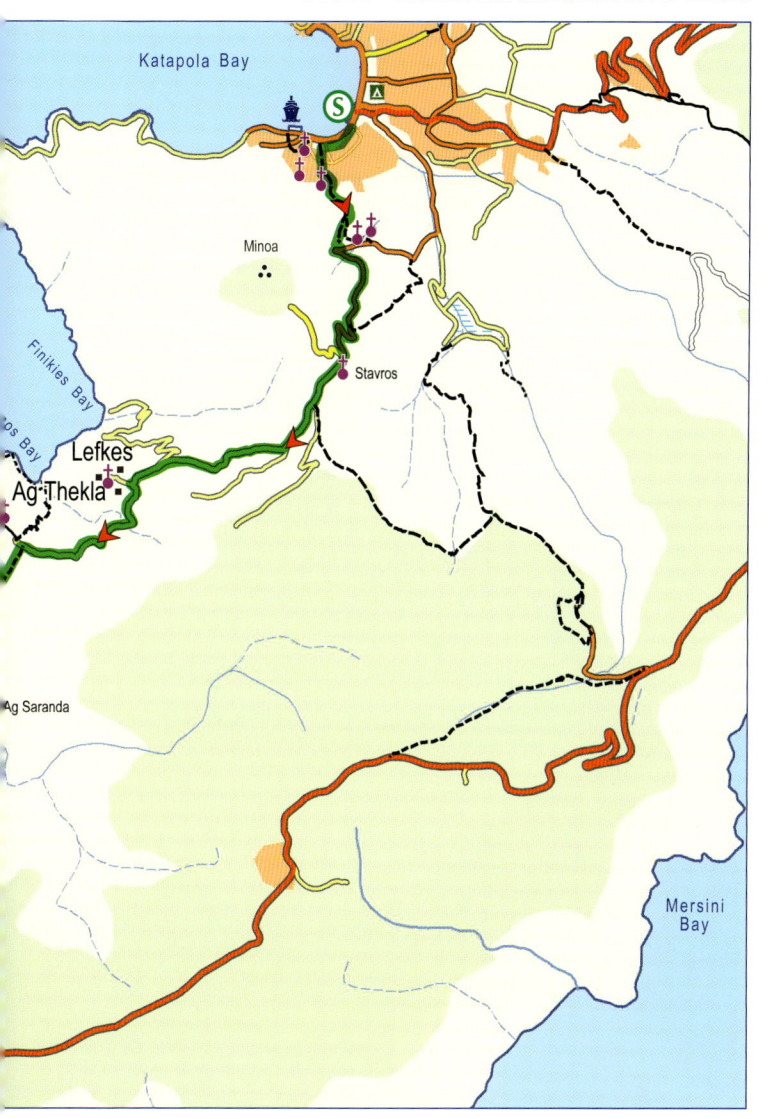

WALK 30 – ROLLERCOASTER ROUTE: KATAPOLA TO VROUTSI

Katapola Bay

Minoa

Finikies Bay

Stavros

Lefkes
Ag Thekla

Ag Saranda

Mersini Bay

207

BC, and were followed by prosperous, sea-trading communities in Cycladic and Mycenean times. The acropolis was fortified in the ninth century BC, when pirates were a serious problem, and a Hellenistic town with many conveniences was built a few hundred years later. Katapola only developed its full potential as a harbour under the Romans, in the second century AD.

Follow the rollercoaster dirt road for about 2km, keeping straight on where other tracks lead off and passing above the crescent of Finikies (palm trees) Bay. ◀ Pass a fork R that ribbons down to Tirokomos (cheesemaker) Bay, and look back to cheese-like modern villas above it. The dirt road ends at **Ag Thekla**, the next huddle of house on a headland, which marked the outer limit of Cycladic settlements that encircled the Minoa acropolis. Turn down the stone path L towards the inlet of **Ag Saranda**, beautiful from a distance but a catchment for wind- and sea-borne rubbish.

Look to the vale below R, where stone-roofed **Ag Pandes** (All Saints) chapel nestles among a wilderness of deceptively soft-toned cushions of spiny shrubs. (A fluted basalt column base from an earlier pagan sanctuary

A short detour R leads to the tiny hamlet of Lefkes – worth a visit for its headland location and spruce traditional houses with green-fingered owners.

Ag Pandes chapel above Ag Saranda Bay

WALK 30 – ROLLERCOASTER ROUTE: KATAPOLA TO VROUTSI

stands on the courtyard wall; you could thread your way down to the beach from here.) Continuing on the main route, the path crosses a wide, dry stream-bed.

> Make a short detour up L to the double **chapel of Ag Saranda**, which has impressive marble doorposts and lintels recycled from a classical temple. Σαραντα (forty) is named for 40 Christian soldiers who were stripped then condemned by their Roman commander to death-by-freezing for not renouncing their faith. They survived the ordeal but were dismembered instead.

The main path is at first bordered by an oleander and olive dell (hiding more marble *spolia*), but then winds relentlessly uphill along the R side of a valley of interlocking spurs. Some 650 metres up, over a small streamcourse, be sure to keep R. You may feel the occasional breath of breeze, but it's another drag uphill before a particle of shade beneath a lonely, dwarfed-by-circumstance juniper.

On the approach to a col, keep up and L and on to **farm** buildings at a dirt road. Turn R at the corner of the building and go through a gate with a new wall just beyond, and head straight down to the wall, to the start of a *monopati* leading L. Descend to a concrete bridge over a dry stream-bed and zig-zag up a splendid path paved with grey rock. Pass a shady junction with a wooden sign, continuing straight up wide steps. (Downhill is a chapel perfectly perched on a knoll overlooking a small, high cultivated valley.) Meet the main road at the four-in-one chapel of **Ag Nikolaos**, which has 14th-century frescos but is locked. ▶ Turn R along the main road, skirting Kamari village, and on to **Vroutsi**.

The far chapel has a fireplace and shelves set into the walls, and was probably inhabited by a lone monk.

WALK 31
Ancient Arkesini and southwest farms

Start/Finish	Bus stop, Arkesini
Distance	11km
Ascent/Descent	520m
Time	4hr
Terrain	Some rough country trails through low scrub along the coast. Lanes, dirt tracks and paths of varying comfort through cultivated highland and villages. Very little shade, and some steep climbs.
Refreshments	Arkesini, Vroutsi
Transport	Limited bus service Chora–Arkesini. Taxi, hitchhike or sleepover!
Accommodation	Arkesini: Pension Marousso, tel +30 22850 72253/72331

Cross from one dramatic coast to the other and look over the arid patchwork landscape of Kato Meria (low places) in the southwest. A cross-country path edging the northern coast leads to the startling citadel of Ancient Arkesini. Traditional paths, some perfectly paved, others ankle-turningly rough, weave through maquis shrubs and rolling high farmland, with the archaeological highlight of a Hellenistic fortified farm.

From the bus stop, go down the main road, past the miniature Ο ΜΑΚΗΣ *kafeneion*, a concrete water catchment area and a row of sickly cypresses. Beyond a chapel and cemetery above R, turn R at a significant **shrine**. At a sharp R bend, go L onto a rough path with a blue signpost for Ammoudi Bay. ◄

You can detour to the small but charming little Ammoudi Bay via a rough path R (1¼hr return).

Follow the wall L, past a new house, and go down to a stream-bed then steeply up the opposite slope, where you pick your way between sparse dwarf shrubs. Swing L to a small concrete hut and rusting mining equipment at the top. Go L through a tangle of wire fence onto the road at a sharp hairpin bend and turn R, and after some 100

WALK 31 – ANCIENT ARKESINI AND SOUTHWEST FARMS

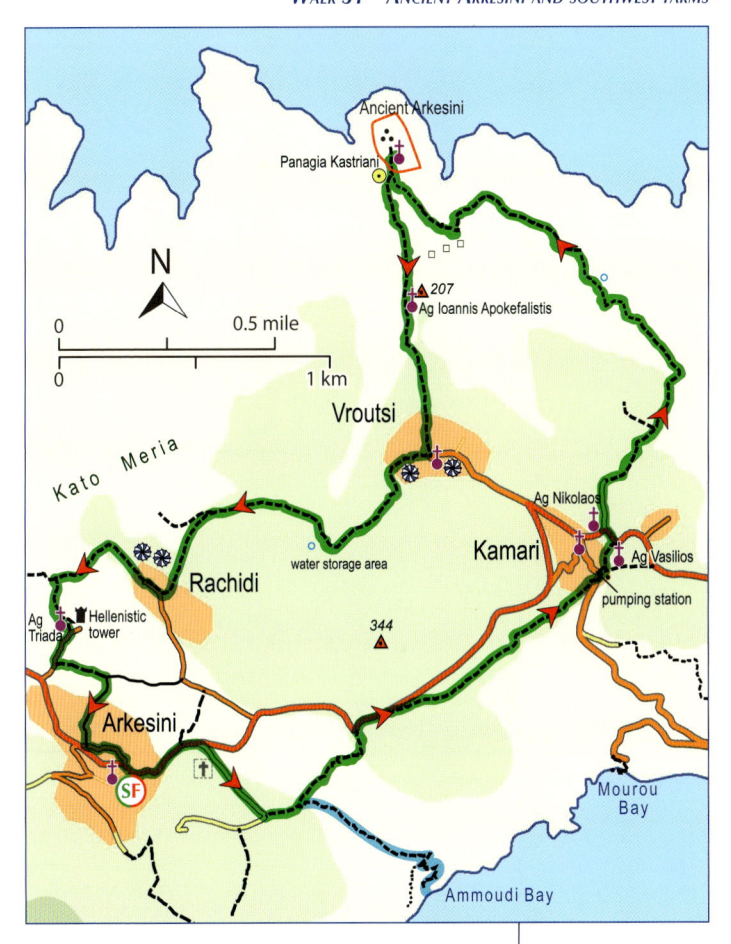

metres turn R onto a *monopati*, which contours round a bulge of land high above the tiny bays of Ammoudi and Mourou, invisible beneath the precipitous land fall.

Continue to a **pumping station** and turn up R to a metalled road. Cross to uneven open ground and go up L to a brief stretch of stony path between walls leading to

Ag Vasilios chapel. Turn L along the main road, and just before **Ag Nikolaos chapel**, with its undulating roof, turn R, soon joining a cobbled path that dips to a shady junction with a wooden signpost, then turn L. Keep R shortly after at the next sign (Βιγλες) and go through a wooden gate waymarked '3'.

The path, bordered by luxuriant stands of *Pistacia lentiscus*, swings seaward and L. At a fork, follow '3' up L, and go L again at another '3' on the wall. Soon go through a wire fence-gate and downhill, over a broken wall, then go L past an outcrop of boulders and through a gap with a rock-slab step. Curve down between walls towards a loop of enclosure with a triangular animal hole, over sloping rocks to a **spring**, and go L uphill past a gate to a prickly pear thicket.

Head generally L and seaward. ◄ Keep to the L of the seaward wall, bear R then head towards and through a gap, from where you see the remains of defensive walls, terraces and fields below the citadel. Drop to **ruined buildings** – the remains of the lower town that skirted the acropolis – at the head of a V-shaped gorge that cuts to a triangle of sea. Continue up the other side, looking half R at a corner to sections of late fourth-century BC wall with characteristic trapezoidal stones.

At the top, go below R of the **threshing circle** on the neck of the headland of **Ancient Arkesini**, towards another Hellenistic wall and a quartered rectangle painted on a rock high above. Pass helmeted, pitted rocks and naturally cemented shale and sand, extended to form dwellings for man and beast, then go up R towards a gap below a curve of wall. Turn immediately up a zig-zag path to reach a blue gate and steps to **Panagia Kastriani chapel** on the summit.

> The high, defensive position overlooking the sea was a natural choice for early Cycladic settlers some 5000 years ago, and there's evidence of habitation during the Iron Age too. The **acropolis** was founded by settlers from Naxos around the eighth century BC, with a sanctuary dedicated to Aphrodite, goddess of

After a large rock outcrop look ahead to Ancient Arkesini with the tiny white spot of the Panagia Kastriani (Virgin of the castle) chapel at its summit.

Stone trough at the foot of Ancient Arkesini acropolis

love. The approach road was then lined with colonnades and inscribed monuments (*steles*). The lower defensive walls and towers were erected during the pirate-ridden Hellenistic years. An underground aqueduct and an arched water cistern were built in Roman times, and occupation appears to have been continuous through the Byzantine period. Alleys lead through the remains of buildings, which include elliptical lodging houses used by pilgrims.

Return to the bottom of the zig-zag path and turn L along the lower terrace, keeping eyes peeled for stone basins, possibly remnants of the Roman water cistern. Join the clearly signed path as it leaves the ancient city boundaries and plods uphill towards the prominent **church of Ag Ioannis Apokefalistis** (the beheaded). At the first house of **Vroutsi**, bear L at the fork then R at the junction into the main 'street'.

Pass Costa's cheerful corner taverna, where you can test the village's legendary hospitality. ▶ Continue past the last house to the junction below a telegraph pole and turn L then immediately R down a country path. This soon widens and sweeps around the gently undulating

An old saying goes: 'Whoso goeth to Vritzi [sic] and does not get drunk is like a pilgrim who goeth to the Holy Sepulchre and doth not worship'.

> Look L to see the commanding position of the Hellenistic fortified farm in the high agricultural valley.

high valley, over a concrete bridge and an open area with concrete-covered **water storage**, before rising gently. Keep straight along the main path at turnoffs R, all the way to the car park of **Rachidi** (so called, they say, because of the good raki made here). Turn R to pass behind and R of the lower chapel, go past a wooden signpost, down a concreted section and keep L beneath a vehicle graveyard. ◄

At an opening of cross-paths, keep L, over ankle-turning loose rocks, and go down to a T-junction. Turn L and keep L uphill past open ground with a concrete cistern, soon after which there's a L turn to **Ag Triada** (Holy Trinity). The official entrance to the **Hellenistic Vasilis Tower** is further along the concrete road, L of a little taverna. (Opening hours are billed as Monday–Friday 8am–3pm, but don't hold your breath out of season.)

> In the fourth-century BC wave of piracy, many watchtowers were built throughout the island. **Vasilis Tower** served as watch- and beacon-tower, refuge for the locals and safe store for produce from the surrounding plains. The original four-storey tower had small windows and a pitched roof surrounded by a walled courtyard. There was a water supply and disposal system (a channel at the east edge of the site leads from the rainwater cistern).

With the taverna behind, go along the white-walled road towards 'new' Arkesini village, in 160 metres turning sharp L and L again onto a stony path between walls and olive groves. At a broad space and junction, turn R up a wide cobbled path to **Arkesini village**. Turn L at the general store, along another white-walled lane, and go past a doctor's surgery and a town council office and wend back to the road and the bus stop.

SANTORINI

Cave dug into volcanic ash and burnt islands in the caldera sea (Walk 33)

WALKING ON THE GREEK ISLANDS – THE CYCLADES

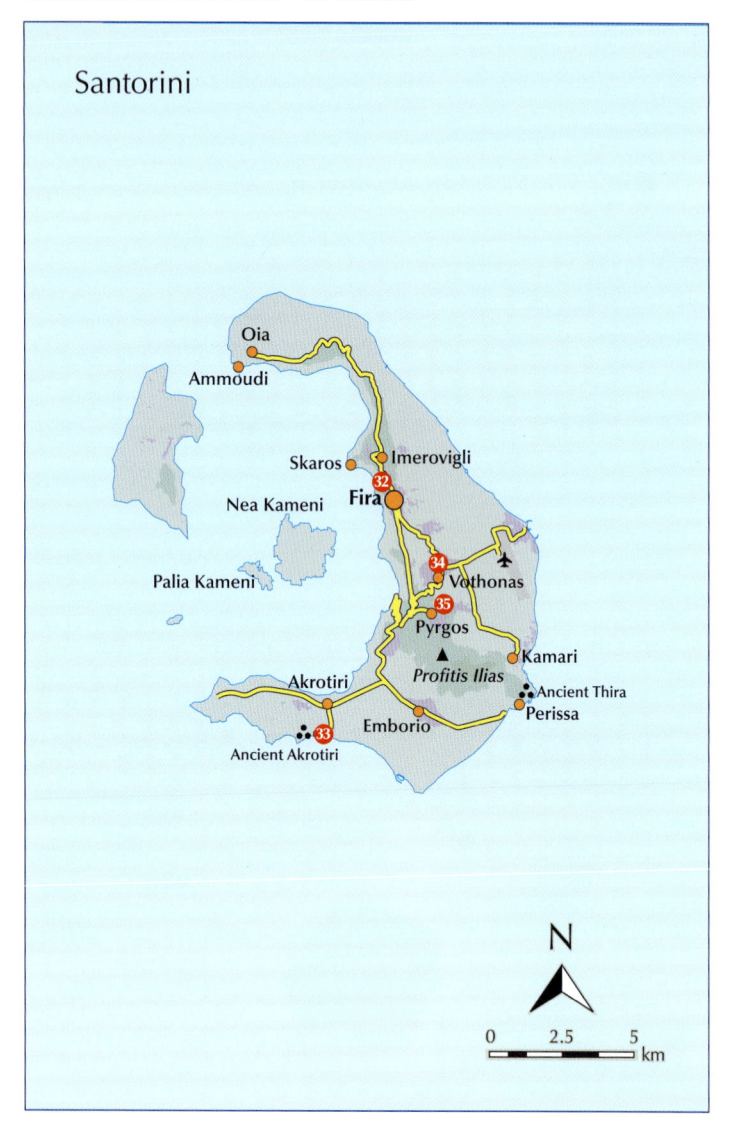

Santorini

Away from caldera tourists, man and mule work the land (Walk 35)

'Living on the edge' sums up Santorini. The island is the rim of a dormant volcano that rears from the world's largest sea-filled caldera in a spectacle of vividly contrasting colours. It has become a bucket-list destination with an almost year-round tourist season – overcrowded, overpriced and definitely not sustainable. But it is nevertheless sensational, and away from the caldera-view stage set are lesser-known and extraordinary landscape and lifestyle features.

The eruption that blasted away the entire centre of the island 3600 years ago and gave Santorini its present form was the biggest eruption in the whole of human history. Scientists have pieced together evidence from around the world to describe its impact. Jets of hot gas and pumice blocks were hurled 36km into the atmosphere, boiling magma hit seawater to produce explosions of steam that widened the vent. There were fast-moving surges of dust and gas, rivers of hot mud and ash that welded into a dense, hard solid. Much of the island was covered in ash several metres thick, and deposits were found 800km away. Clouds of debris, smoke and steam blocked out the sun for long enough to cause frost damage to California, yellow fog in China, and floods and droughts worldwide.

When not serving tourists, islanders make the most of a hard place where ash and pumice pass for soil and drought is common. They've perfected hydroponic techniques and produced world-renowned specialities such as the intensely flavoured, vitamin-packed Santorini tomatoes, and distinctive wines. Hair-frizzing water comes from five desalination plants and wells sunk sometimes 100m into the land. When the rain does come, its effect on the soft volcanic ash and pumice that make up most of the island is devastating. Paths become storm drains, dirt roads and fields turn to gulleys, and cliffs collapse.

Add to that its unstable position bang on the Hellenic ring of fire and it's not surprising that, at times in its history, the island has been deserted. And yet two unique historical sites, the remains of prosperous towns, bear witness to times of prosperity: the 17th-century BC city of Akrotiri with its sophisticated social structure, drainage systems, art and culture, and the ninth-century BC mountain-top capital of Thera.

Santorini's merchant shipping fleet, created initially to export its wine, became the third largest in Greece at the end of the 19th century. It collapsed with the advent of steam power and the opening of the Corinth Canal, plunging the island into economic depression, and depopulation was only reversed by the tourist boom of the 1970s. The island rose again, phoenix-like from its ashes, and today has the highest birth rate in Greece and a population of 25,000 according to a 2017 report, in a 70 sq km area, swelled by an annual influx of 2 million tourists.

Santorini is a small island and you're never far from a roadside supermarket or a town with a year-round life, such as Pyrghos or Emborio. Fira is the main hub for shops and services and has the bus terminal, from where reliable services radiate to the island's main resorts and villages. Your best chance of reasonably priced accommodation is to search online for places in non-tourist areas such as Vourvoulos.

Be prepared for the island's confusion of names. It was dubbed Santorini by the Venetians following their 1207 conquest, for a church in Perissa dedicated to St Irine, a Byzantine empress. Today's Greeks prefer the ancient name of Thera, for the tribal chief who founded the eponymous eighth–ninth-century BC city, and they sometimes use the same name for the island's main town. However, this is also called Fira, or 'Chora'.

WALK 32
Caldera rim: Fira to Ammoudi Bay

Start	Museum of Prehistory, Fira
Finish	Ammoudi Bay
Distance	12km
Ascent	640m
Descent	845m
Time	4½hr including Skaros Rock
Terrain	Alleys through caldera-top villages; wild, exposed cliffs in-between
Refreshments	Fira, Firostefani, Imerovigli, café above Mouzakia cliffs, Oia
Transport	Bus service Oia–Fira

If a visitor does one walk on Santorini, this is it, because of the awe-inspiring perspectives of sea-filled crater rimmed by islands. Fira and Oia are the main log-jams, and in-between are wild heights, chilling drops and fiery rocks. The views are uniquely, sensationally Santorini, even in the villages that ice the volcano-rim layer cake, where steep-raked tiers of Cycladic rooftops fall to deep ocean blues. At the end, beyond the sunset selfie spots, you descend to the farthest end of Ammoudi Bay for a pure Greek harbour-side taverna moment, as the sailing boats come in.

The **Museum of Prehistory** (8.30am–3pm, closed Tuesdays) has incredible artefacts brilliantly displayed and labelled, and giving a superb insight into the island's geological and ancient history. There are originals and reproductions of the wonderful frescos, exquisitely crafted seal stamps and painted pottery from Ancient Akrotiri.

From the **museum**, go N and fork L into souvenir street, then take the first L up an alley and go R at a junction, following 'cable car' signs on steps and walls. At the next

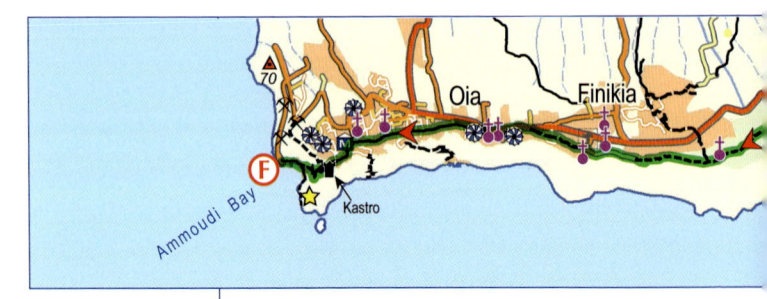

Thirasia, the largest island across the inland sea, is a remnant of the volcano's opposite rim.

junction go R–L, towards an elegant cupola rising ahead. At a small square, with the **archaeological museum** R (open daily 8.30–4pm except Tuesdays), turn L, past the cable car entrance, to go along the cliff edge. ◄

Keep L at the junction, heading towards the Tuscan-red Nomikos Conference Centre. Don't be tempted down dead-ends to tightly packed caldera-view hotels, but follow the main path to a high waist of the island at the conspicuously large **church**.

> **The path may be closed** due to a section falling into the caldera during winter storms. If so, return to the junction and go straight ahead, down the road L, and after the large car park on the bend, turn L and follow the lane to the big church.

Beyond the church, the cobbled path runs to the L of the main road for a while. See on the hill ahead, and soon pass, the mass of 17th-century **Ag Nikolaos Convent**. Follow the path as it climbs, levels then drops to go along the caldera edge, towards another bell-tower and church, then take a L turn downhill signed 'Skaros'.

> A 30-minute **detour to Skaros** takes you beneath gleaming overhangs of solidified lava over a causeway to the butte on which the Venetians astonishingly built their centre of administration after their 1207 conquest. It was the first of five intercommunicating citadels on the island, the others being at

Walk 32 – Caldera rim: Fira to Ammoudi Bay

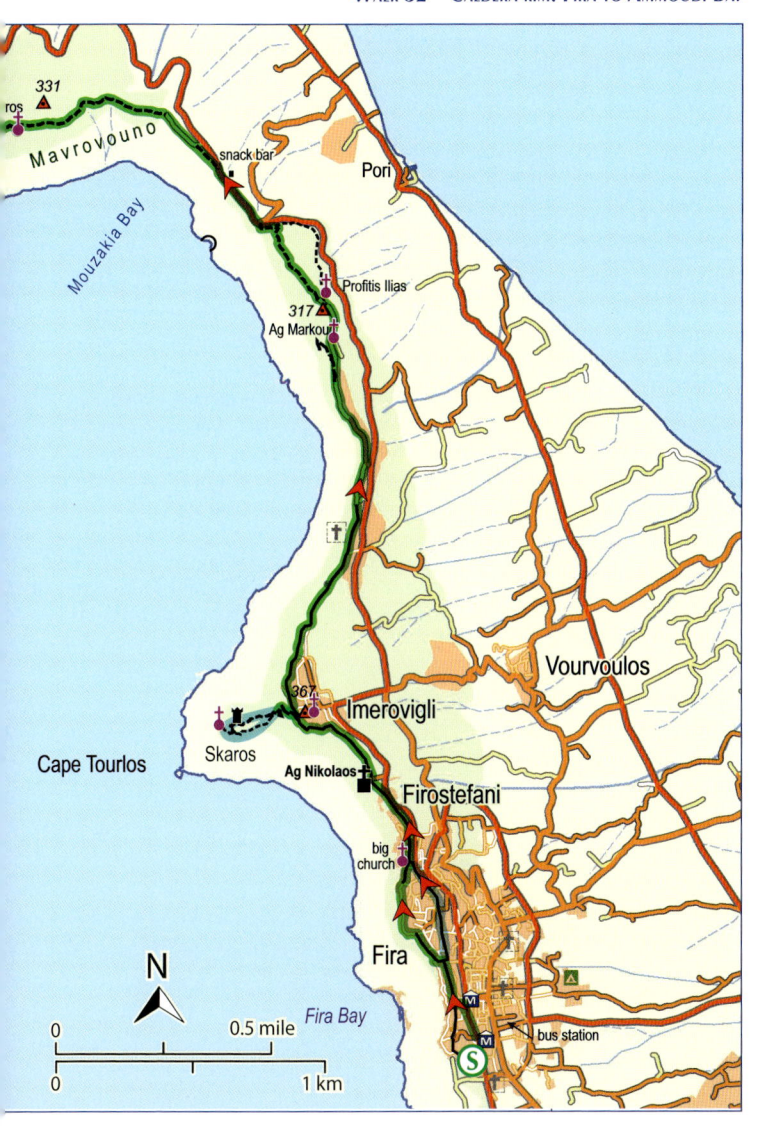

Akrotiri village, Pyrghos, Emborio and Oia. Some 200 people, mostly Venetians and Catholics, lived in buildings that clung on and around this flat-topped cone of unstable rock. It's not surprising that little remains. Follow the main path L from the causeway. Fork R for the summit, which involves a couple of short, vertical climbs. Only a skeletal chapel and cisterns remain, but the view from this volcanic hotspot is predictably jaw-dropping. Retrace your steps, or continue clockwise on a precipitous path that hugs the foot of the citadel then rises to join the causeway.

Wind up from the causeway, past and above a distinctive slice of swimming pool and a R bend, then take the unmarked sharp turn up a path back L. This goes up and N between the village of **Imerovigli** at the highest point of the caldera rim, with a plunge to the deep dark blue more than 300m below. ◄

> The sea inside the crater is so deep that ships can't anchor; they're are moored to buoys chained to weights on the seabed 190–395m below.

The steep-stacked houses eventually peter out altogether on the seaward side, and the path heads up R, then turns to concrete road towards the next sprinkle of hotels. Keep R at a cliff-top car park L, and go straight up

Walking above the world's biggest caldera sea

WALK 32 – CALDERA RIM: FIRA TO AMMOUDI BAY

L at the junction below **Ag Markou chapel**. Now look down another sheer volcano flank to the coastal plain, the miniature harbour of Pori, and the islands of (L–R) Ios, Iraklia, Naxos, Amorgos, Schinousa, Kato and Ano Koufonisia, Donousa and Anafi.

Where an alternative *monopati* leads down R, keep L, to the **church of Profitis Ilias** on a peak. At the far end of the courtyard below the church, take the *monopati* that swings beneath red rock down to the road. Turn L, reach a tiny **snack bar**, and just beyond take the dirt road L uphill, then keep L at the junction. ▶ Soon you're back on the high edges above **Mouzakia Bay**.

> The sometimes rough but well-trodden path offers a brief respite from the exhausting drama of caldera view.

Solidified magma block

WALKING ON THE GREEK ISLANDS – THE CYCLADES

Looking over the **caldera**, you can see its circularity. The island was roughly circular too, until its core imploded around 1600BC. The islands of Thirasia and tiny Aspronisi are the remains of the rim across the inland sea, the channels between them formed by collapsing rocks up to 2km wide. The vent of the volcano was in the centre of the bay, just beyond still-smouldering Nea Kameni (new-burned), a dome of magma that surfaced in 1570, and the smaller Palea Kameni (old-burned), formed in 197BC.

From **Stavros chapel** it's downhill all the way to Oia. If in doubt (at the turnoff to Finikia, for example), keep L, along the S cliff. At the car park, cross to the NW corner to re-find the path, join the road below **two churches**, then just follow the crowds into the sunset, along polished marble paths between designer shops and tourist paraphernalia. Keep L at the square and continue to the 15th-century Venetian *kastro*, whose topless tower is crammed at sunset with camera-toting tourists. It's a relief to walk down the steep, zig-zag way beneath startling red lava cliffs, to the harbours of **Ammoudi**. Continue past the busy first harbour onto the second.

Oia sunset in pastel shades, and returning boats

WALK 33
Ancient Akrotiri and southwest cape

Start/Finish	Car park, Ancient Akrotiri
Distance	9km
Ascent/Descent	390m
Time	3hr
Terrain	Tracks and trails through fields and vineyards of ash and pumice; a steep ravine, where paths may collapse after winter rain, and you can climb round. Wild coastal uplands, then some pebble and sand beach walking. Danger of rockfall on Red Beach.
Refreshments	Akrotiri village, Mesa Pigadia (seasonal), Ancient Akrotiri
Transport	Bus service Fira–Akrotiri village

Akrotiri means 'cape' – specifically the one this walk explores at the southwest tip of the island. It is also the name of the remarkable ancient city excavated from beneath layers of ash, and of a living village topped by a Venetian tower, each of which is en route. Otherwise, this is some of Santorini's most sparsely populated country, with ravines and buttes eroded from the soft ash, and a run of dramatic beaches, each one a different vivid hue of volcanic rock.

From the **car park** entrance take the path NW, signed for Akrotiri village, leading between volcanic rock walls from which caper plants spring. Below the village, where the concrete lane begins, turn R uphill to the main road. Turn L to the village square in **Akrotiri**, straight up the paved path R of the church. On reaching a high concrete wall with 'TO THE CASTLE' painted on it, turn R, and R again up steps, then keep R and up following signs.

Leave the **castle** at the W exit, go straight along the alley and turn L at the road. Take the second path R and kink past a flaking **chapel-like building**. Fork R up steps and follow the alley uphill until it meets a concrete

View north from the Venetian castle in Akrotiri

lane with a mini-market R. Turn L up the concrete lane between the next houses, then leave them at a R bend and fork up R.

At the cross-tracks, with large private houses R, go straight ahead onto a *monopati*, with red- and blue-painted spots on rock R, and swing around the hillside high above the N coast. ◀ Go L for about 50 metres along the road to the small **church** and turn L steeply down to the large **church of Panagia**, with enormous courtyard and neoclassical façade. Go down R past the iron-gated entrance to a path through vine fields.

At the sandy track turn L, and where it bends L, turn off straight ahead down a *monopati* between walls. At a cross-tracks go straight ahead onto a track that runs down a deeply eroded wadi-like valley. Look for a wire fence running at right-angles uphill and go up R beside it where there's a blue spot on a rock (if you see beehives L you've gone too far), soon joining a *monopati* leading to the dirt road. Turn L, then turn L down the dirt track and follow it all the way to the bay of **Mesa Pigadia**, so called for its wells but known to tourists as Black Beach. ◀

Turn NE off the beach approach road up a sand track that cuts inland (although after heavy rain this looks more like a riverbed). At a rough junction at the top, cross up into a field that borders a blocked path, but very soon

Beware: the path crumbles as it goes above, then falls into the asphalt road at a cutting.

The Akro beach bar and restaurant built into the cliff is a tasteful (in every sense) refuelling point.

WALK 33 – ANCIENT AKROTIRI AND SOUTHWEST CAPE

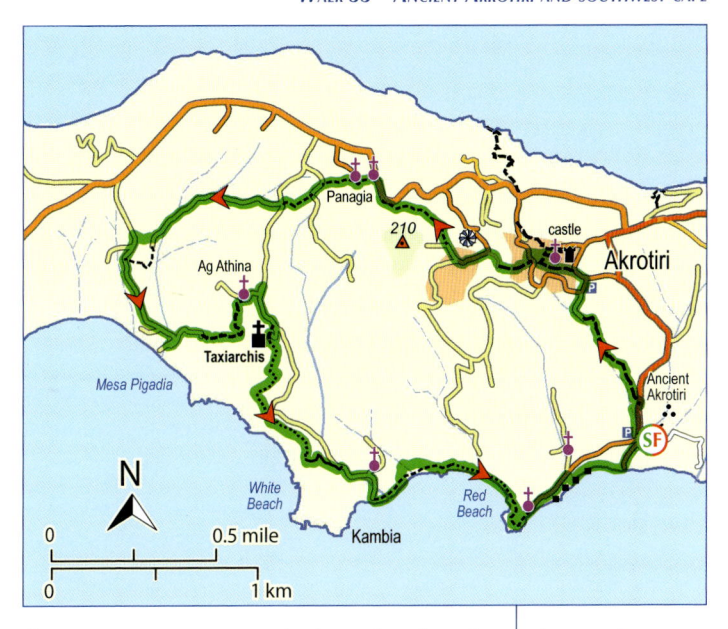

drop R onto it as it turns into a broken trail up the ravine. (If bits have collapsed, scramble above and/or round them, to a crumbling ravine head.) Cross this to the L and go over a narrow band of hard rock above a water-cut drop to reach a path leading to the solitary **church of Ag Athina**. ▶

Turn R, and R again at the dirt road, then fork R and wind up to the **monastery of Taxiarchis** (Archangel Michael) stuck on the side of the cliff. Return to the first bend below the monastery and go S off it onto a scrubland path that passes an ancient arched cistern and then trails off R, winding down a muddle of tracks to a band of white, concrete-like rock. Follow this diagonally down, above and beyond the bend in the dirt road, heading towards a scruffy smallholding on the flank of the hill ahead. Join a vague trail that climbs to a small ridge just above it.

Go L, seeing your way rolling away clearly ahead, with white stacks stark against the dark sea above **White**

This once-fine monopati was destroyed by winter storms, so you may have to climb to the fields above and cross L to the broad, black-cobbled church approach.

WALKING ON THE GREEK ISLANDS – THE CYCLADES

Beach (Aspri Beach), which is accessible only by sea. Eventually drop to a dirt track and turn L down it, keeping L, then go R down the dirt road and L at the fork to reach **Kambia Beach**.

Follow the trail that goes L over giant pebbles and then hugs the cliff. It exits into a small valley, which you cross and ascend the opposite side of. Follow the field past a line of feathery tamarisk trees, turn R through a gap onto a clear trail that takes you to **Red Beach**. ◀

◀ Walk the length of the beach to a well-worn route over the headland, round to a car park, church and tourist shops. If the waves aren't rolling in on a S wind, walk along the beach to **Ancient Akrotiri**: turn R just past the general store between taverna terraces, or farther on opposite a tavern L, down a white-walled path. Otherwise, follow the road back to the start.

The rock, among the oldest lava on the island, was hurled up by a subterranean eruption and oxidised red on exposure.

Keep away from the cliff edge, as rock falls are common.

The 17th-centry BC city of **Akrotiri** lay beneath layers of volcanic ash for more than 3700 years, until excavations began in the late 60s. You can walk through its streets and squares, peer through windows of houses up to four storeys high, see toilets, stairs, and remnants of everyday life such as beds (for very short people) and an ornate table. Yet this is a mere 3–5% of the prehistoric city that has been excavated. What you can't see are the remarkable mosaics, as most of them are in the National Archaeological Museum in Athens, and some in Fira's Museum of Prehistory.

Lava colour palette from Black Beach to Red Beach

WALK 34
Villages and vineyards to Emborio

Start	Vothonas windmill
Finish	Main road, Emborio
Distance	6km
Ascent	290m
Descent	350m
Time	2½hr
Terrain	Steep village alleys, then soft volcanic ash and pumice landscape with vineyards and tomato fields, apart from a steep path in a ravine between Vothonas and Pyrgos, which becomes a water outlet carrying debris after heavy rain
Refreshments	Vothonas, Pyrgos, Emborio
Transport	Bus service Fira to Vothonas, Pyrgos and Emborio

The true heart of Santorini is on the volcano's outer slope, which drops to the coastal plain. Here are captivating inland villages, where real rather than tourist-driven life is lived. Vothonas is a rural backwater with a troglodytic edge. Pyrgos, on its conical bluff in the centre of the island, is smart and arty, while Emborio is a gem of intertwining alleys and charming houses with well-tended yards. They are linked by traditional routes through gulleys and pinnacles eroded from layers of volcanic ash, and the island's main wine-growing region.

Turn R onto the road at the cobbled car park just beyond the **windmill**, and take the first R down the main alley. Turn R at the church, L at the next junction, go past another church (R), then go down to the bottom, at a church opposite a parking area. Turn R then L, between dwellings and storage places cut into the soft tufa cliffs. Caves offer cool respite from summer heat, and warmth in winter, but are unstable unless reinforced. (Many were used for storing wine.)

Walking on the Greek Islands – the Cyclades

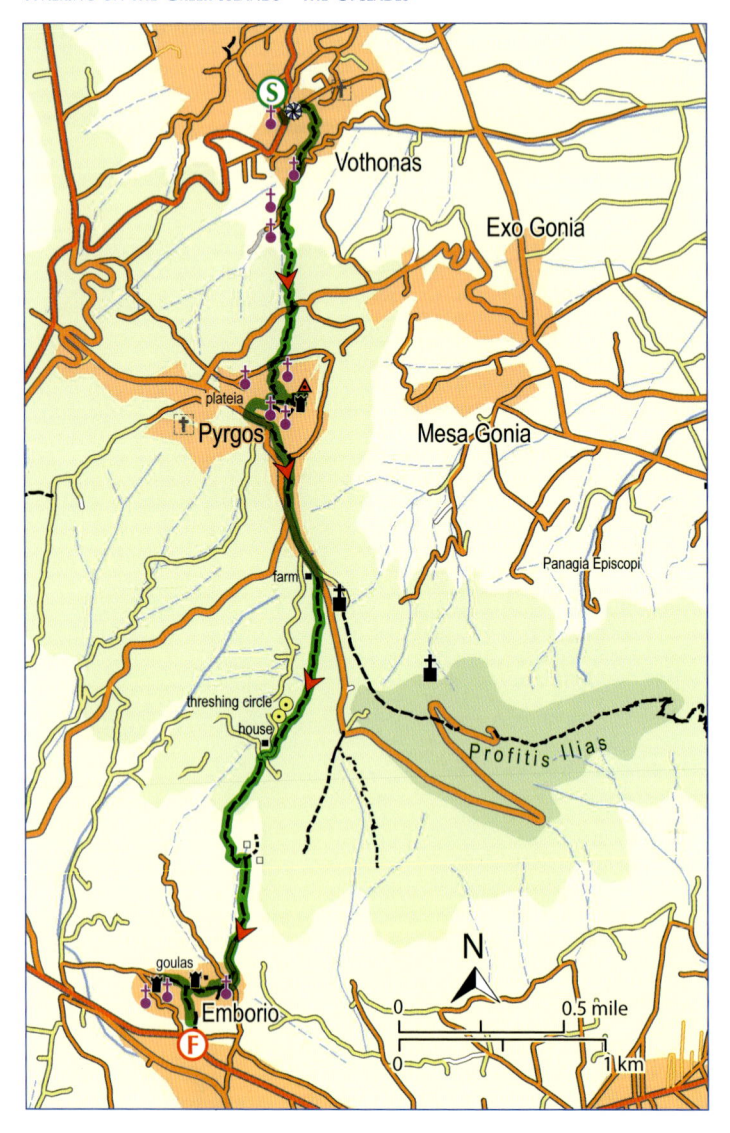

WALK 34 – VILLAGES AND VINEYARDS TO EMBORIO

The wedge of church in the cliff ahead is reached via a collapsible ruler of stairway that replaced the original, which collapsed after a recent stormy winter. ▶ The route continues opposite the wedge of church, up the narrow *monopati* L. This old cobbled path to Pyrgos turns to a broken, rocky gully strewn with vegetation and detritus, which becomes a storm channel after heavy rain. Persevere, though, to the top and cross the main road to a concrete road then footpath. At the next asphalt road, turn R and cross to turn steeply up L into a stepped alley. Just after double doors with a lion-head knocker, turn L and go up through the ruined outer ring of Venetian citadel, towards the domed church. Beyond is a neoclassical house, a gift from an RA (rich Athenian) to his daughter, now a hotel, and a terrace from which you turn L through a covered alley into the *kastro*.

The **Pyrgos kastro** is one of five strongholds built on high points of the island by the Venetians during their governance of Santorini from the early 13th century. The others are at Emborio, Akrotiri, Skaros and Oia. They consisted of a central tower surrounded by an inward-looking girdle of high houses, whose outer walls are defensive.

> To see more of the fissured gorge and a cave chapel, you can go straight ahead at this point for a 15-minute return detour.

Pumice stone 'soil' releases moisture slowly to the koulara vines

WALKING ON THE GREEK ISLANDS – THE CYCLADES

Retrace your steps to the hotel but go L of the **church**, with its splendid bell tower, then L and L again towards caldera-side Santorini, and R down a stepped path to the main road at the bottom. Turn L to the roadside **plateia** (square) on a sharp bend, and go straight across to the signed path, passing briefly above then joining the main avenue to reach a car park with a roundabout. Cross L and turn R onto a footpath below a low wall and go through residential Pyrgos to the main road. Turn L up the road until, after a concrete lane forking straight up L, you go R along a signed *monopati* leading above a track and **farm** with chickens, pigs and chained dogs.

> You are now in a major **wine-producing area**. The idiosyncratic basket-shaped vines (*koulara*), low enough for strong winds to blow over, are crafted by hand using a sickle-like knife. The three strongest shoots are retained and braided into a circle. The leaves grow in spring to form a protective sun-hat over the grapes in the centre.

Keep straight on above a pair of big **threshing circles**, along a cobbled path between walls, which emerges onto a dirt road at a white tufa cliff. Turn L, and L again at the point of the sharp R bend below a large **house**, onto another dapper mule path, passing terraces hedged with invasive Mexican prickly pears, to **Emborio**. Round a weathered ravine pierced with cave dwellings, then go down a lane lined with houses ruined by the 1956 earthquake, some restored. Turn R at the bottom junction, then immediately L up a narrow path with a '2' on a telegraph pole. Wind up painted steps to a smart church and the towering, outwardly defensive houses of the Venetian *kastro*, the entrance to which is via a marble-framed 1831 doorway obliquely up R.

> French author Jean-Paul Sartre visited **Emborio** with his lover Simone de Beauvoir before World War II, and used it as the setting for his play *Les Mouches*. The *kastro* is a warren of dead-end alleys,

Cycladic houses crammed into the Emborio kastro

and beautifully restored buildings. Crammed on the summit with them is the Church of the Panagia, with its open fretwork, wedding-cake tower and mosaic courtyard.

Go down the path opposite the front gates of the Panagia, and turn L then R to the Barber Shop Café. Bear R beside it, go through the tumble of houses, and go R at the junction to a stolidly impressive rhomboid of Venetian tower. Known locally as a **goulas**, this was a 16th-century fortified Venetian family home. Return to the junction and go straight ahead, down towards the big Mitropoleus church, *plateia*, cafés, ATMs and bus stops.

WALKING ON THE GREEK ISLANDS – THE CYCLADES

WALK 35
Highest peak and Ancient Thira to Perissa

Start	Bus stop, Pyrgos
Finish	Perissa Beach
Distance	9km (add 2km for the unmissable Ancient Thira)
Ascent	610m
Descent	920m
Time	4hr
Terrain	Village alleys, dirt roads in ash and pumice vale. Country trails and stone paths over the island's limestone, pre-volcanic mountains; steep descent to coast.
Refreshments	None on route
Transport	Bus service Fira–Perissa

The limestone bulk of Profitis Ilias, at 567m the highest point of the island and the only part that is not volcanic, dominates this walk. The rest of the island falls away from its mighty, ragged cliffs. Below are fields of ash and pumice, gashes of pozzolana quarries, villages lost to earthquakes. And then, a ruined city on a mountaintop, a vertical fall to the flat coast. The history and spectacular views are nothing short of awesome.

Take the path opposite the general store that leads up into the old town. Go R, fork L, then go R towards a four-tier bell tower. Go L signed 'castelli', and L again at facing wrought-iron gate. Pass beneath a terrace with a war memorial (the entrance to the *kastro* is behind). Bear L at the neoclassical hotel and to the R of the **big church**, then follow the path that circuits the castle on the N side, with northern Santorini laid out below.

At tastefully painted double doors (R), turn L down past **Ag Christoforos church,** with the airstrip in your sightline far below. Go down obliquely R across the asphalt road to the next section of path, and obliquely R and down to the next road at the beginning of **Exo Gonia**

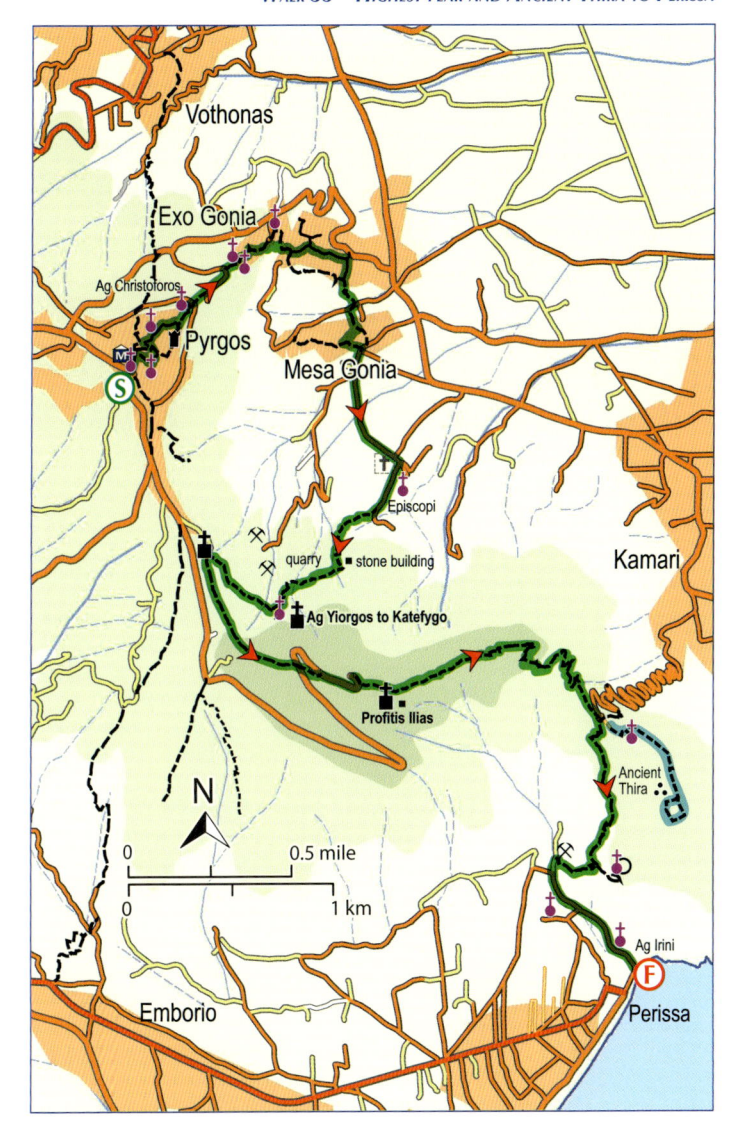

Walk 35 – Highest peak and Ancient Thira to Perissa

Pozzolana quarry, and Pyrgos on its peak

village. Pass a windmill conversion with a tiny chapel extension, take the next R, then keep R as you wind down E until you reach and take a L turn at the road with a clear view to Kamari on the coast.

> **Exo and Mesa Gonia** were prosperous wine-making centres, with many *kanaves* (cellars) built into the soft tufa rock, but after severe damage in the 1956 earthquake many inhabitants moved to Kamari on the coast, sponsored by the monastery on Profitis Ilias.

The neoclassical 'sea captain's house' dates from Santorini's peak merchant shipping days of the 19th century.

After about 20 metres, go R, then R again around a restored neoclassical mansion, continuing down and E to a junction where you turn R. ◄ At the T-junction before the asphalt road (L), turn R – you are now heading mostly S – then go L at the next junction (with impassable *monopati* opposite). At the next junctions, go R and R again, then immediately L into **Mesa Gonia**.

At the tree enclosure, turn L, then fork sharp L to the road and turn R. Fork L onto a dirt road signed 'Παναγεια Επισκοπη'. Continue straight up to a cobbled avenue towards a young church and pass to the L of it, to the island's oldest church, **Episcopi**, beyond.

WALK 35 – HIGHEST PEAK AND ANCIENT THIRA TO PERISSA

As its name suggests, the 11th-century **Panagia Episcopi** (bishop) was the seat of the island's Orthodox bishop in Byzantine times. It is noted for its architecture, 12th-century wall paintings, and a 'priceless' icon of the Virgin Glykophilousa (sweet kissing Madonna).

Go up the road below Episcopi, and just as it begins to dip turn R onto a rough path L of a barbed-wire fence, almost immediately dropping over a gap L to go along the R side of a depression past a fig tree. Follow trails through rough fields at the foot of the crystalline limestone cliffs of Profitis Ilias, up and over gaps in terrace walls, via a small copse with a pistachio nut tree, then towards a **stone building**. The path goes obliquely upslope to the foot of the cliffs, then towards tiny cube building teetering on an edge.

Now head towards a deep vertical cleft and beyond it, R, the 1754 **Ag Yiorgos to Katefygo** (refuge) embedded in the rock face. ▶ At the junction with a classic stepped path snaking L to the monastery, go R above the quarry all the way to a rocky brow and a prospect of Santorini's W side. Turn sharp L just above another **monastery** down R, and follow the straight and narrow cobbled way up **Profitis Ilias**. At the road, cut off a hairpin in it by crossing to a narrow trail to the next bit of road, which you follow R to the next paperclip bend. Cut off L past a rhomboidal building and continue up the road, past the entrance to **Profitis Ilias Monastery**.

Look above to see tiny windows in the rock face; the monks' cells.

The **monastery** (8am–1pm; check in off-season, tel +30 22860 31210) was founded in 1711. In the second half of the 18th century it became one of the wealthiest and best-known monasteries in the Cyclades, with its own ship and founding many educational institutions through the ages. Today a few monks live there and have a shop selling home-grown produce and religious items. Inside are relics of several saints, and clots of blood from toddlers killed by Herod. The icon of the prophet is brought out at times of drought to encourage rain.

Beyond the monastery entrance and just before the abandoned monstrous military buildings, take the signed rock path that drops steeply L. Keep to the ridge over the first col, where Perissa Beach is beneath. At the end of it the route drops to the L of the small peak (look for a red paint spot and a '1' on a rock ahead). Now Kamari and the quarries you circuited earlier are in sight.

Stick to the clearest paths rather than apparent shortcuts, heading straight for Anafi island beyond a headland of pumice, which you skid down almost to the end of before turning sharp R down to the col beneath Mesa Vouna, with Ancient Thira enthrallingly spread over its summit. It's a long flog down to a car park with a roundabout and the road to the entrance of **Ancient Thira**.

Open Tuesday–Sunday 8am–3pm, the **ruins of Ancient Thira** are 360m above sea level, with a choice of a port on either side depending on wind direction. The city was inhabited from the ninth century BC to AD 726, and excavated 1896–1902.

From the car park roundabout, turn L down the signed path to Perissa past an ancient cemetery site. At junction keep R, where you can see the path rounding the spur ahead. Turn down R at the next junction, where the L turn leads to a **quarry**, and wind down to the dirt road. Turn L to the main road into **Perissa**. Just before the beach, look L behind the car park to a scattering of Roman and Hellenistic ruins, and the fifth-century church of **Ag (St) Irini**, from which the island took its name.

APPENDIX A
Route summary table

Walk no	Walk	Distance	Ascent/Descent	Time	Page
Paros					
1	Parikia town to Cape Fokas	9km	160m/170m	3hr	36
2	Northwest coast to Kolimbithres	10km	240m/360m	4hr	43
3	Northwest peninsula eco-park	6.5km	190m	2¼hr	49
4	Naousa port, inland to marble mines	9.5km	325m/180m	3½hr	53
5	West-coast hills to Parikia	9km	280m/445m	3½hr	59
6	Lefkes village and Byzantine Way	12km	445m	4½hr	65
7	South from Lefkes to Dryos port	12.5km	505m/705m	5hr	70
8	Southwest coast: Piso Livadi to Dryos	6.5km	70m/70m	2½hr	75
9	Angeria mountain circular	13km	580m	4½hr	79
Naxos					
10	Naxos town tour	4km	80m	1½hr	87
11	Potamia villages and marble hills	10km	420m	3¼hr	93
12	South coast to Demeter's Temple	8.5km	335m/155m	2½hr	100
13	Rural byways below Profitis Ilias	11.5km	280m	3½hr	104
14	Wild lands around Apalirou	9km	250m	3½hr	108
15	Central villages and Fanari foothills	9.5km	415m	3½hr	114

WALKING ON THE GREEK ISLANDS – THE CYCLADES

Walk no	Walk	Distance	Ascent/Descent	Time	Page
16	Filoti village and Mount Zas	9.5km	730m	4hr	120
17	Apiranthos to emery mines and port	11.5km	315m/905m	4½hr	125
18	Koronos, mountain and east-coast bay	7km	250m/810m	2½hr	132
19	Kynidaros, downriver to Engares	8km	195m/570m	3hr	136
20	Strada 1: Plaka to Kato Potamia	10km	265m/370m	4½hr	142
21	Strada 2: Kato Potamia to Filoti	10.5km	590m/330m	4hr	148
22	Strada 3: Filoti to Apiranthos	8.5km	695m/465m	3hr	155
23	Strada 4: Apiranthos to Koronos	11.5km	760m/785m	4½hr	160
24	Strada 5: Koronos to Apollonas	11km	495m/1035m	4hr	164
Amorgos					
25	Egiali and mountain villages	11km	585m	4hr	172
26	Remote north: monastery and mountains	16km	975m	6½hr	178
27	Along the island spine to Chora	13.5km	930m/645m	5½hr	185
28	Inland capital to Katapola port	9.5km	325m/660m	3½hr	192
29	Old routes inland to the capital	11km	475m	3¾hr	199
30	Rollercoaster route: Katapola to Vroutsi	8km	595m/340m	3hr	205
31	Ancient Arkesini and southwest farms	11km	520m	4hr	210

Appendix A – Route summary table

Walk no	Walk	Distance	Ascent/Descent	Time	Page
Santorini					
32	Caldera rim: Fira to Ammoudi Bay	12km	640m/845m	4½hr	219
33	Ancient Akrotiri and southwest cape	9km	390m	3hr	225
34	Villages and vineyards to Emborio	6km	290m/350m	2½hr	229
35	Highest peak and Ancient Thira to Perissa	9km	610m/920m	4hr	234

APPENDIX B
Useful Greek words and phrases

The following glossary includes a handful of terms used in the book, where the Greek word is more apt than the English, and which are useful for reading maps and signs.

The position of the stress in the word is vital for both meaning and understanding; in the following lists it is denoted with an accent.

The Greek alphabet

Greek	equivalent sound	pronounced as in
Α α	a	drama
Β β	v	valley
Γ γ	y	yard
Δ δ	dh (th)	father
Ε ε	e	egg
Ζ ζ	z	zoo
Η η	i	in
Θ θ	th	path
Ι ι	i	bridge
Κ κ	k	kettle
Λ λ	l	lake
Μ μ	m	manner
Ν ν	n	nature
Ξ ξ	x	box
Ο ο	o	lock
Π π	p	pack
Ρ ρ	r	river
Σ σ	s	sun
Τ τ	t	boat
Υ υ	y	monastery
Φ φ	f	farm
Χ χ	h	loch
Ψ ψ	ps	upside
Ω ω	o	oak

Sound combinations

Greek	equivalent sound	pronounced as in
μπ	b	bear
γκ, γγ	g	goat
ντ	d	door
ει, οι	i	in
αι	e	pen
ου	oo	book
τς	ts	fits
ευ, αυ + vowel	ev, av	clever, savage
ευ, αυ + consonant	ef, af	effect, craft

Greek words for map reading and directions

Greek	English
Ághia (Ag)	female saint
Ághios (Ag)	male saint
Ághioi (Ag)	many saints
akrotíri	cape, headland
áno/epáno	up/upper, high
aristerá	left
chorió	village
dhexiá	right
eftheía	straight ahead
kafeníon	café
kaldherími	mule track, usually paved or cobbled and wide enough for a loaded donkey
karávi	ferry
kástro	castle, usually referring to Venetian fortification
káto	down, lower
koryfí	mountain top
koiládha	valley
kólpos	narrow bay
limáni	port, harbour
límni	lake, lagoon
livádhi	meadow
maghazí	shop, business, taverna
mílos	wind/water mill
monastíri	monastery
monopáti	footpath
naós	temple
nísi	island
órmos	wide bay
óros	mountain
paralía	beach, coast
plátanos	plane tree
plateía/plátsa	village square
potámi	river
pýghi/pyghádi	well, water source, spring

WALKING ON THE GREEK ISLANDS – THE CYCLADES

pýrghos	tower
spolía	architectural salvage, such as bits of temple re-used in later
vounó, ta vouná	mountain, mountains

English–Greek words and phrases

Greetings and pleasantries

English	Greek
hello	yeía sou (singular or informal)/sas (plural or polite)
good morning	kaliméra
good afternoon (noon–3pm)	kaló mesiméri
good evening (4–6pm)	kali spéra
good evening (6–10pm)	kaló vrádhi
good night	kiníchta
how are you?	ti káneis/kánete
excuse me	signóme
please/you're welcome	parakaló
thank you	efcharistó
yes	né
no	óchi
OK	endáxi
cheers ('to us!')	yéia mas!

Practicalities

English	Greek
how much is it?	póso kánei
how far?	póso makriá
when	póte (NB poté means never!)
where is...?	pou eínai...?
which, what?	ti
rooms (used to describe village accommodation, and the rooms themselves)	dhomátia
hotel	xenodochéio

Appendix B – Useful Greek words and phrases

bill	*o loghariazmós*
bus	*leoforío*
bus stop	*stási leoforíou*
car	*aftokínito, máxi*
on foot	*me ta pódia*
petrol	*venzeéni*

Miscellaneous

English	Greek
a little	*lígi*
a lot, many	*polí*
big	*megálo*
cold	*kryo*
good	*kaló*
here	*ethó (hard 'th')*
hot	*zestó*
small	*mikró*
near	*kondá*
there	*ekeí*
today	*símera*
tomorrow	*ávrio*
in a few days	*se líghes méres*

Eating and drinking

English	Greek
beer	*beéra*
bottle	*bookáli*
bread	*psomí*
butter	*voótiro*
cheese	*tyrí*
coffee	*café*
tea	*tsái*

drink(s)	potó, potá
eggs	avghá
ice cubes	pagháki
ice cream	paghotó
oil	ládi
olives	eliés
pasta	zimariká, makarónia
pie	pítta
food	faghitó
fish	psári
fresh juice	frésco xhimó
glass	potíri
greens	chórta
litre	éna kiló
half litre	misó kiló
quarter litre	éna tétarto
milk	ghála
salad	saláta
Greek salad	choriátiki
sausage	loukanikó
slice(s)	fétta, féttes
grilled meat pieces on a stick	souvláki
large chunk of meat, grilled	soúvla
vegetables	lakaniká
vegetarian	chortofághos
vinegar	xídhi
water	neró
bottle of water	bookáli neró
wine	krasí
yoghurt	yaoúrti

APPENDIX C
Bibliography

Early Cycladic Culture, Christos G Doumas (Goulandris Foundation, 2000)

McGilchrist's Greek Islands, Nigel McGilchrist (Genius Loci, 2010)

The Cyclades, John Freely (IB Touris, 2006)

The Cyclades, J Theodore Bent (Archaeopress, 2002)

The First Eden, David Attenborough (Little, Brown, 1987)

The Classical World, Robin Lane Fox (Penguin, 2005)

The Mediterranean in the Ancient World, Fernand Braudel (Penguin, 2002)

Flowers of the Mediterranean, Oleg Polunin & Anthony Huxley (Chatto & Windus, 1978)

Wild Flowers of Greece, Vangelis Papiomitoglou (Mediterraneo Editions, 2006)

Geological Maps of Greece (IGME)

APPENDIX D
Useful contacts

Maps
Anavasi
www.anavasi.gr

Municipality websites
Paros
www.paros.gr/en

Naxos
www.naxos.gr/?lang=en

Amorgos
http://amorgos.gr

Santorini
www.santorini.gr

Airports
Athens
tel +30 21035 30000

Paros
tel +30 22840 92030

Naxos
tel +30 22850 23292

Santorini
tel +30 22860 28400

Airlines
easyJet
www.easyjet.com

Aegean
https://en.aegeanair.com

Port authorities
Piraeus (Athens)
www.olp.gr/en

Paros
tel +30 22840 21240

Naxos
tel +30 22850 22300

Amorgos
Eghiali
tel +30 22850 73620

Katapola
tel +30 22850 71259

Santorini
tel +30 22860 22239

Ferries
GTP (for schedules)
www.gtp.gr

Blue Star
www.bluestarferries.com/en

Seajets
www.seajets.gr

Superfast
www.superfast.com

Hellenic Seaways
https://hellenicseaways.gr/en

Skopelitis
www.smallcycladeslines.gr/en

Taxis
Paros
From Parikia port
tel +30 22840 21500

From Naousa
tel +30 69445 40556

Naxos
tel +30 22850 22444

Appendix D – Useful contacts

Amorgos
From Katapola
tel +30 69321 03077
tel +30 69725 56443
tel +30 69739 88702

Santorini
tel +30 22860 22555

Buses
Athens airport
www.athensairportbus.com/en

Paros
tel +30 22840 21395
https://ktelparou.gr/en

Naxos
tel +30 22850 22291
http://naxosdestinations.com
Groups of five or more can book a mini-bus

Amorgos
tel +30 69366 71033
http://amorgosbuscompany.com/en

Santorini
tel +30 22860 25404

Health
General emergency
tel 112

Paros
Ambulance
tel +30 22840 22500

Health centre
tel +30 22843 60000

Medical centre
tel +30 22840 24410

Naxos
Health centres (and ambulance)

Chora
tel +30 22853 60500

Apiranthos
tel +30 22850 61206

Chalki
tel +30 22850 31206

Komiaki
tel +30 22850 52213

Koronos
tel +30 22850 51280

Melanes
tel +30 22850 62372

Filoti
tel +30 22850 3140

Vivlos
tel +30 22850 41221

Amorgos
Katapola
tel +30 22850 71207

Aegiali
tel +30 22850 73222

Arkesini
tel +30 22850 72250

Santorini
tel +30 22863 60300

Police
Paros
Parikia
tel +30 22840 23333

Naousa
tel +30 22840 51202

Naxos
Chora
tel +30 22850 22100

Filoti
tel +30 22850 31224

Amorgos
tel +30 22850 71210

Santorini
tel +30 22860 22649

Fire
Paros
tel +30 22840 25199

Naxos
tel +30 22850 3219

Amorgos
tel +30 22840 25199

IF YOU ENJOYED THIS GUIDEBOOK YOU MIGHT ALSO BE INTERESTED IN...

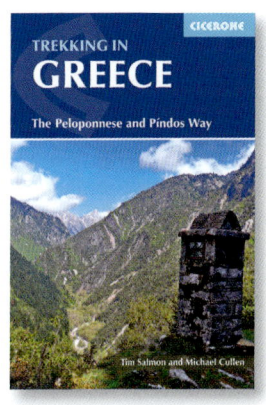

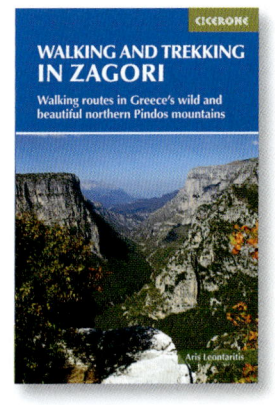

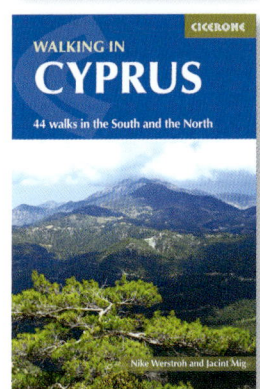

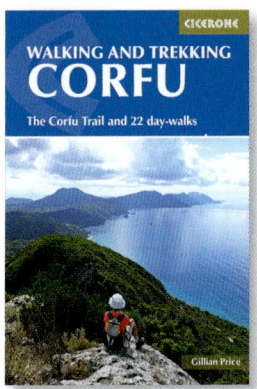

TREKKING IN GREECE
The Peloponnese and Píndos Way

WALKING AND TREKKING IN ZAGORI
Walking routes in Greece's wild and beautiful northern Píndos mountains

WALKING IN CYPRUS
44 walks in the South and the North

WALKING AND TREKKING CORFU
The Corfu Trail and 22 day-walks

visit **www.cicerone.co.uk** for more detail
and our full range of guidebooks

CICERONE

LISTING OF CICERONE GUIDES

SCOTLAND
Backpacker's Britain:
  Northern Scotland
Ben Nevis and Glen Coe
Cycle Touring in Northern Scotland
Cycling in the Hebrides
Great Mountain Days in Scotland
Mountain Biking in Southern and
  Central Scotland
Mountain Biking in West and North
  West Scotland
Not the West Highland Way
Scotland
Scotland's Best Small Mountains
Scotland's Mountain Ridges
The Ayrshire and Arran Coastal Paths
The Border Country
The Borders Abbeys Way
The Cape Wrath Trail
The Great Glen Way
The Great Glen Way Map Booklet
The Hebridean Way
The Hebrides
The Isle of Mull
The Isle of Skye
The Skye Trail
The Southern Upland Way
The Speyside Way
The Speyside Way Map Booklet
The West Highland Way
Walking Highland Perthshire
Walking in Scotland's Far North
Walking in the Angus Glens
Walking in the Cairngorms
Walking in the Ochils, Campsie Fells
  and Lomond Hills
Walking in the Pentland Hills
Walking in the Southern Uplands
Walking in Torridon
Walking Loch Lomond and
  the Trossachs
Walking on Arran
Walking on Harris and Lewis
Walking on Jura, Islay and Colonsay
Walking on Rum and the Small Isles
Walking on the Orkney and
  Shetland Isles
Walking on Uist and Barra
Walking the Corbetts
  Vol 1 South of the Great Glen
Walking the Corbetts
  Vol 2 North of the Great Glen
Walking the Galloway Hills
Walking the Munros Vol 1 –
  Southern, Central and Western
  Highlands
Walking the Munros Vol 2 –
  Northern Highlands and the
  Cairngorms
West Highland Way Map Booklet
Winter Climbs Ben Nevis and
  Glen Coe
Winter Climbs in the Cairngorms

NORTHERN ENGLAND TRAILS
Hadrian's Wall Path
Hadrian's Wall Path Map Booklet
Pennine Way Map Booklet
The Coast to Coast Map Booklet
The Coast to Coast Walk
The Dales Way
The Dales Way Map Booklet
The Pennine Way

LAKE DISTRICT
Cycling in the Lake District
Great Mountain Days in the
  Lake District
Lake District Winter Climbs
Lake District:
  High Level and Fell Walks
Lake District:
  Low Level and Lake Walks
Mountain Biking in the Lake District
Outdoor Adventures with Children –
  Lake District
Scrambles in the Lake District –
  North
Scrambles in the Lake District
  – South
Short Walks in Lakeland Book 2:
  North Lakeland
The Cumbria Way
The Southern Fells
Tour of the Lake District
Trail and Fell Running in the Lake
  District
Walking the Lake District Fells –
  Langdale
Walking the Lake District Fells –
  Wasdale

NORTH WEST ENGLAND AND THE ISLE OF MAN
Cycling the Pennine Bridleway
Cycling the Way of the Roses
Isle of Man Coastal Path
The Lancashire Cycleway
The Lune Valley and Howgills
The Ribble Way
Walking in Cumbria's Eden Valley
Walking in Lancashire
Walking in the Forest of Bowland
  and Pendle
Walking on the Isle of Man
Walking on the West Pennine Moors
Walks in Ribble Country
Walks in Silverdale and Arnside

NORTH EAST ENGLAND, YORKSHIRE DALES AND PENNINES
Cycling in the Yorkshire Dales
Great Mountain Days in the
  Pennines
Mountain Biking in the
  Yorkshire Dales
South Pennine Walks
St Oswald's Way and St Cuthbert's
  Way
The Cleveland Way and the
  Yorkshire Wolds Way
The Cleveland Way Map Booklet
The North York Moors
The Reivers Way
The Teesdale Way
Trail and Fell Running in the
  Yorkshire Dales
Walking in County Durham
Walking in Northumberland
Walking in the North Pennines
Walking in the Yorkshire Dales:
  North and East
Walking in the Yorkshire Dales:
  South and West
Walks in the Yorkshire Dales

WALES AND WELSH BORDERS
Cycle Touring in Wales
Cycling Lon Las Cymru
Glyndwr's Way
Great Mountain Days in Snowdonia
Hillwalking in Shropshire
Hillwalking in Wales – Vol 1
Hillwalking in Wales – Vol 2
Mountain Walking in Snowdonia
Offa's Dyke Map Booklet
Offa's Dyke Path
Pembrokeshire Coast Path
  Map Booklet
Ridges of Snowdonia
Scrambles in Snowdonia
Snowdonia: Low-level and easy
  walks – North
The Cambrian Way
The Ceredigion and Snowdonia
  Coast Paths
The Pembrokeshire Coast Path
The Severn Way
The Snowdonia Way
The Wales Coast Path
The Wye Valley Walk
Walking in Carmarthenshire
Walking in Pembrokeshire
Walking in the Forest of Dean
Walking in the Wye Valley
Walking on the Brecon Beacons
Walking on the Gower
Walking the Shropshire Way

DERBYSHIRE, PEAK DISTRICT AND MIDLANDS
Cycling in the Peak District
Dark Peak Walks
Scrambles in the Dark Peak
Walking in Derbyshire
White Peak Walks:
  The Northern Dales
White Peak Walks:
  The Southern Dales

SOUTHERN ENGLAND
20 Classic Sportive Rides in
  South East England
20 Classic Sportive Rides in
  South West England
Cycling in the Cotswolds
Mountain Biking on the North
  Downs

Mountain Biking on the South Downs
North Downs Way Map Booklet
South West Coast Path Map Booklet – Vol 1: Minehead to St Ives
South West Coast Path Map Booklet – Vol 2: St Ives to Plymouth
South West Coast Path Map Booklet – Vol 3: Plymouth to Poole
Suffolk Coast and Heath Walks
The Cotswold Way
The Cotswold Way Map Booklet
The Great Stones Way
The Kennet and Avon Canal
The Lea Valley Walk
The North Downs Way
The Peddars Way and Norfolk Coast path
The Pilgrims' Way
The Ridgeway Map Booklet
The Ridgeway National Trail
The South Downs Way
The South Downs Way Map Booklet
The South West Coast Path
The Thames Path
The Thames Path Map Booklet
The Two Moors Way
Two Moors Way Map Booklet
Walking Hampshire's Test Way
Walking in Cornwall
Walking in Essex
Walking in Kent
Walking in London
Walking in Norfolk
Walking in Sussex
Walking in the Chilterns
Walking in the Cotswolds
Walking in the Isles of Scilly
Walking in the New Forest
Walking in the North Wessex Downs
Walking in the Thames Valley
Walking on Dartmoor
Walking on Guernsey
Walking on Jersey
Walking on the Isle of Wight
Walking the Jurassic Coast
Walks in the South Downs National Park

BRITISH ISLES CHALLENGES, COLLECTIONS AND ACTIVITIES

The Big Rounds
The Book of the Bivvy
The Book of the Bothy
The C2C Cycle Route
The End to End Cycle Route
The End to End Trail
The Mountains of England and Wales: Vol 1 Wales
The Mountains of England and Wales: Vol 2 England
The National Trails
The UK's County Tops
Three Peaks, Ten Tors

ALPS CROSS-BORDER ROUTES

100 Hut Walks in the Alps
Across the Eastern Alps: E5

Alpine Ski Mountaineering Vol 1 – Western Alps
Alpine Ski Mountaineering Vol 2 – Central and Eastern Alps
Chamonix to Zermatt
The Karnischer Hohenweg
The Tour of the Bernina
Tour of Mont Blanc
Tour of Monte Rosa
Tour of the Matterhorn
Trail Running – Chamonix and the Mont Blanc region
Trekking in the Alps
Trekking in the Silvretta and Ratikon Alps
Trekking Munich to Venice
Walking in the Alps

PYRENEES AND FRANCE/SPAIN CROSS-BORDER ROUTES

Shorter Treks in the Pyrenees
The GR10 Trail
The GR11 Trail
The Pyrenean Haute Route
The Pyrenees
Walks and Climbs in the Pyrenees

AUSTRIA

Innsbruck Mountain Adventures
The Adlerweg
Trekking in Austria's Hohe Tauern
Trekking in the Stubai Alps
Trekking in the Zillertal Alps
Walking in Austria

SWITZERLAND

Switzerland's Jura Crest Trail
The Swiss Alpine Pass Route – Via Alpina Route 1
The Swiss Alps
Tour of the Jungfrau Region
Walking in the Bernese Oberland
Walking in the Engadine – Switzerland
Walking in the Valais

FRANCE

Chamonix Mountain Adventures
Cycle Touring in France
Cycling London to Paris
Cycling the Canal de la Garonne
Cycling the Canal du Midi
Écrins National Park
Mont Blanc Walks
Mountain Adventures in the Maurienne
The GR20 Corsica
The GR5 Trail
The GR5 Trail – Vosges and Jura
The Grand Traverse of the Massif Central
The Loire Cycle Route
The Moselle Cycle Route
The River Rhone Cycle Route
The Robert Louis Stevenson Trail
The Way of St James – Le Puy to the Pyrenees
Tour of the Oisans: The GR54
Tour of the Queyras

Vanoise Ski Touring
Via Ferratas of the French Alps
Walking in Corsica
Walking in Provence – East
Walking in Provence – West
Walking in the Auvergne
Walking in the Briançonnais
Walking in the Cevennes
Walking in the Dordogne
Walking in the Haute Savoie: North
Walking in the Haute Savoie: South
Walks in the Cathar Region

GERMANY

Hiking and Cycling in the Black Forest
The Danube Cycleway Vol 1
The Rhine Cycle Route
The Westweg
Walking in the Bavarian Alps

ICELAND AND GREENLAND

Trekking in Greenland – The Arctic Circle Trail
Walking and Trekking in Iceland

IRELAND

The Wild Atlantic Way and Western Ireland

ITALY

Italy's Sibillini National Park
Shorter Walks in the Dolomites
Ski Touring and Snowshoeing in the Dolomites
The Way of St Francis
Through the Italian Alps
Trekking in the Apennines
Trekking in the Dolomites
Via Ferratas of the Italian Dolomites Vol 1
Via Ferratas of the Italian Dolomites: Vol 2
Walking and Trekking in the Gran Paradiso
Walking in Abruzzo
Walking in Italy's Cinque Terre
Walking in Italy's Stelvio National Park
Walking in Sardinia
Walking in Sicily
Walking in the Dolomites
Walking in Tuscany
Walking in Umbria
Walking Lake Como and Maggiore
Walking Lake Garda and Iseo
Walking on the Amalfi Coast
Walks and Treks in the Maritime Alps

BELGIUM AND LUXEMBOURG

The GR5 Trail – Benelux and Lorraine
Walking in the Ardennes

SCANDINAVIA: NORWAY, SWEDEN, FINLAND

Trekking the Kungsleden
Walking in Norway

POLAND, SLOVAKIA, ROMANIA, HUNGARY AND BULGARIA

The Danube Cycleway Vol 2
The High Tatras
The Mountains of Romania
Walking in Bulgaria's National Parks
Walking in Hungary

SLOVENIA, CROATIA, SERBIA, MONTENEGRO, ALBANIA AND KOSOVO

Mountain Biking in Slovenia
The Islands of Croatia
The Julian Alps of Slovenia
The Mountains of Montenegro
The Peaks of the Balkans Trail
The Slovene Mountain Trail
Walking in Slovenia: The Karavanke
Walks and Treks in Croatia

SPAIN

Camino de Santiago – Camino Frances
Coastal Walks in Andalucia
Cycle Touring in Spain
Cycling the Camino de Santiago
Mountain Walking in Mallorca
Mountain Walking in Southern Catalunya
Spain's Sendero Historico: The GR1
The Andalucian Coast to Coast Walk
The Camino del Norte and Camino Primitivo
The Camino Ingles and Ruta do Mar
The Mountains of Nerja
The Mountains of Ronda and Grazalema
The Northern Caminos
The Sierras of Extremadura
Trekking in Mallorca
Trekking in the Canary Islands
Walking and Trekking in the Sierra Nevada
Walking in Andalucia
Walking in Menorca
Walking in the Cordillera Cantabrica
Walking on Gran Canaria
Walking on La Gomera and El Hierro
Walking on La Palma
Walking on Lanzarote and Fuerteventura
Walking on Tenerife
Walking on the Costa Blanca
Walking the Camino dos Faros

PORTUGAL

Portugal's Rota Vicentina
The Camino Portugues
Walking in Portugal
Walking in the Algarve
Walking on Madeira
Walking on the Azores

GREECE

The High Mountains of Crete
Trekking in Greece
Walking and Trekking in Zagori
Walking and Trekking on Corfu

CYPRUS

Walking in Cyprus

MALTA

Walking on Malta

INTERNATIONAL CHALLENGES, COLLECTIONS AND ACTIVITIES

Canyoning in the Alps
Europe's High Points
The Via Francigena Canterbury to Rome – Part 2

MOROCCO

Mountaineering in the Moroccan High Atlas
The High Atlas
Walks and Scrambles in the Moroccan Anti-Atlas

TANZANIA

Kilimanjaro

SOUTH AFRICA

Walking in the Drakensberg

TAJIKISTAN

Trekking in Tajikistan

JAPAN

Hiking and Trekking in the Japan Alps and Mount Fuji
Japan's Kumano Kodo Pilgrimage

JORDAN

Jordan – Walks, Treks, Caves, Climbs and Canyons
Treks and Climbs in Wadi Rum, Jordan

NEPAL

Annapurna
Everest: A Trekker's Guide
Trekking in the Himalaya

BHUTAN

Trekking in Bhutan

INDIA

Trekking in Ladakh

CHINA

The Mount Kailash Trek

NORTH AMERICA: USA AND CANADA

The John Muir Trail
The Pacific Crest Trail

SOUTH AMERICA: ARGENTINA, CHILE AND PERU

Aconcagua and the Southern Andes
Hiking and Biking Peru's Inca Trails
Torres del Paine

TECHNIQUES

Fastpacking
Geocaching in the UK
Lightweight Camping
Map and Compass
Outdoor Photography
Polar Exploration
Rock Climbing
Sport Climbing
The Mountain Hut Book

MINI GUIDES

Alpine Flowers
Avalanche!
Navigation
Pocket First Aid and Wilderness Medicine
Snow

MOUNTAIN LITERATURE

8000 metres
A Walk in the Clouds
Abode of the Gods
Fifty Years of Adventure
The Pennine Way – the Path, the People, the Journey
Unjustifiable Risk?

For full information on all our guides, books and eBooks, visit our website: **www.cicerone.co.uk**

Explore the world with Cicerone

walking • trekking • mountaineering • climbing • mountain biking • cycling • via ferratas • scrambling • trail running • skills and techniques

For over 50 years, Cicerone have built up an outstanding collection of nearly 400 guides, inspiring all sorts of amazing experiences.

www.cicerone.co.uk – where adventures begin

- Our **website** is a treasure-trove for every outdoor adventurer. You can buy books or read inspiring articles and trip reports, get technical advice, check for updates, and view videos, photographs and mapping for routes and treks.

- **Register this book** or any other Cicerone guide in your member's library on our website and you can choose to automatically access updates and GPX files for your books, if available.

- Our **fortnightly newsletters** will update you on new publications and articles and keep you informed of other news and events. You can also follow us on Facebook, Twitter and Instagram.

We hope you have enjoyed using this guidebook. If you have any comments you would like to share, please contact us using the form on our website or via email, so that we can provide the best experience for future customers.

CICERONE

Juniper House, Murley Moss Business Village, Oxenholme Road, Kendal LA9 7RL

info@cicerone.co.uk   cicerone.co.uk